The *New* Daily Study Bible

The Letters to
Timothy, Titus, and Philemon

The *New* Daily Study Bible

The Letters to
Timothy, Titus, and Philemon

William Barclay

Westminster John Knox Press
LOUISVILLE • LONDON

© The William Barclay Estate, 1975, 2003

First edition published in 1956 as *The Daily Study Bible: The Letters to Timothy and Titus* and in 1957 as *The Daily Study Bible: The Letter to Philemon*
Revised edition published in 1975
This third edition fully revised and updated by Saint Andrew Press and published as *The New Daily Study Bible: The Letters to Timothy, Titus, and Philemon* in 2003

Published in the United States by
Westminster John Knox Press
Louisville, Kentucky

PRINTED IN THE UNITED STATES OF AMERICA

03 04 05 06 07 08 09 10 11 12 – 10 9 8 7 6 5 4 3 2 1

Library of Congress Cataloging-in-Publication Data is on file at the Library of Congress, Washington, D.C.

ISBN 0–664–22677–9

To

R.G.M.

A GREAT ENCOURAGER

CONTENTS

I TIMOTHY

TIMOTHY, TITUS AND PHILEMON

2 TIMOTHY

TITUS

PHILEMON

SERIES FOREWORD
(by Ronnie Barclay)

My father always had a great love for the English language and its literature. As a student at the University of Glasgow, he won a prize in the English class – and I have no doubt that he could have become a Professor of English instead of Divinity and Biblical Criticism. In a pre-computer age, he had a mind like a computer that could store vast numbers of quotations, illustrations, anecdotes and allusions; and, more remarkably still, he could retrieve them at will. The editor of this revision has, where necessary, corrected and attributed the vast majority of these quotations with considerable skill and has enhanced our pleasure as we read quotations from Plato to T. S. Eliot.

There is another very welcome improvement in the new text. My mother was one of five sisters, and my grandmother was a commanding figure as the Presbyterian minister's wife in a small village in Ayrshire in Scotland. She ran that small community very efficiently, and I always felt that my father, surrounded by so many women, was more than some-what overawed by it all! I am sure that this is the reason why his use of English tended to be dominated by the words 'man', 'men' and so on, with the result that it sounded very male-orientated. Once again, the editor has very skilfully improved my father's English and made the text much more readable for all of us by amending the often one-sided language.

It is a well-known fact that William Barclay wrote at break-neck speed and never corrected anything once it was on paper – he took great pride in mentioning this at every possible opportunity! This revision, in removing repetition and correcting the inevitable errors that had slipped through, has produced a text free from all the tell-tale signs of very rapid writing. It is with great pleasure that I commend this revision to readers old and new in the certainty that William Barclay speaks even more clearly to us all with his wonderful appeal in this new version of his much-loved *Daily Study Bible*.

Ronnie Barclay
Bedfordshire
2001

GENERAL INTRODUCTION

(by William Barclay, from the 1975 edition)

The Daily Study Bible series has always had one aim – to convey the results of scholarship to the ordinary reader. A. S. Peake delighted in the saying that he was a 'theological middle-man', and I would be happy if the same could be said of me in regard to these volumes. And yet the primary aim of the series has never been academic. It could be summed up in the famous words of Richard of Chichester's prayer – to enable men and women 'to know Jesus Christ more clearly, to love him more dearly, and to follow him more nearly'.

It is all of twenty years since the first volume of *The Daily Study Bible* was published. The series was the brain-child of the late Rev. Andrew McCosh, MA, STM, the then Secretary and Manager of the Committee on Publications of the Church of Scotland, and of the late Rev. R. G. Macdonald, OBE, MA, DD, its Convener.

It is a great joy to me to know that all through the years *The Daily Study Bible* has been used at home and abroad, by minister, by missionary, by student and by layman, and that it has been translated into many different languages. Now, after so many printings, it has become necessary to renew the printer's type and the opportunity has been taken to restyle the books, to correct some errors in the text and to remove some references which have become outdated. At the same time, the Biblical quotations within the text have been changed to use the Revised Standard Version, but my own original translation of the New Testament passages has been retained at the beginning of each daily section.

There is one debt which I would be sadly lacking in courtesy if I did not acknowledge. The work of revision and correction has been done entirely by the Rev. James Martin, MA, BD, Minister of High Carntyne Church, Glasgow. Had it not been for him this task would never have been undertaken, and it is impossible for me to thank him enough for the selfless toil he has put into the revision of these books.

It is my prayer that God may continue to use *The Daily Study Bible* to enable men better to understand His word.

William Barclay
Glasgow
1975
(Published in the 1975 edition)

GENERAL FOREWORD

(by John Drane)

I only met William Barclay once, not long after his retirement from the chair of Biblical Criticism at the University of Glasgow. Of course I had known about him long before that, not least because his theological passion – the Bible – was also a significant formative influence in my own life and ministry. One of my most vivid memories of his influence goes back to when I was working on my own doctoral research in the New Testament. It was summer 1971, and I was a leader on a mission team working in the north-east of Scotland at the same time as Barclay's Baird Lectures were being broadcast on national television. One night, a young Ph.D. scientist who was interested in Christianity, but still unsure about some things, came to me and announced: 'I've just been watching William Barclay on TV. He's convinced me that I need to be a Christian; when can I be baptized?' That kind of thing did not happen every day. So how could it be that Barclay's message was so accessible to people with no previous knowledge or experience of the Christian faith?

I soon realised that there was no magic ingredient that enabled this apparently ordinary professor to be a brilliant communicator. His secret lay in who he was, his own sense of identity and purpose, and above all his integrity in being true to himself and his faith. Born in the far north of Scotland, he was brought up in Motherwell, a steel-producing town south of Glasgow where his family settled when he was only five, and this was the kind of place where he felt most at home. Though his association with the University of Glasgow provided a focus for his life over almost fifty years, from his first day as a student in 1925 to his retirement from the faculty in 1974, he never became an ivory-tower academic, divorced from the realities of life in the real world. On the contrary, it was his commitment to the working-class culture of industrial Clydeside that enabled him to make such a lasting contribution not only to the world of the university but also to the life of the Church.

He was ordained to the ministry of the Church of Scotland at the age of twenty-six, but was often misunderstood even by other Christians. I doubt that William Barclay would ever have chosen words such as 'missionary' or 'evangelist' to describe his own ministry, but he accomplished what few others have done, as he took the traditional Presbyterian emphasis on spirituality-through-learning and transformed it into a most effective vehicle for evangelism. His own primary interest was in the history and language of the New Testament, but William Barclay was never only a historian or literary critic. His constant concern was to explore how these ancient books, and the faith of which they spoke, could continue to be relevant to people of his own time. If the Scottish churches had known how to capitalize on his enormous popularity in the media during the 1960s and 1970s, they might easily have avoided much of the decline of subsequent years.

Connecting the Bible to life has never been the way to win friends in the world of academic theology, and Barclay could undoubtedly have made things easier for himself had he been prepared to be a more conventional academic. But he was too deeply rooted in his own culture – and too seriously committed to the gospel – for that. He could see little purpose in a belief system that was so wrapped up in arcane and complicated terminology that it was accessible only to experts. Not only did he demystify Christian theology, but he also did it for working people, addressing the kind of things that mattered to ordinary folks in their everyday lives. In doing so, he also challenged the elitism that has often been deeply ingrained in the twin worlds of academic theology and the Church, with their shared assumption that popular culture is an inappropriate vehicle for serious thinking. Professor Barclay can hardly have been surprised when his predilection for writing books for the masses – not to mention talking to them on television – was questioned by his peers and even occasionally dismissed as being 'unscholarly' or insufficiently 'academic'. That was all untrue, of course, for his work was soundly based in reliable scholarship and his own extensive knowledge of the original languages of the Bible. But like One many centuries before him (and unlike most of his peers, in both Church and academy), 'the common people heard him gladly' (Mark 12:37), which no doubt explains why his writings are still inspirational – and why it is a particular pleasure for me personally to commend them to a new readership in a new century.

John Drane
University of Aberdeen
2001

EDITOR'S PREFACE
(by Linda Foster)

When the first volume of the original *Daily Bible Readings*, which later became *The Daily Study Bible* (the commentary on Acts), was published in 1953, no one could have anticipated or envisaged the revolution in the use of language which was to take place in the last quarter of the twentieth century. Indeed, when the first revised edition, to which William Barclay refers in his General Introduction, was completed in 1975, such a revolution was still waiting in the wings. But at the beginning of the twenty-first century, inclusive language and the concept of political correctness are well-established facts of life. It has therefore been with some trepidation that the editing of this unique and much-loved text has been undertaken in producing *The New Daily Study Bible*. Inevitably, the demands of the new language have resulted in the loss of some of Barclay's most sonorous phrases, perhaps best remembered in the often-repeated words 'many a man'. Nonetheless, this revision is made in the conviction that William Barclay, the great communicator, would have welcomed it. In the discussion of Matthew 9:16–17 ('The Problem of the New Idea'), he affirmed the value of language that has stood the test of time and in which people have 'found comfort and put their trust', but he also spoke of 'living in a changing and expanding world' and questioned the wisdom of reading God's word to twentieth-century men and women in Elizabethan English. It is the intention of this new edition to heed that warning and to bring

William Barclay's message of God's word to readers of the twenty-first century in the language of their own time.

In the editorial process, certain decisions have been made in order to keep a balance between that new language and the familiar Barclay style. Quotations from the Bible are now taken from the New Revised Standard Version, but William Barclay's own translation of individual passages has been retained throughout. Where the new version differs from the text on which Barclay originally commented, because of the existence of an alternative reading, the variant text is indicated by square brackets. I have made no attempt to guess what Barclay would have said about the NRSV text; his commentary still refers to the Authorized (King James) and Revised Standard Versions of the Bible, but I believe that the inclusive language of the NRSV considerably assists the flow of the discussion.

For similar reasons, the dating conventions of BC and AD – rather than the more recent and increasingly used BCE (before the common era) and CE (common era) – have been retained. William Barclay took great care to explain the meanings of words and phrases and scholarly points, but it has not seemed appropriate to select new terms and make such explanations on his behalf.

One of the most difficult problems to solve has concerned monetary values. Barclay had his own system for translating the coinage of New Testament times into British currency. Over the years, these equivalent values have become increasingly out of date, and often the force of the point being made has been lost or diminished. There is no easy way to bring these equivalents up to date in a way that will continue to make sense, particularly when readers come from both sides of the Atlantic. I have therefore followed the only known yardstick that gives any feel for the values concerned, namely that a *denarius* was a day's wage for a working man, and I have made alterations to the text accordingly.

One of the striking features of *The Daily Study Bible* is the range of quotations from literature and hymnody that are used by way of illustration. Many of these passages appeared without identification or attribution, and for the new edition I have attempted wherever possible to provide sources and authors. In the same way, details have been included about scholars and other individuals cited, by way of context and explanation, and I am most grateful to Professor John Drane for his assistance in discovering information about some of the more obscure or unfamiliar characters. It is clear that readers use *The Daily Study Bible* in different ways. Some look up particular passages while others work through the daily readings in a more systematic way. The descriptions and explanations are therefore not offered every time an individual is mentioned (in order to avoid repetition that some may find tedious), but I trust that the information can be discovered without too much difficulty.

Finally, the 'Further Reading' lists at the end of each volume have been removed. Many new commentaries and individual studies have been added to those that were the basis of William Barclay's work, and making a selection from that ever-increasing catalogue is an impossible task. It is nonetheless my hope that the exploration that begins with these volumes of *The New Daily Study Bible* will go on in the discovery of new writers and new books.

Throughout the editorial process, many conversations have taken place – conversations with the British and American publishers, and with those who love the books and find in them both information and inspiration. Ronnie Barclay's contribution to this revision of his father's work has been invaluable. But one conversation has dominated the work, and that has been a conversation with William Barclay himself through the text. There has been a real sense of listening to his voice in all the questioning and in the searching for new words to convey the meaning of that text. The aim of *The New Daily Study Bible* is to make clear his message, so that the distinctive voice, which has spoken to so many in past years, may continue to be heard for generations to come.

Linda Foster
London
2001

A GENERAL INTRODUCTION
TO THE LETTERS OF PAUL

The Letters of Paul

There is no more interesting body of documents in the New Testament than the letters of Paul. That is because, of all forms of literature, a letter is most personal. Demetrius, one of the ancient Greek literary critics, once wrote: 'Everyone reveals his own soul in his letters. In every other form of composition it is possible to discern the writer's character, but in none so clearly as the epistolary' (Demetrius, *On Style*, 227). It is precisely because he left us so many letters that we feel we know Paul so well. In them, he opened his mind and heart to the people he loved so much; and in them, to this day, we can see that great mind grappling with the problems of the early Church, and feel that great heart throbbing with love for men and women, even when they were misguided and mistaken.

The Difficulty of Letters

At the same time, there is often nothing so difficult to understand as a letter. Demetrius (*On Style*, 223) quotes a saying of Artemon, who edited the letters of Aristotle. Artemon said that a letter ought to be written in the same manner as a dialogue, because it was one of the two sides of a discussion. In other words, reading a letter is like listening to one side of a telephone conversation. So, when we read the letters of

Paul, we often find ourselves in difficulty. We do not possess the letter which he was answering, we do not fully know the circumstances with which he was dealing, and it is only from the letter itself that we can deduce the situation which prompted it. Before we can hope to understand fully any letter Paul wrote, we must try to reconstruct the situation that produced it.

The Ancient Letters

It is a great pity that Paul's letters were ever called *epistles*. They are in the most literal sense *letters*. One of the great lights shed on the interpretation of the New Testament has been the discovery and the publication of the *papyri*. In the ancient world, *papyrus* was the substance on which most documents were written. It was composed of strips of the pith of a certain bulrush that grew on the banks of the Nile. These strips were laid one on top of the other to form a substance very like brown paper. The sands of the Egyptian desert were ideal for preservation; for papyrus, although very brittle, will last forever as long as moisture does not get at it. As a result, from the Egyptian rubbish heaps, archaeologists have rescued hundreds of documents – marriage contracts, legal agreements, government forms and, most interesting of all, private letters. When we read these private letters, we find that there was a pattern to which nearly all conformed, and we find that Paul's letters reproduce exactly that pattern. Here is one of these ancient letters. It is from a soldier, called Apion, to his father Epimachus. He is writing from Misenum to tell his father that he has arrived safely after a stormy passage.

> Apion sends heartiest greetings to his father and lord Epimachus. I pray above all that you are well and fit; and that things are going well with you and my sister

and her daughter and my brother. I thank my Lord Serapis [his god] that he kept me safe when I was in peril on the sea. As soon as I got to Misenum I got my journey money from Caesar – three gold pieces. And things are going fine with me. So I beg you, my dear father, send me a line, first to let me know how you are, and then about my brothers, and thirdly, that I may kiss your hand, because you brought me up well, and because of that I hope, God willing, soon to be promoted. Give Capito my heartiest greetings, and my brothers and Serenilla and my friends. I sent you a little picture of myself painted by Euctemon. My military name is Antonius Maximus. I pray for your good health. Serenus sends good wishes, Agathos Daimon's boy, and Turbo, Gallonius's son. (G. Milligan, *Selections from the Greek Papyri*, 36)

Little did Apion think that we would be reading his letter to his father some 2,000 years after he had written it. It shows how little human nature changes. The young man is hoping for promotion quickly. Who will Serenilla be but the girl he left behind? He sends the ancient equivalent of a photograph to the family and friends at home. Now, that letter falls into certain sections. (1) There is a greeting. (2) There is a prayer for the health of the recipients. (3) There is a thanksgiving to the gods. (4) There are the special contents. (5) Finally, there are the special salutations and the personal greetings. Practically every one of Paul's letters shows exactly the same sections, as we now demonstrate.

(1) *The greeting*: Romans 1:1; 1 Corinthians 1:1; 2 Corinthians 1:1; Galatians 1:1; Ephesians 1:1; Philippians 1:1; Colossians 1:1–2; 1 Thessalonians 1:1; 2 Thessalonians 1:1.

(2) *The prayer*: in every case, Paul prays for the grace of God on the people to whom he writes: Romans 1:7; 1 Corinthians 1:3; 2 Corinthians 1:2; Galatians 1:3; Ephesians

1:2; Philippians 1:3; Colossians 1:2; 1 Thessalonians 1:1; 2 Thessalonians 1:2.

(3) *The thanksgiving*: Romans 1:8; 1 Corinthians 1:4; 2 Corinthians 1:3; Ephesians 1:3; Philippians 1:3; 1 Thessalonians 1:3; 2 Thessalonians 1:3.

(4) *The special contents*: the main body of the letters.

(5) *The special salutations and personal greetings*: Romans 16; 1 Corinthians 16:19; 2 Corinthians 13:13; Philippians 4:21–2; Colossians 4:12–15; 1 Thessalonians 5:26.

When Paul wrote letters, he wrote them on the pattern which everyone used. The German theologian Adolf Deissmann says of them: 'They differ from the messages of the homely papyrus leaves of Egypt, not as letters but only as the letters of Paul.' When we read Paul's letters, we are reading things which were meant to be not academic exercises and theological treatises, but human documents written by a friend to his friends.

The Immediate Situation

With a very few exceptions, Paul's letters were written to meet an immediate situation. They were not systematic arguments which he sat down to write in the peace and silence of his study. There was some threatening situation in Corinth, or Galatia, or Philippi, or Thessalonica, and he wrote a letter to meet it. He was not in the least thinking of us when he wrote, but solely of the people to whom he was writing. Deissmann writes: 'Paul had no thought of adding a few fresh compositions to the already extant Jewish epistles; still less of enriching the sacred literature of his nation . . . He had no presentiment of the place his words would occupy in universal history; not so much that they would be in existence in the next generation, far less that one day people would look at them as Holy Scripture.' We must always remember that a thing need not be of only passing interest because it was written to meet an immediate situation. Every one of the great love songs of the world was written at a particular time for one person; but they live on for the benefit and enjoyment of all. It is precisely because Paul's letters were written to meet a threatening danger or a pressing need that they still throb with life. And it is because human need and the human situation do not change that God speaks to us through them today.

The Spoken Word

There is one other thing that we must note about these letters. Paul did what most people did in his day. He did not normally pen his own letters, but dictated them to a secretary and then added his own authenticating signature. (We actually know the name of one of the people who did the writing for him. In Romans 16:22, Tertius, the secretary, slips in his own greeting before the letter draws to an end.) In 1 Corinthians 16:21, Paul says in effect: 'This is my own signature, my autograph, so that you can be sure this letter comes from me' (cf. Colossians 4:18; 2 Thessalonians 3:17).

This explains a great deal. Sometimes Paul is hard to understand, because his sentences begin and never finish; his grammar breaks down and the construction becomes complicated. We must not think of him sitting quietly at a desk, carefully polishing each sentence as he writes. We must think of him striding up and down some little room, pouring out a torrent of words, while his secretary races to get them down. When Paul composed his letters, he had in his mind's eye a vision of the people to whom he was writing, and he was pouring out his heart to them in words that fell over each other in his eagerness to help.

INTRODUCTION TO THE
LETTERS TO TIMOTHY AND TITUS

Personal Letters

The two letters to Timothy and the letter to Titus have always
been regarded as forming a separate group, different from
the other letters of Paul. The most obvious difference is that
they, along with the little letter to Philemon, are written to
individuals, whereas all other Pauline letters are written to
churches. The Muratorian Canon, which was the earliest
official list of New Testament books, says that they were
written 'from personal feeling and affection'. They are private
rather than public letters.

Ecclesiastical Letters

But it very soon began to be seen that, though these are
personal and private letters, they have a significance and a
relevance far beyond the immediate. In 1 Timothy 3:15, their
aim is set down. They are written to Timothy 'that you may
know how one ought to behave in the household of God,
which is the church of the living God'. So, it came to be seen
that these letters have not only a personal significance but
also what one might call an *ecclesiastical* significance. The
Muratorian Canon says of them that, though they are personal
letters written out of personal affection, 'they are still hallowed
in the respect of the Catholic Church, and *in the arrangement
of ecclesiastical discipline*'. The early Christian theologian

Tertullian said that Paul wrote 'two letters to Timothy and one to Titus, which were composed *concerning the state of the Church (de ecclesiastico statu)*'. It is not then surprising that the first name given to them was *Pontifical Letters*, that is, written by the *pontifex*, the priest, the controller of the church.

Pastoral Letters

Bit by bit, they came to acquire the name by which they are still known – the Pastoral Epistles. In writing about 1 Timothy, the philosopher and theologian Thomas Aquinas, as long ago as 1274, said: 'This letter is as it were *a pastoral rule* which the Apostle delivered to Timothy.' In his introduction to the second letter, he writes: 'In the first letter he gives Timothy instructions concerning ecclesiastical order; in this second letter he deals with a *pastoral care* which should be so great that it will even accept martyrdom for the sake of the care of the flock.' But this title, the Pastoral Epistles, really became attached to these letters in 1726 when a great scholar named Paul Anton gave a series of famous lectures on them under that title.

These letters, then, deal with the care and organization of the flock of God; they tell men and women how to behave within the household of God; and they give instructions as to how God's house should be administered, as to what kind of people the leaders and pastors of the Church should be, and as to how the threats which endanger the purity of Christian faith and life should be dealt with.

The Growing Church

The main interest of these letters is that in them we get a picture of the infant Church. In those early days, it was an island in a sea of idolatry. The people in it were only one remove from their origins in the ancient religions. It would have been so easy for them to lapse into the standards from which they had come; the tarnishing atmosphere was all around. It is most significant that missionaries have reported that, of all letters, the Pastoral Epistles speak most directly to the situation of the younger churches. The situation with which they deal has been re-enacted in India, in Africa and in China. They can never lose their interest, because in them we see, as nowhere else, the problems which continually confronted and pressed upon the growing Church.

The Ecclesiastical Background of the Pastorals

From the beginning, these letters have presented problems to New Testament scholars. There are many who have felt that, as they stand, they cannot have come directly from the hand and pen of Paul. That this is no new feeling may be seen from the fact that Marcion (a second-century heretic, who in spite of his unacceptable beliefs was the first person to draw up a list of New Testament books) did not include them among Paul's letters. Let us then see what makes people doubt their direct Pauline authorship.

In these letters, we are confronted with the picture of a church with a fairly highly developed ecclesiastical organization. There are *elders* (1 Timothy 5:17–19; Titus 1:5–6), there are *bishops*, superintendents or overseers (1 Timothy 3:1–7; Titus 1:7–16), and there are *deacons* (1 Timothy 3:8–13). From 1 Timothy 5:17–18, we learn that, by that time, elders were even paid officials. The elders who rule well are to be counted worthy of a double reward, and the Church is urged to remember that the labourer deserves to be paid. There is at least the beginning of the order of widows who became so prominent later on in the early Church (1 Timothy 5:3–

16). There is clearly here a quite elaborate structure within the Church – too elaborate, some would claim, for the early days in which Paul lived and worked.

The Days of Creeds

It is even claimed that in these letters we can see the days of creeds emerging. The word *faith* changed its meaning. In the earliest days, it is always *faith in a person*; it is the most intimate possible personal connection of love and trust and obedience with Jesus Christ. In later days, it became *faith in a creed*; it became the acceptance of certain doctrines. It is said that in the Pastoral Epistles we can see this change emerging.

In the later days, some will come who will depart from the *faith* and pay attention to teachings of demons (1 Timothy 4:1). A good servant of Jesus Christ must be nourished in the words of *faith and sound teaching* (1 Timothy 4:6). The heretics are people of corrupt minds and counterfeit *faith* (2 Timothy 3:8). The duty of Titus is to rebuke people that they may be sound in the *faith* (Titus 1:13).

This comes out particularly in an expression peculiar to the Pastorals. As the Revised Standard Version has it, Timothy is urged to keep hold of 'the truth that has been entrusted to you' (2 Timothy 1:14). The word for *that has been entrusted* is *parathēkē*. *Parathēkē* means a *deposit* which has been entrusted to a banker or someone else for safe-keeping. It is essentially something which must be handed back or handed on absolutely unchanged. That is to say, the stress is on *orthodoxy*. Instead of being a close, personal relationship to Jesus Christ, as it was in the thrilling, pulsating days of the early Church, faith has become the acceptance of a creed. It is even held that in the Pastorals we have echoes of the earliest creeds.

4

> He was revealed in flesh,
> vindicated in spirit,
> seen by angels,
> proclaimed among Gentiles,
> believed in throughout the world,
> taken up in glory. (1 Timothy 3:16)

That indeed sounds like the fragment of a creed which is to be recited.

> Remember Jesus Christ, raised from the dead, a descendant
> of David – that is my gospel. (2 Timothy 2:8)

That sounds like a reminder of a sentence from an accepted creed.

Within the Pastorals, there undoubtedly are indications that the time of insistence on acceptance of a creed has begun, and that the days of the first thrilling personal discovery of Christ are beginning to fade.

A Dangerous Heresy

It is clear that in the forefront of the situation against which the Pastoral Epistles were written there was a dangerous heresy which was threatening the welfare of the Christian Church. If we can distinguish the various characteristic features of that heresy, we may be able to go on to identify it.

It was characterized by *speculative intellectualism*. It produced questions (1 Timothy 1:4); those involved in it had a craving for questions (1 Timothy 6:4); it dealt in stupid and senseless questions (2 Timothy 2:23); its stupid questions are to be avoided (Titus 3:9). The word used in each case for *questions* is *ekzētēsis*, which means *speculative discussion*. This heresy was obviously one which was a playground of the intellectuals, or rather the pseudo-intellectuals of the Church.

It was characterized by *pride*. The heretics are proud, although in reality they know nothing (1 Timothy 6:4). There are indications that these intellectuals set themselves on a level above ordinary Christians; in fact, they may well have said that complete salvation was outside the grasp of the ordinary man or woman and open only to them. At times, the Pastoral Epistles stress the word *all* in a most significant way. The grace of God, which brings salvation, has appeared to *all* (Titus 2:11). It is God's will that *all* should be saved and come to a knowledge of the truth (1 Timothy 2:4). The intellectuals tried to make the greatest blessings of Christianity the exclusive possession of a chosen few; and, in complete contrast, the true faith stresses the all-embracing love of God.

There were within that heresy two opposite tendencies. There was a tendency to *self-denial*. The heretics tried to lay down special food laws, forgetting that everything God has made is good (1 Timothy 4:4–5). They listed many things as impure, forgetting that to the pure all things are pure (Titus 1:15). It is not impossible that they regarded sex as something unclean and belittled marriage, and even tried to persuade those who were married to renounce it, for in Titus 2:4 the simple duties of married life are stressed as being binding on Christians.

But this heresy also resulted in *immorality*. The heretics even went into private houses and led away weak and foolish women who were swayed by all kinds of desires (2 Timothy 3:6). They claimed to know God, but denied him by their actions (Titus 1:16). They were out to impose upon people and to make money out of their false teaching. To them, gain was godliness (1 Timothy 6:5); they taught and deceived for sordid gain (Titus 1:11).

On the one hand, this heresy produced an un-Christian self-denial, and on the other it produced an equally un-

6

Christian immorality. It was characterized, too, by *words* and *tales* and *genealogies*. It was full of godless chatter and useless controversies (1 Timothy 6:20). It produced endless genealogies (1 Timothy 1:4; Titus 3:9). It produced myths and fables (1 Timothy 1:4; Titus 1:14).

It was at least in some way and to some extent tied up with *Jewish legalism*. Among its devotees were those 'of the circumcision' (Titus 1:10). The aim of the heretics was to be teachers of the law (1 Timothy 1:7). It pressed on people Jewish myths and the commandments of those who reject the truth (Titus 1:14).

Finally, these heretics denied *the resurrection of the body*. They said that any resurrection that a Christian was going to experience had been experienced already (2 Timothy 2:18). This is probably a reference to those who held that the only resurrection Christians experienced was a spiritual one when they died with Christ and rose again with him in the experience of baptism (Romans 6:4).

The Beginnings of Gnosticism

Is there any heresy which fits all this material? There is, and its name is *Gnosticism*. The basic idea behind Gnosticism was that all matter is essentially evil and that spirit alone is good. That basic belief had certain consequences.

The Gnostics believed that matter is as eternal as God, and that when God created the world he had to use this essentially evil matter. That meant that, to them, God could not be the direct creator of the world. In order to touch this flawed matter, he had to send out a series of emanations or divine powers – they called them *aeons* – each one more and more distant from himself until at last there came an emanation or aeon so distant that it could deal with matter and create the world. Between human beings and God there stretched a series of these emanations, each one containing an individual's name and genealogy. So Gnosticism literally had endless myths and endless genealogies. If men and women were ever to get to God, they must, as it were, climb this ladder of emanations; and, to do that, they needed a very special kind of knowledge including all kinds of passwords to get them past each stage. Only a person of the highest intellectual ability could hope to acquire this knowledge and know these passwords and so get to God.

Further, if matter was totally evil, the body was altogether evil. From that, two opposite possible consequences sprang. Either the body must be held in check so that a rigorous self-discipline resulted, in which the needs of the body were as far as possible eliminated and its instincts, especially the sexual drive, as far as possible destroyed; or it could be held that, since it was evil, it did not matter what was done with the body, and its instincts and desires could be given full rein. The Gnostics therefore became either people who denied themselves all physical comforts or people to whom morality had ceased to have any relevance at all.

Still further, if the body was evil, clearly there could be no such thing as its resurrection. It was not the resurrection of the body but its destruction to which the Gnostics looked forward.

All this fits accurately the situation of the Pastoral Epistles. In Gnosticism, we see the intellectualism, the intellectual arrogance, the myths and the genealogies, the self-denial and the immorality, the refusal to contemplate the possibility of a bodily resurrection, which were part and parcel of the heresy against which the Pastoral Epistles were written.

One element in the heresy has not yet been fitted into place – the Judaism and the legalism of which the Pastoral Epistles speak. That too finds its place. Sometimes Gnosticism and Judaism joined hands. We have already said that the Gnostics insisted that to climb the ladder to God a very special knowledge was necessary, and that some of them insisted that for the good life a strict self-discipline was essential. It was the claim of certain of the Jews that it was precisely the Jewish law and the Jewish food regulations which provided that special knowledge and necessary self-discipline, and so there were times when Judaism and Gnosticism went hand in hand.

It is quite clear that the heresy behind the Pastoral Epistles was Gnosticism. Some have used that fact to try to prove that Paul could have had nothing to do with the writing of these letters, because, they say, Gnosticism did not emerge until much later than Paul. It is quite true that the great formal systems of Gnosticism, connected with such names as Valentinus and Basilides, did not arise until the second century; but these great figures only systematized what was already there. The basic ideas of Gnosticism were there in the atmosphere which surrounded the early Church, even in the days of Paul. It is easy to see their attraction, and also to see that, if they had been allowed to flourish unchecked, they could have turned Christianity into a speculative philosophy and wrecked it. In facing Gnosticism, the Church was facing one of the gravest dangers which ever threatened the Christian faith.

The Language of the Pastorals

The most impressive argument against the direct Pauline origin of the Pastorals is a fact which is quite clear in the Greek but not so clear in any English translation. The total number of words in the Pastoral Epistles is 902, of which fifty-four are proper names; and of these 902 words, no fewer than 306 never occur in any other of Paul's letters. That is to say, more than a third of the words in the Pastoral Epistles are totally absent from Paul's other letters. In fact, 175 words in the Pastoral Epistles occur nowhere else in the New Testament at all, although it is only fair to say that there are fifty words in the Pastoral Epistles which occur in Paul's other letters and nowhere else in the New Testament.

Further, when the other letters of Paul and the Pastorals say the same thing, they say it in different ways, using different words and different turns of speech to express the same idea.

Again, many of Paul's favourite words are entirely absent from the Pastoral Epistles. The words for the *cross* (*stauros*) and *to crucify* (*stauroun*) occur twenty-seven times in Paul's other letters, and never in the Pastorals. *Eleutheria* and the kindred words which have to do with *freedom* occur twenty-nine times in Paul's other letters, and never in the Pastorals. *Huios*, *son*, and *huiothesia*, *adoption*, occur forty-six times in Paul's other letters, and never in the Pastorals.

What is more, Greek has many more of those little words called *particles* and *enclitics* than English has. Sometimes they indicate little more than a tone of voice; every Greek sentence is joined to its predecessor by one of them; and they are often virtually untranslatable. Of these particles and enclitics, there are 112 which Paul uses altogether 932 times in his other letters that never occur in the Pastorals.

There is clearly something which has to be explained here. The vocabulary and the style make it hard to believe that Paul wrote the Pastoral Epistles in the same sense as he wrote his other letters.

Paul's Activities in the Pastorals

But perhaps the most obvious difficulty of the Pastorals is that they show Paul engaged in activities for which there is no room in his life as we know it from the Acts of the Apostles. He has clearly conducted a mission in Crete (Titus 1:5). And he proposes to spend a winter in Nicopolis, which is in Epirus (Titus 3:12). In Paul's life as we know it, that particular mission and that particular winter just cannot be fitted in. But it may well be that just here we have stumbled on the solution to the problem.

Was Paul Released from his Roman Imprisonment?

Let us sum up. We have seen that the church organization of the Pastorals is more elaborate than in any other Pauline letter. We have seen that the stress on orthodoxy sounds like second- or third-generation Christianity, when the thrill of the new discovery is wearing off and the Church is on the way to becoming an institution. We have seen that Paul is depicted as carrying out a mission or missions which cannot be fitted into the scheme of his life as we have it in Acts. But Acts leaves the question of what happened to Paul in Rome unresolved. It ends by telling us that he lived for two whole years in a kind of semi-captivity, preaching the gospel without hindrance (Acts 28:30–1). But it does not tell us how that captivity ended, whether in Paul's release or his execution. It is true that the general assumption is that it ended in his condemnation and death; but there is a by no means negligible stream of tradition which tells that it ended in his release, his liberty for two or three further years, his reimprisonment and finally his execution about the year AD 67.

Let us look at this question, for it is of considerable interest. First, it is clear that, when Paul was in prison in Rome, he did not regard release as impossible; in fact, it looks as if he expected it. When he wrote to the Philippians, he said that he was sending Timothy to them, and goes on: 'And I trust in the Lord that I will also come soon' (Philippians 2:24). When he wrote to Philemon, sending back the runaway Onesimus, he says: 'One thing more – prepare a guest room for me, for I am hoping through your prayers to be restored to you' (Philemon 22). Clearly he was prepared for release, whether or not it ever came.

Second, let us remember a plan that was very dear to Paul's heart. Before he went to Jerusalem on that journey on which he was arrested, he wrote to the church at Rome, and in that letter he is planning a visit to Spain. 'When I go to Spain . . . I do hope to see you on my journey', he writes. 'I will set out by way of you', he writes, 'to Spain' (Romans 15:24, 15:28). Was that visit ever paid?

The letter known as 1 Clement, which was sent from the Roman church to the Christians at Corinth in about AD 90, said of Paul that he preached the gospel in the east and in the west, that he instructed the whole world (that is, the Roman Empire) in righteousness, and that he went to the extremity (*terma*, the terminus) of the west before his martyrdom. What did Clement mean by *the extremity of the west*? There are many who argue that he meant nothing more than Rome. Now, it is true that someone writing some distance away in the east in Asia Minor would probably think of Rome as *the extremity of the west*. But Clement was writing from Rome, and it is difficult to see that for anyone in Rome *the extremity of the west* could be anything other than Spain. It certainly seems that Clement believed that Paul reached Spain.

The greatest of all the early Church historians was Eusebius, who was writing early in the fourth century. In his account of Paul's life, he writes: 'Luke, who wrote the Acts of the Apostles, brought his history to a close at this point, after stating that Paul had spent two whole years at Rome as a prisoner at large, and preached the word of God without constraint. Thus, after he had made his defence, it is said that the Apostle was sent again on the ministry of preaching, and that on coming to the same city a second time he suffered martyrdom' (*Ecclesiastical History*, 2:22:2). Eusebius has nothing to say about Spain, but he did know the story that Paul had been released from his first Roman imprisonment.

The Muratorian Canon, that first list of New Testament books, describes Luke's scheme in writing Acts: 'Luke related to Theophilus events of which he was an eyewitness, as also, in a separate place, he evidently declares the martyrdom of Peter [he probably refers to Luke 22:31–2]; but omits the journey of Paul from Rome to Spain.'

In the fifth century, two of the great Christian fathers are definite about this journey. John Chrysostom in his sermon on 2 Timothy 4:20 says: 'Saint Paul after his residence in Rome departed to Spain.' Jerome in his *Catalogue of Writers* says that Paul 'was dismissed by Nero that he might preach Christ's gospel in the west'.

Beyond doubt, there was a stream of tradition which held that Paul journeyed to Spain.

This is a matter on which we will have to come to our own decision. The one thing which makes us doubt the historicity of that tradition is that in Spain itself there is not, and never was, any tradition that Paul had worked and preached there – no stories about him, no places connected with his name. It would be very strange if the memory of such a visit had become totally obliterated. It could well be that the whole story of Paul's release and journey to the west arose simply as a deduction from his expressed intention to visit Spain (Romans 15). Most New Testament scholars do not think that Paul was released from his imprisonment; the general consensus of opinion is that his only release was by death.

Paul and the Pastoral Epistles

What then shall we say of Paul's connection with these letters? If we can accept the tradition of his release, and of his return to preaching and teaching, and of his death as late as AD 67, we might well believe that as they stand they came from his hand. But, if we cannot believe that – and the evidence is on the whole against it – are we to say that they have no connection with Paul at all?

We must remember that the ancient world did not think of these things as we do. It would see nothing wrong in issuing a letter under the name of a great teacher if it was sure that the letter said the things which that teacher would say under the same circumstances. To the ancient world, it was natural and entirely appropriate that a disciple should write in his master's name. No one would have seen anything wrong in one of Paul's disciples meeting a new and threatening situation with a letter under Paul's name. To regard that as forgery is to misunderstand the thinking in the ancient world. Are we then to swing completely to the other extreme and say that one of Paul's disciples issued these letters in Paul's name years after he was dead, and at a time when the Church was much more highly organized than it ever was during his lifetime?

As we see it, the answer is no. It is incredible that any disciple would put into Paul's mouth a claim to be the chief of sinners (1 Timothy 1:15); the tendency would be to stress Paul's holiness, not to talk about his sin. It is incredible that anyone writing in the name of Paul would give Timothy the homely advice to drink a little wine for the sake of his health (1 Timothy 5:23). The whole of 2 Timothy 4 is so personal and so full of intimate, loving details that no one but Paul could have written it.

Where can we find the solution? It may well be that something like this happened. It is quite obvious that many letters of Paul were lost. Apart from his great public letters, he must have had a continuous private correspondence, and of that we possess only the little letter to Philemon. It may well be that in the later days there were some fragments of Paul's correspondence in the possession of some Christian teacher. This teacher saw the church of his day and his locality in Ephesus threatened on every side. It was threatened with heresy from outside and from within. It was threatened with a fall away from its own high standards of purity and truth. The quality of its members and the standard of its office-bearers were degenerating. He had in his possession little letters of Paul which said exactly the things that should be said; but, as they stood, they were too short and too fragmentary to publish. So he amplified them and made them supremely relevant to the contemporary situation and sent them out to the church.

In the Pastoral Epistles, we are still hearing the voice of Paul, and often hearing it speak with a unique personal intimacy; but we think that the form of the letters is the work of a Christian teacher who summoned the help of Paul when the church of the day needed the guidance which only he could give.

The Letters to Timothy

1 TIMOTHY

THE ROYAL COMMAND

1 Timothy 1:1–2

> Paul, an apostle of Christ Jesus, by the royal command
> of God, our Saviour, and of Jesus Christ, our Hope,
> writes this letter to Timothy, his true child in the faith.
> Grace, mercy and peace be to you from our Lord Jesus
> Christ.

No one ever laid such weight of importance on a commission
as Paul did. He did not do this through pride; he emphasized
the value of his role in wonder that God had chosen him for a
task like that. Twice in the opening words of this letter, he
speaks of the greatness of his privilege.

(1) First, he calls himself *an apostle of Christ Jesus*.
Apostle is the Greek word *apostolos*, from the verb
apostellein, which means *to send out*; an *apostolos* was *one
who was sent out*. As far back as the time of the Greek
historian Herodotus, it means an *envoy*, an *ambassador*, one
who is sent out to represent both country and monarch. Paul
always regarded himself as the envoy and ambassador of
Christ. And, in truth, that is the office of every Christian. It is
the first duty of all ambassadors to form a liaison between
the country to which they are sent and the country from which
they have come. They form the connecting link. And the first

duty of Christians is to be a connecting link between other people and Jesus Christ.

(2) Second, he says that he is an apostle *by the royal command of God*. The word he uses is *epitagē*. This is the word in Greek for the orders which some absolutely binding law gives to an individual; for direct royal command; and above all for the instructions which come to individuals either directly or by some oracle from God. For instance, a man in an inscription dedicates an altar to the goddess Cybele *kat'epitagēn*, in accordance with the command of the goddess, which, he tells us, had come to him in a dream. Paul thought of himself as a man holding the royal commission.

If we can arrive at this consciousness of being sent out by God, a new splendour enters into life. However humble our part may be in it, we are on royal service. As the Methodist writer Rita Snowden's poem 'Through Open Windows' says:

> Life can never be dull again
> When once we've thrown our windows open wide
> And seen the mighty world that lies outside,
> And whispered to ourselves this wondrous thing,
> 'We're wanted for the business of the King!'

It is always a privilege to do even the most menial things for someone whom we love and respect and admire. Throughout life, Christians are on the business of the King.

Paul goes on to give to God and to Jesus two great titles. He speaks of God, *our Saviour*. This is a new way of speaking. We do not find this title for God in any of Paul's earlier letters. There are two elements behind this title.

(1) It comes from an Old Testament background. It is Moses' charge against Israel that Jeshurun 'abandoned God who made him, and scoffed at *the Rock of his salvation*' (Deuteronomy 32:15). The psalmist sings of how the good

will receive righteousness from *the God of their salvation* (Psalm 24:5). It is Mary's song, 'My soul magnifies the Lord, and my spirit rejoices in *God my Saviour*' (Luke 1:46–7). When Paul called God *Saviour*, he was going back to an idea which had always been dear to Israel.

(2) There is a Gentile background. It so happened that, just at this time, the title *sōtēr*, saviour, was a familiar one. It had always been used. In the old days, the Romans had called Scipio, their great general, 'our hope and our salvation'. But, at this particular time, it was the title which the Greeks gave to Aesculapius, the god of healing. And it was one of the titles which Nero, the Roman emperor, had taken for himself. So, in this opening sentence, Paul is taking the title which was repeatedly on the lips of a seeking and a wistful world and giving it to the only person to whom it belonged by right.

We must never forget that Paul called God *Saviour*. It is possible to understand the atonement in quite the wrong way. Sometimes people speak of it in a way which indicates that something Jesus did pacified the anger of God. The idea they present is that God was set on our destruction and that somehow his wrath was turned to love by Jesus. Nowhere in the New Testament is there any support for that. It was because God *loved* the world so much that he sent Jesus into the world (John 3:16). God is Saviour. We must never think or preach or teach of a God who had to be pacified and persuaded into loving us, for everything begins from his love.

THE HOPE OF THE WORLD

I Timothy I:I–2 *(contd)*

PAUL uses a title which was to become one of the great titles of Jesus – 'Christ Jesus, *our hope*'. Long ago, the psalmist had demanded: 'Why are you cast down, O my soul?' and had answered: 'Hope in God' (Psalm 43:5). Paul himself speaks of 'Christ in you, the hope of glory' (Colossians 1:27). John speaks of the dazzling prospect which confronted Christians – the prospect of being like Christ – and goes on to say: 'All who have this hope in him purify themselves, just as he is pure' (1 John 3:3).

In the early Church, this was to become one of the most precious titles of Christ. Ignatius, the first-century Bishop of Antioch, when on his way to execution in Rome, writes to the church in Ephesus: 'Be of good cheer in God the Father and in Jesus Christ our common hope' (*To the Ephesians*, 21:2). Polycarp, the second-century Bishop of Smyrna, writes: 'Let us therefore persevere in our hope and the earnest of our righteousness, who is Jesus Christ' (*Epistle of Polycarp*, 8).

(1) People found in Christ *the hope of moral victory and of self-conquest*. The ancient world was well aware of its sin. The Greek philosopher Epictetus had spoken wistfully of 'our weakness in necessary things'. Seneca, the Roman philosopher and statesman, had said that 'we hate our vices and love them at the same time'. He said: 'We have not stood bravely enough by our good resolutions; despite our will and resistance we have lost our innocence. Nor is it only that we have acted amiss; we shall do so to the end.' Persius, the Roman poet, wrote poignantly: 'Let the guilty see virtue, and pine that they have lost her forever.' Persius talks of 'filthy Natta benumbed by vice'. The ancient world knew its moral helplessness only too well; and Christ came, not only telling men and women what was right, but also giving them the power to do it. Christ gave to those who had lost it the hope of moral victory instead of defeat.

(2) People found in Christ *the hope of victory over circumstances*. Christianity came into the world in an age of the

most terrible personal insecurity. When Tacitus, the Roman historian, came to write the history of that very age in which the Christian Church came into being, he began by saying: 'I am entering upon the history of a period rich in disaster, gloomy with wars, rent with seditions; nay, savage in its very hours of peace. Four emperors perished by the sword; there were three civil wars; there were more with foreigners, and some had the character of both at once . . . Rome wasted by fires; its oldest temples burned; the very Capitol set in flames by Roman hands; the defilement of sacred rites; adultery in high places; the sea crowded with exiles; island rocks drenched with murder; yet wilder was the frenzy in Rome; nobility, wealth, the refusal of office, its acceptance, everything was a crime, and virtue was the surest way to ruin. Nor were the rewards of the informers less odious than their deeds. One found his spoils in a priesthood or a consulate; another in a provincial governorship, another behind the throne. All was one delirium of hate and terror; slaves were bribed to betray their masters, freedmen their patrons; and he who had no foe was betrayed by his friend' (*Histories*, 1-2). As the classical scholar Gilbert Murray said, the whole age was suffering from 'the failure of nerve'. People were longing for some defence to keep 'the advancing chaos of the world' at bay. It was Christ who in such times gave men and women the strength to live, and the courage, if need be, to die. In the certainty that nothing on earth could separate them from the love of God in Christ Jesus, Christians discovered the means of victory over the terrors of the age.

(3) People found in Christ *the hope of victory over death*. They found in him, at one and the same time, strength for mortal things and the immortal hope: Christ, our hope, was – and still should be – the rallying call of the Church.

TIMOTHY, MY SON

1 Timothy 1:1–2 (*contd*)

It is to Timothy that this letter is sent; and Paul was never able to speak of him without affection in his voice.

Timothy was a native of Lystra in the province of Galatia. It was a Roman colony; it called itself 'the most brilliant colony of Lystra', but in reality it was a little place on the edges of civilization. Its importance was that there was a resident Roman garrison there to keep control of the wild tribes of the Isaurian mountains which lay beyond. It was on the first missionary journey that Paul and Barnabas arrived there (Acts 14:8–21). At that time, there is no mention of Timothy; but it has been suggested that, when Paul was in Lystra, he found a lodging in Timothy's home, in view of the fact that he knew well the faith and devotion of Timothy's mother Eunice and of his grandmother Lois (2 Timothy 1:5).

On that first visit, Timothy must have been very young; but the Christian faith took hold of him, and Paul became his hero. It was at Paul's visit to Lystra on the second missionary journey that life began for Timothy (Acts 16:1–3). Young as he was, he had become a valuable member of the Christian church in Lystra. There was such a charm and enthusiasm in the young man that everyone spoke well of him. To Paul, he seemed the ideal person to be his assistant. Maybe even then he had dreams that this young man was the one to train to take over his work when the time came.

Timothy was the child of a mixed marriage: his mother was a Jew, and his father a Greek (Acts 16:1). Paul circumcised him. It was not that Paul was a slave to the Jewish law, or that he saw in circumcision any special virtue; but he knew that, if Timothy was to work among the Jews, there would be an initial prejudice against him if he was uncircumcised, and so he took this step as a practical measure to increase Timothy's usefulness as an evangelist.

From that time forward, Timothy was Paul's constant companion. He was left behind at Beroea with Silas when Paul escaped to Athens, and later joined him there (Acts 17:14–15, 18:5). He was sent as Paul's messenger to Macedonia (Acts 19:22). He was there when the collection from the churches was being taken to Jerusalem (Acts 20:4). He was with Paul in Corinth when Paul wrote his letter to Rome (Romans 16:21). He was Paul's messenger to Corinth when there was trouble in that unruly church (1 Corinthians 4:17, 16:10). He was with Paul when he wrote 2 Corinthians (2 Corinthians 1:1, 1:19). It was Timothy whom Paul sent to see how things were going in Thessalonica; and he was with Paul when he wrote his letter to that church (1 Thessalonians 1:1, 3:2, 3:6). He was with Paul in prison when he wrote to Philippi; and Paul was planning to send him to Philippi as his representative (Philippians 1:1, 2:19). He was with Paul when he wrote to the church at Colossae and to Philemon (Colossians 1:1; Philemon 1:1). Timothy was constantly by Paul's side; and, when Paul had a difficult job to do, Timothy was the one sent to do it.

Over and over again, there is affection in Paul's voice when he speaks of Timothy. When he is sending him to that sadly divided church at Corinth, he writes: 'I sent you Timothy, who is my beloved and faithful child in the Lord' (1 Corinthians 4:17). When he is planning to send him to Philippi, he writes: 'I have no one like him . . . like a son with a father he has served with me in the work of the gospel' (Philippians 2:20, 2:22). Here he calls him 'his true child'. The word that he uses for *true* is *gnēsios*. It has two meanings. It was the normal word for a *legitimate* child, as distinct from illegitimate. It was also the word for *genuine*, as opposed to counterfeit.

Timothy was the man whom Paul could trust and could send anywhere, knowing that he would go. Happy indeed is the leader who possesses a follower like that. Timothy is our example of how we should serve in the faith. Christ and his Church need servants like that.

GRACE, MERCY AND PEACE

1 Timothy 1:1-2 (*contd*)

PAUL always began his letters with a blessing (Romans 1:7; 1 Corinthians 1:3; 2 Corinthians 1:2; Galatians 1:3; Ephesians 1:2; Philippians 1:2; Colossians 1:2; 1 Thessalonians 1:1; 2 Thessalonians 1:2; Philemon 3). In all these other letters, only *grace* and *peace* occur. It is only in the letters to Timothy that *mercy* is used (2 Timothy 1:2; Titus 1:4). Let us look at these three great words.

(1) In *grace*, there are always three dominant ideas.

(a) In classical Greek, the word means outward grace or favour, beauty, attractiveness, sweetness. Usually, although not always, it is applied to persons. The English word *charm* comes near to expressing its meaning. Grace is characteristically a lovely and an attractive thing.

(b) In the New Testament, there is always the idea of sheer generosity. Grace is something unearned and undeserved. It is the opposite of a *debt*. Paul says that, if it is a case of earning things, the reward is a matter not of grace but of debt (Romans 4:4). It stands in opposition to *works*. Paul says that God's election of his chosen people is the consequence not of works but of grace (Romans 11:6).

(c) In the New Testament, there is always the idea of sheer *universality*. Again and again, Paul uses the word *grace* in

connection with the reception of the Gentiles into the family
of God. He thanks God for the grace given to the Corinthians
in Jesus Christ (1 Corinthians 1:4). He talks of the grace of
God bestowed on the churches of Macedonia (2 Corinthians
8:1). He talks of the Galatians being called into the grace of
Christ (Galatians 1:6). The hope which came to the
Thessalonians came through grace (2 Thessalonians 2:16). It
was God's grace which made Paul an apostle to the Gentiles
(1 Corinthians 15:10). It was by the grace of God that he
moved among the Corinthians (2 Corinthians 1:12). It was
by grace that God called him and set him apart before birth
(Galatians 1:15). It is the grace given to him by God which
enables him to write boldly to the church at Rome (Romans
15:15). To Paul, the great demonstration of the grace of God
was the reception of the Gentiles into the Church and his
apostleship to them.

Grace is a lovely thing; it is a free thing; and it is a universal
thing. As the New Testament scholar F. J. A. Hort wrote so
beautifully: 'Grace is a comprehensive word, gathering up
all that may be supposed to be expressed in the smile of a
heavenly king, looking down upon his people.'

(2) *Peace* was the normal Jewish word of greeting; and,
in Hebrew thought, it expresses not simply the negative
absence of trouble but 'the most comprehensive form of
wellbeing'. It is everything which makes for our highest good.
It is the state that we are in when we are within the love of
God. Hort writes: 'Peace is the antithesis to every kind of
conflict and war and molestation, to enmity without and
distraction within.' As John Newton's hymn has it:

> Bowed down beneath a load of sin,
>   By Satan sorely pressed,
> By war without and fears within,
>   I come to thee for rest.

(3) *Mercy* is the new word in the apostolic blessing. In Greek the word is *eleos*, and in Hebrew *chesedh*. Now *chesedh* is the word which in the Old Testament is often translated as *loving kindness*; and, when Paul prayed for *mercy* on Timothy, he is saying, to put it very simply: 'Timothy, may God be good to you.' But there is more to it than that. *Chesedh* is used in the Psalms no fewer than 127 times. And, time and time again, it has the meaning of *help in time of need*. It denotes, as the commentator R. St John Parry puts it, 'God's active intervention to help'. As Hort puts it, 'It is the coming down of the Most High to help the helpless.' In Psalm 40:11, the psalmist rejoices: 'Your steadfast love and your faithfulness keep me safe for ever.' In Psalm 57:3, he says: 'He will send from heaven and save me . . . God will send forth his steadfast love and his faithfulness.' In Psalm 86:14–16, he thinks of the forces of the evil people which rise against him, and comforts himself with the thought that God is 'abounding in steadfast love and faithfulness'. It is by God's abundant mercy that he has given us the living hope of the resurrection (1 Peter 1:3). The Gentiles should glorify God for that mercy which has rescued them from sin and hopelessness (Romans 15:9). God's mercy is God active to save. It may well be that Paul added *mercy* to his two usual words, *grace* and *peace*, because Timothy was up against it and Paul wanted in one word to tell him that the Most High was the help of the helpless.

ERROR AND HERESY

1 Timothy 1:3–7

> I am writing to you now to reinforce the plea that I already made to you, when I urged you to stay in

Ephesus while I went to Macedonia, that you might
pass on the order to some of the people there, not to
teach erroneous novelties, nor to give their attention to
idle tales and endless genealogies, which only succeed
in producing empty speculations rather than the
effective administration of God's people, which should
be based on faith. The instruction which I gave you is
designed to produce love which issues from a pure heart,
a good conscience and an undissembling faith. But some
of these people of whom I am talking have never even
tried to find the right road, and have turned aside out of
it to empty and useless discussions, in their claim to
become teachers of the law, although they do not know
what they are talking about, nor do they realize the real
meaning of the things about which they dogmatize.

It is clear that behind the Pastoral Epistles there is some
heresy which is endangering the Church. Right at the
beginning, we should try to see what this heresy is. We will
therefore collect the facts about it now.

This passage brings us face to face with two of its main
characteristics. It dealt in *idle tales* and *endless genealogies*.
These two things were not peculiar to this heresy but were
deeply ingrained in the thought of the ancient world.

First, the *idle tales*. One of the characteristics of the ancient
world was that the poets and even the historians loved to
work out romantic and fictitious tales about the foundation
of cities and of families. They would tell how some god came
to earth and founded the city or took in marriage a mortal
woman and founded a family. The ancient world was full of
stories like that.

Second, the *endless genealogies*. The ancient world had
a passion for genealogies. We can see this even in the Old
Testament with its chapters of names and in the New

Testament with the genealogies of Jesus with which Matthew and Luke begin their gospels. A man like Alexander the Great had a completely artificial pedigree constructed in which he traced his lineage back on the one side to Achilles and Andromache and on the other to Perseus and Hercules.

It would be the easiest thing in the world for Christianity to get lost in endless fables and stories about origins and in elaborate and imaginary genealogies. That was a danger which was fundamental to the situation in which Christian thought was developing.

It was peculiarly threatening from two directions.

It was threatening from the *Jewish* direction. To the Jews, there was no book in the world like the Old Testament. Their scholars spent a lifetime studying it and expounding it. In the Old Testament, many chapters and many sections are long genealogies; and one of the favourite occupations of the Jewish scholars was to construct an imaginary and inspiring biography for every name in the list! People could go on doing that forever; and it may be that that was what was partly in Paul's mind. He may be saying: 'When you ought to be working at the Christian life, you are working out imaginary biographies and genealogies. You are wasting your time on trivia when you should be getting down to life and living.' This may be a warning to us never to allow Christian thinking to get lost in speculations which do not matter.

THE SPECULATIONS OF THE GREEKS

1 Timothy 1:3–7 (*contd*)

BUT this danger came with an even greater threat from the *Greek* side. At this time in history, a Greek line of thought was developing which came to be known as *Gnosticism*. We find it especially in the background of the Pastoral Epistles, the Letter to the Colossians and the Fourth Gospel.

Gnosticism was entirely speculative. It began with the problem of the origin of sin and of suffering. If God is altogether good, he could not have created them. How then did they get into the world? The Gnostic answer was that creation was not creation out of nothing; before time began, *matter* existed. They believed that this matter was essentially imperfect and evil; and out of this essentially evil matter the world was created.

No sooner had they reached this point than they ran into another difficulty. If matter is essentially evil and God is essentially good, matter could not have been touched by God. So they began another set of speculations. They said that God put out an emanation, a divine power, and that this emanation put out another emanation, and the second emanation put out a third emanation, and so on and on until there came into being an emanation so distant from God that he could handle matter; and that it was not God but this emanation who created the world.

They went further. They held that each successive emanation knew less about God, so that there came a stage in the series of emanations when the emanations were completely ignorant of him – and, more, there was a final stage when the emanations were not only ignorant of God but actively hostile to him. So they arrived at the thought that the god who created the world was quite ignorant of and hostile to the true God. Later on, they went even further and identified the God of the Old Testament with this creating god, and the God of the New Testament with the true God.

They further provided each one of the emanations with a complete biography. And so they built up an elaborate mythology of gods and emanations, each with a story, a biography and a genealogy. There is no doubt that the ancient world was riddled with that kind of thinking, and that it even entered the Church itself. It made Jesus merely the greatest of the emanations, the divine power closest to God. It placed him as the highest link in the endless chain between God and human beings.

This Gnostic line of thought had certain characteristics which appear all through the Pastoral Epistles as the characteristics of those whose heresies were threatening the Church and the purity of the faith.

(1) Gnosticism was obviously highly speculative, and it was therefore intensely intellectually snobbish. It believed that all this intellectual speculation was quite beyond the mental grasp of ordinary people and was for a chosen few, the elite of the Church. So, Timothy is warned against 'profane chatter and contradictions of what is falsely called knowledge' (1 Timothy 6:20). He is warned against a religion of speculative questions instead of humble faith (1 Timothy 1:4). He is warned against the one who is conceited but really understands nothing and who loves controversy and disputes about words (1 Timothy 6:4). He is told to shun 'profane chatter', for it can produce only ungodliness (2 Timothy 2:16). He is told to avoid 'stupid and senseless controversies' which in the end can only lead to strife (2 Timothy 2:23). Further, the Pastoral Epistles go out of their way to stress the fact that this idea of an intellectual aristocracy is quite wrong, for God's love is universal. God wants *everyone* to be saved and *everyone* to come to a knowledge of the truth (1 Timothy 2:4). God is the Saviour of *all*, especially those who believe (1 Timothy 4:10). The Christian Church would have nothing to do with any kind of faith which was founded on intellectual speculation and which set up an arrogant intellectual elite.

(2) Gnosticism was concerned with this long series of emanations. It gave to each of them a biography and a pedigree and an importance in the chain between God and human beings. These Gnostics were concerned with 'endless genealogies' (1 Timothy 1:4). They went in for 'profane myths' about them (1 Timothy 4:7). They turned their ears away from the truth to myths (2 Timothy 4:4). They dealt in fables like the Jewish myths (Titus 1:14). Worst of all, they thought in terms of two gods and of Jesus as one of a whole series of mediators between God and human beings, whereas 'there is one God; there is also one mediator between God and humankind, Christ Jesus, himself human' (1 Timothy 2:5). There is only one King of the ages, immortal, invisible; there is only one God (1 Timothy 1:17). Christianity had to renounce a religion which took the unique place from God and from Jesus Christ.

THE ETHICS OF HERESY

1 Timothy 1:3–7 (*contd*)

THE danger of Gnosticism was not only intellectual. It also had serious moral and ethical consequences. We must remember that its basic belief was that matter was essentially evil and that spirit alone was good. That had two opposite results.

(1) If matter is evil, the body is evil; and the body must be despised and held in check. Therefore Gnosticism could and did result in strict abstinence. It forbade marriage, for the instincts of the body were to be suppressed. It laid down strict food laws, for the needs of the body must as far as possible be eliminated. So the Pastorals speak of those who forbid marriage and who demand abstinence from foods (1 Timothy

4:3). The answer to these people is that everything which God has created is good and is to be received with thanksgiving (1 Timothy 4:4). The Gnostics looked on creation as an evil thing, the work of an evil god; Christians look on creation as a fine thing, the gift of a good God. Christians live in a world where all things are pure; the Gnostics lived in a world where all things were corrupt (Titus 1:15).

(2) But Gnosticism could result in precisely the opposite ethical belief. If the body is evil, it does not matter what is done with it. Therefore, let people satisfy their appetites. These things are of no importance; therefore people can use their bodies in the most promiscuous way and it makes no difference. So the Pastorals speak of those who lead away weak women until they are overwhelmed by sin and become the victims of all kinds of desires (2 Timothy 3:6). Such people profess to know God, but they deny him by their actions (Titus 1:16). They used their religious beliefs as an excuse for immorality.

(3) Gnosticism had another consequence. Christians believe in the resurrection of the body. That is not to say that they ever believed that we are resurrected with this mortal, human body; but they always believed that, after resurrection from the dead, people would have spiritual bodies, provided by God. Paul discusses this whole question in 1 Corinthians 15. The Gnostics held that there was no such thing as the resurrection of the body (2 Timothy 2:18). After death, the individual would be a kind of disembodied spirit. The basic difference is that the Gnostics believed in the body's destruction; Christians believe in its redemption. The Gnostics believed in what they would call *soul salvation*; Christians believe in *whole salvation*.

So, behind the Pastoral Epistles there are dangerous heretics who gave their lives to intellectual speculations, who saw this as an evil world and saw the creating god as evil, who put between the world and God an endless series of emanations and lesser gods and spent their time equipping each of them with endless fables and genealogies, who reduced Jesus to the position of a link in a chain and took away his uniqueness, who lived either in rigorous self-denial or unrestrained immorality, and who denied the resurrection of the body. It was to combat their heretical beliefs that the Pastorals were written.

THE MIND OF THE HERETIC

1 Timothy 1:3–7 (*contd*)

IN this passage, there is a clear picture of the mind of the dangerous heretic. There is a kind of heresy in which people differ from orthodox belief because they have honestly thought things out and cannot agree with it. They do not take any pride in being different; they are different simply because they have to be. Such a heresy does not spoil a person's character but rather enhances it, because the individual has really thought out a personal faith and is not living on a second-hand orthodoxy. But that is not the kind of heretic whose picture is drawn here. Here, five characteristics of dangerous heretics are distinguished.

(1) They are driven by the desire for novelty. They are like people who must be part of the latest fashion and the latest craze. They despise old things for no better reason than that they are old, and desire new things for no better reason than that they are new. Christianity always has the problem of presenting old truth in a new way. The truth does not change, but every age must find its own way of presenting it. Every teacher and preacher must speak in language which is

easily understood. The old truth and the new presentation must always go hand in hand.

(2) They praise the intellect at the expense of the heart. Their conception of religion is speculation and not experience. Christianity has never demanded that people should stop thinking for themselves, but it does demand that their thinking should be dominated by a personal experience of Jesus Christ.

(3) They deal in argument instead of action. They are more interested in obscure discussion than in the effective administration of the household of the faith. They forget that the truth is not only something to be accepted with the mind but is also something which must be translated into action. Long ago, the distinction between Greeks and Jews was drawn. The Greeks loved argument for the sake of argument; there was nothing that they liked better than to sit with a group of friends, indulge in a series of mental acrobatics and enjoy 'the stimulus of a mental hike'. But they were not particularly interested in reaching conclusions or in evolving a principle of *action*. The Jews, too, liked argument; but they wanted every argument to end in a decision which demanded action. There is always a danger of heresy when we fall in love with words and forget deeds, for deeds are the acid test by which every argument must be tested.

(4) They are moved by arrogance rather than by humility. They look down with a certain contempt on people who cannot follow their flights of intellectual speculation. They regard those who do not share their conclusions as ignorant fools. Christians somehow have to combine an immovable certainty with a gentle humility.

(5) They are guilty of dogmatism without knowledge. They do not really know what they are talking about nor really understand the significance of the things about which they are so dogmatic. The strange thing about religious argument

is that we all think that we have a right to express a dogmatic opinion. In all other fields, we demand that people should have a certain level of knowledge before they lay down the law. But there are those who dogmatize about the Bible and its teaching although they have never even tried to find out what the experts in language and history have said. It may well be that the Christian cause has suffered more from ignorant dogmatism than from anything else.

When we think of the characteristics of those who were troubling the church at Ephesus, we can see that their descendants are still with us.

THE MIND OF THE CHRISTIAN THINKER

1 Timothy 1:3-7 (*contd*)

As this passage draws the picture of the thinker who disturbs the Church, it also draws the picture of those who are true Christian thinkers. Again, there are five characteristics.

(1) Their thinking is based on *faith*. Faith means taking God at his word; it means believing that he is as Jesus proclaimed him to be. That is to say, Christian thinkers begin from the principle that Jesus Christ has given the full revelation of God.

(2) Their thinking is motivated by *love*. Paul's whole purpose is to produce love. To think in love will always save us from certain things. It will save us from *arrogant* thinking. It will save us from *contemptuous* thinking. It will save us from *condemning* either that with which we do not agree or that which we do not understand. It will save us from expressing our views in such a way that we hurt other people. Love saves us from *destructive thinking* and *destructive speaking*. To think in love is always to think in sympathy. Those who

argue in love argue not to defeat an opponent but to win that opponent over.

(3) Their thinking comes from a *pure heart*. Here, the word used is very significant. It is *katharos*, which originally simply meant *clean* as opposed to *soiled* or *dirty*. Later, it came to have certain more specific uses. It was used of corn that had been winnowed and cleansed of all chaff. It was used of an army which had been purified of all cowardly and un-disciplined soldiers until there was nothing left but first-class fighting men. It was used of something which was without any contaminating impurity. So, a pure heart is a heart whose motives are absolutely pure and absolutely unmixed. In the hearts of Christian thinkers, there is no desire to show how clever they are, no desire to win a purely debating victory, no desire to show up the ignorance of opponents. Their only desire is to help and to shed light and to lead others nearer to God. Christian thinkers are moved only by love of truth and love for others.

(4) Their thinking comes from a *good conscience*. The Greek word for *conscience* is *suneidēsis*. It literally means a *knowing with*. The real meaning of conscience is a *knowing with oneself*. To have a good conscience is to be able to look in the face the knowledge which one shares with no one but oneself and not to be ashamed. The American essayist Ralph Waldo Emerson remarked of Seneca that he said the loveliest things, if only he had had the right to say them. Christian thinkers are men and women whose thoughts and whose actions give them the right to say what they do – and that is the most acid test of all.

(5) Christian thinkers are men and women of *undis-sembling faith*. The phrase literally means the faith *in which there is no hypocrisy*. That simply means that the great characteristic of Christian thinkers is *sincerity*. They are

sincere both in their desire to find the truth and in their desire to communicate it.

THOSE WHO NEED NO LAW

1 Timothy 1:8–11

> We know that the law is good, if a man uses it legiti-mately, in the awareness that the law was not instituted to deal with good men, but with the lawless and the undisciplined, the irreverent and the sinners, the impious and the polluted, those who have sunk so low that they strike their fathers and their mothers, murderers, fornicators, homosexuals, slave-dealers and kidnappers, liars, perjurers, and all those who are guilty of anything which is the reverse of sound teaching, that teaching which is in accordance with the glorious gospel of the blessed God, that gospel which has been entrusted to me.

This passage begins with what was a favourite thought in the ancient world. The place of the law is to deal with evildoers. The good do not need any law to control their actions or to threaten them with punishments; and, in a world where everyone was good, there would be no need for laws at all.

Antiphanes, the Greek, had it: 'He who does no wrong needs no law.' It was the claim of Aristotle that 'philosophy enables a man to do without external control that which others do because of fear of the laws'. Ambrose, the great fourth-century Bishop of Milan, wrote: 'The just man has the law of his own mind, of his own equity and of his own justice as his standard; and therefore he is not recalled from fault by terror of punishment, but by the rule of honour.' Both Christians and non-Christians regarded true goodness as something which had its source in the human heart – as something which was not dependent on the rewards and punishments of the law.

But in one thing they differed. The non-Christians looked back to an ancient golden age when all things were good and no law was needed. Ovid, the Roman poet, drew one of the most famous pictures of that ancient golden age (*Metamorphoses*, 1:90–112). 'Golden was that first age, which, with no one to compel, without a law, of its own will, kept faith and did the right. There was no fear of punishment; no threatening words were to be read on brazen tablets; no suppliant throng gazed fearfully upon the judge's face; but without judges men lived secure. Not yet had the pine tree, felled on its native mountains, descended thence into the watery plain to visit other lands; men knew no shores except their own. Nor yet were cities begirt with steep moats; there were no trumpets of straight, no horns of curving brass, no swords or helmets. There was no need at all of armed men; for nations, secure from war's alarms, passed the years in gentle peace.' Tacitus, the Roman historian, had the same picture (*Annals*, 3:26). 'In the earliest times, when men had as yet no evil passions, they led blameless, guiltless lives, without either punishment or restraint. Led by their own nature to pursue none but virtuous ends, they required no rewards; and as they desired nothing contrary to the right, there was no need for pains and penalties.' The ancient world looked back and longed for the days that were gone. But the Christian faith does not look back to a lost golden age; it looks forward to the day when the only law will be the love of Christ within an individual's heart, for it is certain that the day of law cannot end until the day of love dawns.

There should be only one controlling factor in the lives of every one of us. Our goodness should come not from fear of the law, not even from fear of judgment, but from fear of disappointing the love of Christ and of grieving the fatherly heart of God. The driving force for Christians comes from the fact that they know that sin is not only breaking God's law but also breaking his heart. It is not the law of God but the love of God which urges us on.

THOSE WHOM THE LAW CONDEMNS

1 Timothy 1:8–11 (contd)

IN an ideal state, when the kingdom comes, there will be no need for any law other than the love of God within our hearts; but, as things are, the case is very different. And here Paul sets out a catalogue of sins which the law must control and condemn. The interest of the passage is that it shows us the background against which Christianity grew up. This list of sins is in fact a description of the world in which the early Christians lived and moved and had their being. Nothing shows us so well how the Christian Church was a little island of purity in a vicious world. We talk about it being hard to be a Christian in modern civilization; we have only to read a passage like this to see how infinitely harder it must have been in the circumstances in which the Church first began. Let us take this terrible list and look at the items on it.

There are the *lawless* (*anomoi*). They are those who know the laws of right and wrong and who break them open-eyed. No one can blame people for breaking a law they do not know exists; but the *lawless* are those who deliberately violate the laws in order to satisfy their own ambitions and desires.

There are the *undisciplined* (*anhupotaktoi*). They are the unruly and the insubordinate, those who refuse to obey any authority. They are like soldiers who mutinously disobey the word of command. They are either too proud or too lacking in self-restraint to accept any control.

There are the *irreverent* (*asebeis*). *Asebēs* is a terrible word. It describes not indifference nor the lapse into sin. It describes 'positive and active irreligion', the spirit which defiantly withholds from God that which is his right. It describes human nature 'in direct conflict with God'.

There are the *sinners* (*hamartōloi*). In its most common usage, this word describes character. It describes the person who has no moral standards left.

There are the *impious* (*anosioi*). *Hosios* is a noble word. The things which are *hosios* are part of the very constitution of the universe, the things which all held sacred. The Greeks, for instance, declared with a shudder that the Egyptian custom where brother could marry sister and the Persian custom where son could marry mother were *anosia*, *unholy*. The person who is *anosios* is worse than a mere law-breaker, because such a person violates the ultimate decencies of life.

There are the *polluted* (*bebēloi*). *Bebēlos* is an ugly word with a strange history. It originally meant simply *that which can be trodden upon*, as against that which is sacred to some god and therefore untouchable. It came to mean *profane* in opposition to *sacred*, and then the one who profanes the sacred things, the person who desecrates God's day, disobeys his laws and belittles his worship. Everything touched by the one who is *bebēlos* becomes contaminated.

There are *those who strike or even kill their parents* (*patralōai* and *mētralōai*). Under Roman law, a son who struck his parents could be put to death. The words describe sons or daughters who have no sense of gratitude, respect or even shame. And it must always be remembered that this most cruel of blows can be one not upon the body but upon the heart.

There are the *murderers* (*androphonoi*), literally *man-slayers*. Paul is thinking of the Ten Commandments and of how the breaking of these laws characterizes the Gentile world. We must not think that this has nothing to do with us, for Jesus widened the commandment to include not only the act of murder but also the feeling of anger against a brother or sister.

There are the *fornicators and the homosexuals* (*pornoi* and *arsenokoitai*). It is difficult for us to realize the state of the ancient world in matters of sexual morality. There was a great deal of promiscuity. One of the extraordinary things was the actual connection of immorality and religion. The Temple of Aphrodite, goddess of love, at Corinth had attached to it 1,000 priestesses who were sacred prostitutes and who in the evening came down to the city streets and plied their trade. It is said that Solon was the first law-maker in Athens to legalize prostitution and that, with the profits of the public brothels that he instituted, a new temple was built to Aphrodite, the goddess of love.

It is an extraordinary thing that, outside Christianity, time and time again, immorality and obscenity flourish under the very protection of religion. It has often been said, and said truly, that chastity was the one completely new virtue which Christianity brought into this world. It was no easy thing in the early days to endeavour to live according to the Christian ethic in a world like that.

There are the *andrapodistai*. The word may either mean *slave-dealers* or *slave-kidnappers*. Possibly both meanings are involved here. It is true that slavery was an integral part of the ancient world. It is true that Aristotle declared that civilization was founded on slavery, that certain men and women existed only to perform the menial tasks of life for the convenience of the cultured classes. But, even in the ancient world, voices were raised against slavery. The Jewish writer Philo spoke of slave-dealers as those 'who despoil men of their most precious possession, their freedom'.

But this more probably refers to those who kidnapped slaves. Slaves were valuable property. An especially accomplished slave would fetch three or four times as much as an ordinary slave with no special gifts. Beautiful youths were in special demand as pages and cupbearers. Marcus Antonius is said to have paid the equivalent of several thousand pounds for two well-matched youths who were wrongly represented to be twins. In the days when Rome was especially eager to learn the arts of Greece, slaves who were skilled in Greek literature and music and art were particularly valuable. The result was that, frequently, valuable slaves were either seduced from their masters or kidnapped. The kidnapping of especially beautiful or especially accomplished slaves was a common feature of ancient life.

Finally, there are *liars* (*pseustai*) and *perjurers* (*epiorkoi*), those who did not hesitate to twist the truth to achieve dishonourable ends.

Here is a vivid picture of the atmosphere in which the ancient Church grew up. It was against an infection like that that the writer of the Pastorals sought to protect the Christians in his charge.

THE CLEANSING WORD

1 Timothy 1:8–11 (*contd*)

INTO this world came the Christian message; and this passage tells us four things about it.

(1) It is *sound* teaching. The word used for sound (*hugiainein*) literally means *health-giving*. Christianity is an

ethical religion. It demands the living of a good life. It must always be remembered that Christianity does not mean observing a ritual, even if that ritual consists of Bible-reading and church-going; it means living a good life. Christianity, if it is real, is health-giving; it is the moral antiseptic which alone can cleanse life.

(2) It is a *glorious gospel*; that is to say, it is *glorious good news*. It is good news of forgiveness for past sins and of power to conquer sin in the days to come, good news of God's mercy, God's cleansing and God's grace.

(3) It is good news *which comes from God*. The Christian gospel is not something which people discovered for themselves; it is something revealed by God. It does not only offer mutual support and assistance; it offers the power of God.

(4) That good news *comes through men and women*. It was entrusted to Paul to bring it to others. God makes his offer, and he needs his messengers. Real Christians are people who have themselves taken up the offer of God and have realized that they cannot keep such good news to themselves but must share it with others who have not yet found it.

SAVED TO SERVE

I Timothy 1:12–17

> I give thanks to Jesus Christ, our Lord, who has filled me with his power, that he showed that he believed that he could trust me, by appointing me to his service, although I was formerly an insulter, a persecutor and a man of insolent and brutal violence. But I received mercy from him, because it was in ignorance that I acted thus, in the days when I did not believe. But the grace of our Lord rose higher than my sin, and I found it in the faith and love of those whose lives are lived in Jesus

Christ. This is a saying on which we can rely, and which
we are completely bound to accept, that Christ Jesus
came into the world to save sinners – of whom I am
chief. This was why I received mercy – so that in me
Jesus Christ might display all that patience of his,
so that I might be the first outline sketch of those
who would one day come to believe in him, that they
might find eternal life. To the King, eternal, immortal,
invisible, to the only God, be honour and glory for ever
and ever. Amen.

THIS passage begins with a joyful pouring forth of thanks.
There were four tremendous things for which Paul wished to
thank Jesus Christ.

(1) He thanked Jesus because Jesus *chose* him. Paul never
had the feeling that he had chosen Christ, but always that
Christ had chosen him. It was as if, when he was heading
straight for destruction, Jesus Christ had laid his hand upon
his shoulder and stopped him in his tracks. It was as if, when
he was busy throwing away his life, Jesus Christ had suddenly
brought him to his senses.

In the days of the Second World War, I knew a Polish
airman. He had crowded more thrilling and close escapes
from death and from worse into a few years than the vast
majority of people do into a lifetime. Sometimes he would
tell the story of escape from occupied Europe, of parachute
descents from the air, of rescue from the sea – and, at the end
of this amazing account of his exploits, he would always say,
with a look of wonder in his eyes: 'And now I belong to
God.' That is how Paul felt; he was Christ's man, for Christ
had chosen him.

(2) He thanked Jesus because Jesus *trusted* him. It was
to Paul an amazing thing that he, the chief persecutor,
had been chosen as the missionary of Christ. It was not

only that Jesus Christ had forgiven him; it was that Christ trusted him. Sometimes we forgive people who have made mistakes or been guilty of some sin, but we make it very clear that their past makes it impossible for us to trust them again with any responsibility. But Christ had not only forgiven Paul; he entrusted him with work to do. The man who had been Christ's persecutor had been made his ambassador.

(3) He thanked Jesus because Jesus had *appointed* him. We must be very careful to note to what purpose Paul felt he had been appointed. He was appointed to *service*. Paul never thought of himself as appointed to honour, or to leadership within the Church. He was saved to serve. Plutarch tells that, when a Spartan won a victory in the games, his reward was that he might stand beside his king in battle. A Spartan wrestler at the Olympic Games was offered a very considerable bribe to abandon the struggle, but he refused. Finally, after a terrific effort, he won his victory. Someone said to him: 'Well, Spartan, what have you got out of this costly victory you have won?' He answered: 'I have won the privilege of standing in front of my king in battle.' His reward was to serve and, if need be, to die for his king. It was for service, not honour, that Paul knew that he had been chosen.

(4) He thanked Jesus because Jesus had *empowered* him. Paul had long since discovered that Jesus Christ never gives anyone a task to do without also giving the power to do it. Paul would never have said: 'See what I have done', but always 'See what Jesus Christ has enabled me to do.' No one is good enough, or strong enough, or pure enough, or wise enough to be the servant of Christ. But, if we give ourselves to Christ, we will go forward not in our own strength but in the strength of our Lord.

THE MEANS OF CONVERSION

1 Timothy 1:12–17 (*contd*)

THERE are two further interesting things in this passage.

Paul's Jewish background comes out. He says that Jesus Christ had mercy on him because he had committed his sins against Christ and his Church in the days of his ignorance. We often think that the Jewish viewpoint was that sacrifice atoned for sin; people sinned, that sin broke the relationship with God, then sacrifice was made, and God's anger was appeased and the relationship restored.

It may well have been that that was in fact the popular, devalued view of sacrifice. But the highest Jewish thought insisted on two things. First, it insisted that sacrifice could never atone for deliberate sin but only for the sins committed in ignorance or in a moment of passion. Second, the highest Jewish thought insisted that no sacrifice could atone for any sin unless there was sorrow and remorse in the heart of the one who brought it. Here, Paul is speaking out of his Jewish background. His heart had been broken by the mercy of Christ; his sins had been committed in the days before he knew Christ and his love. And, for these reasons, he felt that there was mercy for him.

There is a still more interesting matter, which is pointed out by E. F. Brown in his commentary. Verse 14 is difficult. In the Revised Standard Version, it runs: 'The grace of our Lord overflowed for me with the faith and love that are in Christ Jesus.' The first part is not difficult; it simply means that the grace of God rose higher than Paul's sin. But what exactly is the meaning of the phrase 'with the faith and love that are in Christ Jesus'? Brown suggests that it means that the work of the grace of Christ in Paul's heart was helped by the faith and the love he found in the members of the Christian

Church. The effect of the grace of Christ was aided by things like the sympathy and the understanding and the kindness he received from men like Ananias, who opened his eyes and called him *brother* (Acts 9:10–19), and Barnabas, who stood by him when the rest of the Church regarded him with bleak suspicion (Acts 9:26–8). That is a very lovely idea. And, if it is correct, we can see that there are three factors which co-operate in the conversion of any individual.

(1) First, there is God. It was the prayer of Jeremiah: 'Restore us to yourself, O Lord' (Lamentations 5:21). As St Augustine had it, we would never even have begun to seek for God unless he had already found us. The prime mover is God; behind the first desire for goodness felt by anyone, there is his seeking love.

(2) There is the human response. The Authorized Version renders Matthew 18:3 entirely passively: 'Except ye *be converted* and become as little children, ye shall not enter into the kingdom of heaven.' The Revised Standard Version gives a much more active rendering: 'Unless you *turn* and become like children, you will never enter the kingdom of heaven.' There must be human response to divine appeal. God gave us free will, and we can use it either to accept or to refuse his offer.

(3) There is the influence and intervention of a Christian. It is Paul's conviction that he is sent to open the eyes of the Gentiles, 'that they may turn from darkness to light and from the power of Satan to God, so that they may receive forgiveness of sins' (Acts 26:18). It is James' belief that anyone who converts the sinner from error 'will save the sinner's soul from death and will cover a multitude of sins' (James 5:20). So, there is a double duty laid upon us. It has been said that a saint is someone who makes it easier to believe in God, and that a saint is someone in whom Christ

lives again. We must give thanks for those who showed us Christ, whose words and example brought us to him, and we must strive to be the influence which brings others to him.

In this matter of conversion, the initiative of God, the response of the individual and the influence of Christians all combine.

THE UNFORGOTTEN SHAME
AND THE UNDYING INSPIRATION

1 Timothy 1:12–17 (contd)

THE thing which stands out in this passage is Paul's insistence on remembering his own sin. He piles up his words on top of one another to show the awfulness of what he had done to Christ and the Church. He was an *insulter* of the Church; he had flung hot and angry words at the Christians, accusing them of crimes against God. He was a *persecutor*; he had taken every means open to him under the Jewish law to annihilate the Christian Church. Then comes a terrible word; he had been *a man of insolent and brutal violence*. The word in Greek is *hubristēs*. It indicates a kind of arrogant sadism; it describes someone who is out to inflict pain for the sheer joy of inflicting it. The corresponding abstract noun is *hubris*, which Aristotle defines: '*Hubris* means to hurt and to grieve people, in such a way that shame comes to the man who is hurt and grieved, and not that the person who inflicts the hurt and injury may gain anything else in addition to what he already possesses, but simply that he may find delight in his own cruelty and in the suffering of the other person.'

That is what Paul was once like with regard to the Christian Church. Not content with words of insult, he went to the limit of legal persecution. Not content with legal persecution, he went to the limit of sadistic brutality in his attempt to stamp out the Christian faith. He remembered that; and to the end of the day he continued to regard himself as the chief of sinners. It is not that he *was* the chief of sinners; he still *is*. True, he could never forget that he was a forgiven sinner; but neither could he ever forget that he was a sinner. Why should he remember his sin with such vividness?

(1) The memory of his sin was the surest way to keep him from pride. There could be no such thing as spiritual pride for someone who had done the things that he had done. John Newton was one of the great preachers and the supreme hymn-writers of the Church of the eighteenth century, but he had sunk to the lowest depths to which anyone can sink in the days when he had sailed the seas in a slave-trader's ship. So, when he became a converted man and a preacher of the gospel, he wrote a text in great letters and fastened it above the mantelpiece of his study where he could not fail to see it: 'Thou shalt remember that thou wast a bondman in the land of Egypt and the Lord thy God redeemed thee.' He also composed his own epitaph: 'John Newton, Clerk, once an Infidel and Libertine, a Servant of Slaves in Africa, was, by the Mercy of our Lord and Saviour Jesus Christ, Preserved, Restored, Pardoned, and Appointed to Preach the Faith he had so long laboured to destroy.' John Newton never forgot that he was a forgiven sinner; neither did Paul. Neither must we. It does us good to remember our sins; it saves us from spiritual pride.

(2) The memory of his sin was the surest way to keep his gratitude burning. To remember what we have been forgiven is the surest way to keep awake our love to Jesus Christ. The old Puritan Thomas Goodwin wrote a letter to his son: 'When I was threatening to become cold in my ministry, and when I

felt Sabbath morning coming and my heart not filled with amazement at the grace of God, or when I was making ready to dispense the Lord's Supper, do you know what I used to do? I used to take a turn up and down among the sins of my past life, and I always came down again with a broken and a contrite heart, ready to preach, as it was preached in the beginning, the forgiveness of sins. I do not think I ever went up the pulpit stair that I did not stop for a moment at the foot of it and take a turn up and down among the sins of my past years. I do not think that I ever planned a sermon that I did not take a turn round my study table and look back at the sins of my youth and of all my life down to the present; and many a Sabbath morning, when my soul had been cold and dry, for the lack of prayer during the week, a turn up and down in my past life before I went into the pulpit always broke my hard heart and made me close with the gospel for my own soul before I began to preach.' When we remember how we have hurt God, hurt those who love us and hurt others, and when we remember how God and our neighbours have forgiven us, that memory must awake the flame of gratitude within our hearts.

(3) The memory of his sin was the constant urge to greater effort. It is quite true that we can never earn the approval of God, or deserve his love; but it is also true that we can never stop trying to do something to show how much we appreciate the love and the mercy which have made us what we are. Whenever we love anyone, we cannot help trying always to demonstrate our love. When we remember how much God loves us and how little we deserve it, when we remember that it was for us that Jesus Christ hung and suffered on Calvary, it must compel us to effort that will tell God that we realize what he has done for us and will show Jesus Christ that his sacrifice was not in vain.

(4) The memory of his sin was bound to be a constant encouragement to others. Paul uses a vivid picture. He says that what happened to him was a kind of outline sketch of what was going to happen to those who would accept Christ in the days to come. The word he uses is *hupotupōsis*, which means an outline, a sketch-plan, a first draft, a preliminary model. It is as if Paul were saying: 'Look what Christ has done for me! If someone like me can be saved, there is hope for everyone.' Suppose someone was seriously ill and had to go through a dangerous operation, it would be the greatest encouragement to that person to meet and talk with another person who had undergone the same operation and had emerged completely cured. Paul did not conceal his record; he broadcast it so that others might take courage and be filled with hope that the grace which had changed him could change them too.

In John Bunyan's *The Pilgrim's Progress*, Greatheart said to Christian's boys: 'You must know that Forgetful Green is the most dangerous place in all these parts.' Paul's sin was something which he refused to forget – for, every time he remembered the greatness of his sin, he remembered the still greater greatness of Jesus Christ. It was not that he brooded over his sin in an unhealthy way; it was that he remembered it to rejoice in the wonder of the grace of Jesus Christ.

THE SUMMONS WHICH CANNOT BE DENIED

1 Timothy 1:18–20

> I entrust this charge to you, Timothy lad, because it is the natural consequence of the messages which came to the prophets from God, and which marked you out as the very man for this work, so that, in obedience to

these messages, you may wage a fine campaign, maintaining your faith and a good conscience all the time; and there are some who, in matters of the faith, have repelled the guidance of conscience, and have come to shipwreck. Among them are Hymenaeus and Alexander, whom I have handed over to Satan, that they may be disciplined out of their insults to God and his Church.

THE first section of this passage is highly compressed. What lies behind it is this. There must have been a meeting of the prophets of the Church. They were people known to be within God's confidence and to know his intentions. 'Surely the Lord God does nothing without revealing his secret to his servants the prophets' (Amos 3:7). This meeting considered the situation which was threatening the Church and came to the conclusion that Timothy was the person to deal with it. We can see the prophets acting in exactly the same way in Acts 13:1–3. The Church was faced with the great decision whether or not to take the gospel out to the Gentiles, and it was to the prophets that there came the message of the Holy Spirit, saying: 'Set apart for me Barnabas and Saul for the work to which I have called them' (Acts 13:2). That was what had happened to Timothy. He had been marked out by the prophets as the one to deal with the situation in the Church. It may well have been that he shrank from the greatness of the task which faced him – and here Paul encourages him with certain considerations.

(1) Paul says to him: 'You are a man who has been chosen, and you cannot refuse your task.' Something like that happened to the Scottish reformer John Knox. He had been teaching in St Andrews. His teaching was supposed to be private, but many came to it, for he was obviously a man with a message. So, the people urged him 'that he would take

the preaching place upon him. But he utterly refused, alleging that he would not run where God had not called him . . . Whereupon they privily among themselves advising, having with them in council Sir David Lindsay of the Mount, they concluded that they would give a charge to the said John, and that publicly by the mouth of their preacher.'

So Sunday came, and Knox was in church, and John Rough was preaching. 'The said John Rough, preacher, directed his words to the said John Knox, saying: "Brother, ye shall not be offended, albeit that I speak unto you that which I have in charge, even from all those that are here present, which is this: in the name of God, and of his Son Jesus Christ, and in the name of these that presently call you by my mouth, I charge you that you refuse not this holy vocation, but . . . that you take upon you the public office and charge of preaching, even as you look to avoid God's heavy displeasure, and desire that he shall multiply his graces with you." And in the end he said to those that were present: "Was not this your charge to me? And do ye not approve this vocation?" They answered: "It was: and we approve it." Whereat the said John, abashed, burst forth in most abundant tears, and withdrew himself to his chamber. His countenance and behaviour, from that day till the day that he was compelled to present himself to the public place of preaching, did sufficiently declare the grief and trouble of his heart; for no man saw any sign of mirth in him, neither yet had he pleasure to accompany any man, many days together.'

John Knox was chosen; he did not want to answer the call; but he had to, for the choice had been made by God. Years afterwards, the Regent of Scotland, James Morton, uttered his famous epitaph by Knox's graveside: 'In respect that he bore God's message, to whom he must make account for the same, he (albeit he was weak and an unworthy creature, and

a fearful man) feared not the faces of men.' The consciousness of being chosen gave him courage.

So, Paul says to Timothy: 'You have been chosen; you
cannot let down God and you cannot let us down.' To every
one of us, there comes God's choosing; and, when we are
summoned to some work for him, we dare not refuse it.

(2) It may be that Paul was saying to Timothy: 'Be true to
your name.' *Timothy* – its full form is *Timotheos* – is composed of two Greek words, *timē*, which means *honour* and
theos, which means *God*, and so means *honour to God*. If we
are called by the name *Christian*, one of Christ's people, to
that name we must be true.

(3) Finally, Paul says to Timothy: 'I entrust this charge to
you.' The word which he uses for *to entrust* is *paratithesthai*,
which is the word used of entrusting something valuable to
someone's safe-keeping. It is used, for instance, of making a
deposit in a bank, or of entrusting someone to another's care.
It always implies that a trust has been placed in someone for
which that person will be called to account. So, Paul says:
'Timothy, into your hands I am placing a sacred trust. See
that you do not fail.' God places his trust in us; into our hands
he puts his honour and his Church. We too must see to it that
we do not fail.

DESPATCHED ON GOD'S CAMPAIGN

1 Timothy 1:18–20 (*contd*)

WHAT then is entrusted to Timothy? He is despatched to fight
a *good campaign*. The picture of life as a campaign is one
which has always held immense fascination. Maximus of Tyre
said: 'God is the general; life is the campaign; man is the
soldier.' Seneca said: 'For me to live, my dear Lucilius, is to

be a soldier.' When a man became a follower of the goddess Isis and was initiated into the mysteries connected with the goddess's name, the summons to him was: 'Enrol yourself in the sacred soldiery of Isis.'

There are three things to be noted.

(1) It is not to a *battle* that we are summoned; it is to a *campaign*. Life is one long campaign, a service from which there is no release – not a short, sharp struggle after which we can lay down our weapons and rest in peace. To change the metaphor, life is not a sprint; it is a marathon race. It is there that the danger enters in. It is necessary always to be on the watch. As the Irish orator John Philpot Curran had it: 'Eternal vigilance is the price of liberty.' The temptations of life never cease their search for a chink in a Christian's armour. It is one of the most common dangers in life to proceed in a series of spasms. We must remember that we are summoned to a campaign which goes on as long as life continues.

(2) It is to a *fine* campaign that Timothy is summoned. Here again, we have the word *kalos*, of which the Pastorals are so fond. It does not mean only something which is good and strong; it means something which is also attractive and lovely. The soldier of Christ is not a conscript who serves grimly and grudgingly, but a volunteer who serves with a certain courage and gallantry. Christ's soldiers are not slaves of duty, but servants of joy.

(3) Timothy is commanded to take with him two weapons of equipment. (a) He is to take *faith*. Even when things are at their darkest, he must have faith in the essential rightness of his cause and in the ultimate triumph of God. It was faith which gave strength to John Knox when he was in despair. Once, when he was a slave on the galleys, the ship came in sight of St Andrews. He was so weak that he had to be lifted

up bodily in order to see. They showed him the church steeple and asked if he knew it. 'Yes,' he said, 'I know it well: and I am fully persuaded, how weak that ever I now appear, that I shall not depart this life till that my tongue shall glorify his godly name in the same place.' He describes his feelings in 1554 when he had to flee the country to escape the vengeance of Mary Tudor. 'Not only the ungodly, but even my faithful brethren, yea, and my own self, that is, all natural under-standing, judged my cause to be irremediable. The frail flesh, oppressed with fear and pain, desireth deliverance, ever abhorring and drawing back from obedience giving. O Christian brethren, I write by experience ... I know the grudging and murmuring complaints of the flesh; I know the anger, wrath and indignation which it conceiveth against God, calling all his promises in doubt, and being ready every hour utterly to fall from God. *Against which remains only faith.*' In the darkest hour, Christian soldiers need the faith that will not shrink.

(b) He is to take the defence of a *good conscience*. That is to say, Christian soldiers must at least try to live in accordance with their own beliefs. The message loses its strength and value when conscience condemns the one who speaks.

A STERN REBUKE

1 Timothy 1:18–20 (*contd*)

THE passage closes with a stern rebuke to two members of the Church who have injured the Church, grieved Paul and ruined their own lives. Hymenaeus is mentioned again in 2 Timothy 2:17; and Alexander may well be the Alexander who is referred to in 2 Timothy 4:14. Paul has three com-plaints against them.

(1) They had rejected the guidance of conscience. They had allowed their own desires to speak with more persuasiveness than the voice of God.

(2) They had lapsed into evil practices. Once they had abandoned God, life had become tainted and debased. When God went from life, beauty went along with him.

(3) They had taken to false teaching. Again, it was almost inevitable. When people take the wrong way, their first instinct is to find excuses for themselves. They take the Christian teaching and twist it to suit themselves. Out of the right, they find distorted arguments to justify what is wrong. They find arguments in the words of Christ to justify the ways of the devil. The moment people disobey the voice of conscience, their conduct becomes debased and their thinking twisted.

So, Paul goes on to say that he has 'handed them over to Satan'. What is the meaning of this terrible phrase? There are three possibilities.

(1) He may be thinking of the Jewish practice of excommunication. According to synagogue practice, if a man was an evildoer he was first publicly rebuked. If that was ineffective, he was banished from the synagogue for a period of thirty days. If he was still stubbornly unrepentant, he was put under the ban, which made him a person who was damned, debarred from the society of others and the fellowship of God. In such a case, it might well be said that someone had been handed over to Satan.

(2) He may be saying that he has barred them from the Church and turned them loose in the world. In a non-Christian society, it was inevitable that people should draw a hard and fast line between the Church and the world. The Church was God's territory; the world was Satan's; and to be debarred from the Church was to be handed over to that territory which was under the sway of Satan. The phrase may mean that these

two men who had caused trouble in the Church were abandoned to the world.

(3) The third explanation is the most likely of the three. Satan was held to be responsible for human suffering and pain. A man in the Corinthian church had been guilty of the terrible sin of incest. Paul's advice was that he should be delivered to Satan 'for the destruction of the flesh, so that his spirit may be saved on the day of the Lord' (1 Corinthians 5:5). The idea is that the Church should pray for some physical punishment to fall on that man so that by physical pain he might be brought to his senses. In Job's case, it was Satan who brought the physical suffering upon him (Job 2:6–7). In the New Testament itself, we have the terrible end of Ananias and Sapphira (Acts 5:5, 5:10), and the blindness which fell upon Elymas because of his opposition to the gospel (Acts 13:11). It may well be that it was Paul's prayer that these two men should be subjected to some painful condition which would be a punishment and a warning.

That is all the more likely because it is Paul's hope that they will be not obliterated and destroyed, but disciplined out of their evil ways. To him, as it ought to be to us, punishment was never mere vindictive vengeance but always remedial discipline, never meant simply to hurt but always to cure.

THE UNIVERSALITY OF THE GOSPEL

1 Timothy 2:1–7

> So, then, the first thing I urge you to do is to offer your requests, your prayers, your petitions, your thanksgivings for all men. Pray for kings and for all who are in authority, that they may enjoy a life that is tranquil

and undisturbed, and that they may act in all godliness
and reverence. That is the fine way to live, the way
which meets with the approval of God, our Saviour,
who wishes all men to be saved, and to come to a full
knowledge of the truth. For there is one God, and one
mediator, between God and man, the man Jesus Christ,
who gave himself a ransom for all. It was thus he bore
his witness to God in his own good times, a witness to
which I have been appointed a herald and an envoy (I
am speaking the truth: I do not lie), a teacher to the
Gentiles, a teacher whose message is based on faith and
truth.

BEFORE we study this passage in detail, we must note one
thing which shines out from it in a way that no one can fail
to see. Few passages in the New Testament so stress the
universality of the gospel. Prayer is to be made for *all*; God
is the Saviour who wants *all* to be saved; Jesus gave his life a
ransom for *all*. As Walter Lock writes in his commentary:
'God's will to save is as wide as his will to create.'

This is a note which sounds in the New Testament again
and again. Through Christ, God was reconciling the *world*
to himself (2 Corinthians 5:18–19). God so loved the
world that he gave his Son (John 3:16). It was Jesus' confidence that, if he was lifted up on his cross, sooner or later
he would draw *all* people to him (John 12:32).

E. F. Brown calls this passage 'the charter of missionary
work'. He says that it is the proof that all are *capax Dei*,
capable of receiving God. They may be lost, but they can be
found; they may be ignorant, but they can be enlightened;
they may be sinners, but they can be saved. George Wishart,
the reformer and martyr, and forerunner of John Knox, writes
in his translation of the First Swiss Confession: 'The end and
intent of the Scripture is to declare that God is benevolent

and friendly-minded to mankind; and that he hath declared that kindness in and through Jesus Christ, his only Son; the which kindness is received by faith.' That is why prayer must be made for all. God wants all men and women, and so, therefore, must his Church.

(1) The gospel includes *high and low*. Both the emperor in his power and slaves in their helplessness were included in the sweep of the gospel. Both the philosophers in their wisdom and ordinary men and women in their ignorance need the grace and truth that the gospel can bring. Within the gospel, there are no class distinctions. Monarch and commoner, rich and poor, employer and employee are all included in its limitless embrace.

(2) The gospel includes *good and bad*. A strange malady has sometimes afflicted the Church in modern times, causing it to insist that people must be respectable before they are allowed in, and to look askance at sinners who seek entry to its doors. But the New Testament is clear that the Church exists not only to improve and instruct the good but also to welcome and save the sinner. The missionary C. T. Studd used to repeat four lines of doggerel:

> Some want to live within the sound
>   Of Church or Chapel bell;
> I want to run a rescue shop
>   Within a yard of hell.

One of the great saints of modern times, and indeed of all time, was Toyohiko Kagawa. He went to Shinkawa in Japan to find men and women for Christ, and he lived there in the filthiest and most depraved slums in the world. His biographer W. J. Smart describes the situation: 'His neighbours were unregistered prostitutes, thieves who boasted of their power to outwit all the police in the city, and murderers who were not only proud of their murder record but always ready to add to their local prestige by committing another. All the people, whether sick, or feeble-minded or criminal, lived in conditions of abysmal misery, in streets slippery with filth, where rats crawled out of open sewers to die. The air was always filled with stench. An idiot girl who lived next door to Kagawa had vile pictures painted on her back to decoy lustful men to her den. Everywhere human bodies rotted with syphilis.' Kagawa wanted people like that – and so does Jesus Christ, for he wants *all* people, good and bad alike.

(3) The gospel embraces *Christian and non-Christian*. Prayer is to be made for *all* men and women. The emperors and rulers for whom this letter bids us pray were not Christians; they were in fact hostile to the Church, and yet they were to be carried to the throne of grace by the prayers of the Church. For true Christians, there is no such thing as an enemy in all this world. No one is outside our prayers, for no one is outside the love of Christ, and no one is outside the purpose of God, who wants *all* to be saved.

THE WAY OF PRAYER

1 Timothy 2:1–7 (*contd*)

Four different words for prayer are grouped together. It is true that they are not to be sharply distinguished; nevertheless, each has something to tell us about the way of prayer.

(1) The first is *deēsis*, which we have translated as *request*. It is not exclusively a religious word; it can be used of a request made either to another person or to God. But its fundamental idea is a sense of need. No one will make a request unless a sense of need has already wakened a desire. Prayer begins with a sense of need. It begins with the conviction

that we cannot deal with life ourselves. That sense of human weakness is the basis of all approach to God. As Joseph Hart's hymn 'Come ye sinners' has it:

> Let not conscience make you linger,
>   Nor of fitness fondly dream;
> All the fitness he requireth
>   Is to feel your need of him.

(2) The second is *proseuchē*, which we have translated as *prayer*. The basic difference between *deēsis* and *proseuchē* is that *deēsis* may be addressed either to others or to God, but *proseuchē* is never used of anything else but approach to God. There are certain needs which only God can satisfy. There is a strength which he alone can give; a forgiveness which he alone can grant; a certainty which he alone can bestow. It may well be that our weakness remains with us because we so often take our needs to the wrong place.

(3) The third is *enteuxis*, which we have translated as *petition*. Of the three words, this is the most interesting. It is the noun from the verb *entugchanein*. This originally meant simply *to meet* or *to fall in* with a person; it went on to mean *to hold intimate conversation with a person*; then it acquired a special meaning and meant *to enter into a king's presence and to submit a petition to him*. That tells us a great deal about prayer. It tells us that the way to God stands open and that we have the right to bring our petitions to one who is a king. As John Newton wrote in the hymn 'Come my soul, thy suit prepare':

> Thou art coming to a King;
> Large petitions with thee bring;
> For his grace and power are such,
> None can ever ask too much.

It is impossible to ask too much from this king.

(4) The fourth is *eucharistia*, which we have translated as *thanksgiving*. Prayer does not mean only asking God for things; it also means thanking God for things. For too many of us, prayer is an exercise in complaint when it should be an exercise in thanksgiving. Epictetus, not a Christian but a Stoic philosopher, used to say: 'What can I, who am a little old lame man, do, except give praise to God?' We have the right to bring our needs to God, but we have also the duty of bringing our thanksgivings to him.

PRAYER FOR THOSE IN AUTHORITY

1 Timothy 2:1–7 (*contd*)

THIS passage distinctly commands prayer for kings and emperors and all who are set in authority. This was a principle of prime importance for communal Christian prayer. Emperors might be persecutors, and those in authority might be determined to stamp out Christianity. But the Christian Church never, even in the times of the most bitter persecution, ceased to pray for them.

It is extraordinary to trace how, all through its early days, those days of bitter persecution, the Church regarded it as an absolute duty to pray for the emperor and his subordinate kings and governors. 'Fear God', said Peter. 'Honour the emperor' (1 Peter 2:17) – and we must remember that that emperor was none other than Nero, that monster of cruelty. The early Christian theologian Tertullian insists that, for the emperor, Christians pray for 'long life, secure dominion, a safe home, a faithful senate, a righteous people, and a world at peace' (*Apology*, 30). 'We pray for our rulers,' he wrote, 'for the state of the world, for the peace of all things and for the postponement of the end' (*Apology*, 39). He writes: 'The Christian is the enemy of no man, least of all of the emperor, for we know that, since he has been appointed by God, it is necessary that we should love him, and reverence him, and honour him, and desire his safety, together with that of the whole Roman Empire. Therefore we sacrifice for the safety of the emperor' (*Ad Scapulam*, 2). Cyprian, Bishop of Carthage in the third century, writing to Demetrianus, speaks of the Christian Church as 'sacrificing and placating God night and day for your peace and safety' (*Ad Demetrianum*, 20). In AD 311, the Emperor Galerius actually asked for the prayers of the Christians, and promised them mercy and tolerant treatment if they prayed for the state. The second-century Christian writer Tatian says: 'Does the emperor order us to pay tribute? We willingly offer it. Does the ruler order us to render service or servitude? We acknowledge our servitude. But a man must be honoured as befits a man, but only God is to be reverenced' (*Apology*, 4). In the same period, Theophilus of Antioch writes: 'The honour that I will give the emperor is all the greater, because I will not worship him, but I will pray for him. I will worship no one but the true and real God, for I know that the emperor was appointed by him ... Those give real honour to the emperor who are well-disposed to him, who obey him, and who pray for him' (*Apology*, 1:11). And the second-century Christian scholar, Justin Martyr, writes: 'We worship God alone, but in all other things we gladly serve you, acknowledging kings and rulers of men, and praying that they may be found to have pure reason with kingly power' (*Apology*, 1:14, 17).

The greatest of all the prayers for the emperor is in Clement of Rome's First Letter to the church at Corinth, which was written in about AD 90 when the savagery of Domitian was still fresh in people's minds: 'Thou, Lord and Master, hast given our rulers and governors the power of sovereignty through thine excellent and unspeakable might, that we, knowing the glory and honour which thou hast given them, may submit ourselves unto them, in nothing resisting thy will. Grant unto them, therefore, O Lord, health, peace, concord, stability, that they may administer the government which thou hast given them without failure. For thou, O heavenly Master, King of the Ages, givest to the sons of men glory and honour and power over all things that are upon the earth. Do thou, Lord, direct their counsel according to that which is good and well-pleasing in thy sight, that, administering the power which thou hast given them in peace and gentleness with godliness, they may obtain thy favour. O thou, who alone art able to do these things, and things far more exceeding good than these for us, we praise thee through the High Priest and Guardian of our souls, Jesus Christ, through whom be the glory and the majesty unto thee both now and for all generations, and for ever and ever. Amen' (1 Clement 61).

The Church always regarded it as a duty and an obligation to pray for those set in authority over the kingdoms of the earth, and brought even its persecutors before the throne of grace.

THE GIFTS OF GOD

1 Timothy 2:1–7 (*contd*)

THE Church prayed for certain things for those in authority.

(1) It prayed for 'a life that is tranquil and undisturbed'. That was the prayer for freedom from war, from rebellion and from anything which would disturb the peace of the realm. That is the prayer of good citizens for their country.

(2) But the Church prayed for much more than that. It prayed for 'a life that is lived in godliness and reverence'. Here, we are confronted with two great words which are keynotes of the Pastoral Epistles and describe qualities which not only the ruler but every Christian must long to possess.

First, there is *godliness, eusebeia*. This is one of the great and almost untranslatable Greek words. It describes reverence towards both God and other people. It describes that attitude of mind which respects others and honours God. Eusebius, the early Church historian, defined it as 'reverence towards the one and only God, and the kind of life that he would wish us to lead'. To the Greeks, the great example of *eusebeia* was Socrates, whom the Greek historian Xenophon describes in the following terms: 'So pious and devoutly religious that he would take no step apart from the will of heaven; so just and upright that he never did even a trifling injury to any living soul; so self-controlled, so temperate, that he never at any time chose the sweeter in place of the bitter; so sensible and wise and prudent that in distinguishing the better from the worse he never erred' (*Memorabilia*, 4:8:11). *Eusebeia* comes very near to that great Latin word *pietas*, which the classical scholar Warde Fowler describes in this way: 'The quality known to the Romans as *pietas* rises, in spite of trial and danger, superior to the enticements of individual passion and selfish ease. Aeneas's *pietas* became a sense of duty to the will of the gods, as well as to his father, his son and his people; and this duty never leaves him.' Clearly, *eusebeia* is a tremendous thing. It never forgets the reverence due to God; it never forgets the rights due to others; it never forgets the respect due to self. It describes the character of those who never fail God, other people or themselves.

Second, there is *reverence, semnotēs*. Here again, we are in the realm of the untranslatable. The corresponding adjective *semnos* is constantly applied to the gods. R. C. Trench, who was Archbishop of Dublin, says that the one who is *semnos* 'has on him a grace and a dignity, not lent by earth'. He says that such a person 'without demanding it challenges and inspires reverence'. Aristotle was the great ethical teacher of the Greeks. He had a way of describing every virtue as the mid-point between two extremes. On the one side there was an extreme of excess and on the other an extreme of want, and in between there was the mid-point, the happy medium, in which virtue lay. Aristotle says that *semnotēs* is the mid-point between *areskeia*, *subservience*, and *authadeia*, *arrogance*. It may be said that for the person who is *semnos* all life is one act of worship; all life is lived in the presence of God; such a person moves through the world, as it has been put, as if it were the temple of the living God, never forgetting the holiness of God or the dignity of others.

These two great qualities are regal qualities which everyone must long to possess and for which everyone must pray.

ONE GOD AND ONE SAVIOUR

1 Timothy 2:1–7 (*contd*)

PAUL concludes with a statement of the greatest truths of the Christian faith.

(1) There is one God. We are not living in a world such as the Gnostics produced, with their theories of two gods hostile to each other. We are not living in a world in which there is a horde of gods, often in competition with one another. One of the greatest sources of relief which Christianity brings to those who have worshipped many gods is the conviction that there is only one God. To those who have lived in constant fear of the gods, it is a liberation to discover that there is

one God only whose name is Father and whose nature is love.

(2) There is one mediator. Even the Jews would have said that there are many mediators between God and human beings. A mediator is one who stands between two parties and acts as go-between. To the Jews, the angels were mediators. The Testament of Dan (6:2) has it: 'Draw near unto God, and unto the angel who intercedes for you, for he is a mediator between God and man.' To the Greeks, there were all kinds of mediators. Plutarch said it was an insult to God to think that he was in any way directly involved in the world; he was involved in the world only through angels and demons and demi-gods who were, so to speak, his liaison officers.

Neither in Jewish nor in Greek thought did people have *direct* access to God. But, through Jesus Christ, Christians have that direct access, with nothing to bar the way between. Further, there is only *one* mediator. Unless there is one God and one mediator, there can be no such thing as mutual fellowship. If there are many gods and many mediators competing for their allegiance and their love, religion becomes something which divides people instead of uniting them. It is because there is one God and one mediator that people are joined in fellowship with one another.

Paul goes on to call Jesus the one who gave his life as a ransom for all. That simply means that it cost God the life and death of his Son to bring men and women back to himself. There was a man who lost a son in the Second World War. He had lived a most careless and even a godless life; but his son's death brought him face to face with God as never before. He became a changed man. One day, he was standing in front of the local war memorial, looking at his son's name on it. And, very gently, he said: 'I guess he had to go down to lift me up.' That is what Jesus did; it cost his life and death to tell us of the love of God and to bring us home to him.

Then Paul claims for himself four roles.

(1) He is a *herald* of the story of Jesus Christ. A herald is someone who makes a statement and who says: 'This is true.' Heralds bring not a personal proclamation but one which comes from the king.

(2) He is a *witness* to the story of Christ. Witnesses are people who say: 'This is true, and I know it' and also say: 'It works.' They tell not only the story of Christ but also the story of what Christ has done for them.

(3) He is an *envoy*. Envoys are people whose duty is to commend their country in a foreign land. Envoys in the Christian sense are therefore people who commend the story of Christ to others. They want to communicate that story to others, so that it will mean as much to others as it does to them.

(4) He is a *teacher*. The *herald* is the person who proclaims the facts; the *witness* is the person who proclaims the power of the facts; the *envoy* is the person who commends the facts; the *teacher* is the person who leads people into the meaning of the facts. It is not enough to know that Christ lived and died; we must think out what that meant. We must not only feel the wonder of the story of Christ; we must think out its meaning for ourselves and for the world.

BARRIERS TO PRAYER

1 Timothy 2:8–15

> So, then, it is my wish that men should pray everywhere, lifting up holy hands, with no anger in their hearts and no doubts in their minds. Even so, it is my wish that

women should modestly and wisely adorn themselves in seemly dress. This adornment should not consist in braided hair, and ornaments of gold, and pearls, but – as befits women who profess to reverence God – they should adorn themselves with good works. Let a woman learn in silence and with all submission. I do not allow a woman to teach or to dictate to a man. Rather, it is my advice that she should be silent. For Adam was formed first, and then Eve; and Adam was not deceived, but the woman was deceived, and so became guilty of transgression. But women will be saved through child-bearing, if they continue in faith and love, and if they wisely walk the road that leads to holiness.

THE early Church took over the Jewish way of praying, which was to pray standing, with hands outstretched and the palms upwards. Later, Tertullian was to say that this depicted the attitude of Jesus upon the cross.

The Jews had always known about the barriers which kept people's prayers from God. Isaiah heard God say to the people: 'When you stretch out your hands, I will hide my eyes from you; even though you make many prayers, I will not listen; your hands are full of blood' (Isaiah 1:15). Here, too, certain things are demanded.

(1) Those who pray must stretch out holy hands. They must hold up to God hands which do not touch the forbidden things. This does not mean for one moment that sinners are barred from God; but it does mean that there is no reality in the prayers of people who then go out to soil their hands with forbidden things, as if they had never prayed. It is not thinking of anyone who is helplessly in the grip of some passion and desperately fighting against it, bitterly conscious of failure. It is thinking of those whose prayers are a mere formality.

(2) Those who pray must have no anger in their hearts. It has been said that 'forgiveness is indivisible'. Human and divine forgiveness go hand in hand. Again and again, Jesus stresses the fact that we cannot hope to receive the forgiveness of God as long as there is hostility between us and our neighbours. 'So when you are offering your gift at the altar, if you remember that your brother or sister has something against you, leave your gift there before the altar and go; first be reconciled to your brother or sister, and then come and offer your gift' (Matthew 5:23-4). 'If you do not forgive others, neither will your Father forgive your trespasses' (Matthew 6:15). Jesus tells how the unforgiving servant himself found no forgiveness, and ends: 'So my heavenly Father will also do to every one of you, if you do not forgive your brother or sister from your heart' (Matthew 18:35). To be forgiven, we must be forgiving. The *Didache*, the earliest Christian book on public worship, which dates from about AD 100, has it: 'Let no one who has a quarrel with his neighbour come to us, until they are reconciled.' The bitterness in people's hearts is a barrier which hinders their prayers from reaching God.

(3) Those who pray must have no doubts in their minds. This phrase can mean two things. The word used is *dialogismos*, which can mean both an *argument* and a *doubt*. If we take it in the sense of *argument*, it simply repeats what has gone before and restates the fact that bitterness and quarrels and venomous debates are a hindrance to prayer. It is better to take it in the sense of *doubt*. Before prayer is answered, there must be belief that God will answer. If people pray pessimistically and with no real belief that it is any use, their prayers fall to the ground. Before we can be cured, we must believe that we can be cured; before we can take to ourselves the grace of God, we must believe in that grace.

We must take our prayers to God in the complete confidence that he hears and answers prayer.

WOMEN IN THE CHURCH

1 Timothy 2:8–15 (*contd*)

THE second part of this passage deals with the place of women in the Church. It cannot be read out of its historical context, for it springs entirely from the situation in which it was written.

(1) It was written against a Jewish background. No nation ever gave a bigger place to women in the home and in family matters than the Jews did; but officially the position of a woman was very low. In Jewish law, she was not a person but a thing; she was entirely at the disposal of her father or of her husband. She was forbidden to learn the law; to instruct a woman in the law was to cast pearls before swine. Women had no part in the synagogue service; they were shut apart in a section of the synagogue, or in a gallery, where they could not be seen. A man came to the synagogue to *learn*, but, at the most, a woman came to *hear*. In the synagogue, the lesson from Scripture was read by members of the congregation – but not by women, for that would have been to lessen 'the honour of the congregation'. It was absolutely forbidden for a woman to teach in a school; she might not even teach the youngest children. A woman was exempt from the stated demands of the law. She had no obligation to attend the sacred feasts and festivals. Women, slaves and children were classed together. In the Jewish morning prayer, a man thanked God that God had not made him 'a Gentile, a slave or a woman'. In the *Sayings of the Fathers*, Rabbi Josē ben Johanan is quoted as saying: '"Let your house be opened

wide, and let the poor be your household, and talk not much with a woman." Hence the wise have said: "Everyone that talks much with a woman causes evil to himself, and desists from the works of the Law, and his end is that he inherits Gehenna."' A strict Rabbi would never greet a woman on the street, not even his own wife or daughter or mother or sister. It was said of woman: 'Her work is to send her children to the synagogue; to attend to domestic concerns; to leave her husband free to study in the schools; to keep house for him until he returns.'

(2) It was written against a Greek background. The Greek background made things doubly difficult, as the place of women in Greek religion was low. The Temple of Aphrodite in Corinth had 1,000 priestesses who were sacred prostitutes and plied their trade every evening on the city streets. The Temple of Diana in Ephesus had its hundreds of priestesses called the *Melissae*, which means the *bees*, whose function was the same. The respectable Greek woman led a very confined life. She lived in her own quarters into which no one but her husband came. She did not even appear at meals. She never at any time appeared on the street alone; she never went to any public assembly. The fact is that, if in a Greek town Christian women had taken an active and a speaking part in its work, the church would inevitably have gained the reputation of being a place frequented by loose women.

Further, in Greek society there were women whose whole life consisted in elaborate dressing and braiding of the hair. In Rome, Pliny, the Governor of Bithynia, tells us of the Emperor Caligula's wife having a dress covered entirely in pearls and emeralds. Even the Greeks and the Romans were shocked at the love of dress and of adornment which characterized some of their women. The great Greek religions were called the mystery religions, and they had precisely the same regulations about dress as Paul has here. There is an inscription which reads: 'A consecrated woman shall not have gold ornaments, nor rouge, nor face-whitening, nor a head-band, nor braided hair, nor shoes, except those made of felt or of the skins of sacrificed animals.' The early Church did not lay down these regulations as in any sense permanent, but as being necessary in the situation in which it found itself.

In any event, there is much on the other side. In the Genesis story, it was the woman who was created second and who fell to the seduction of the serpent tempter; but it was Mary of Nazareth who bore and who trained the child Jesus; it was Mary of Magdala who was first to see the risen Lord; it was four women who of all the disciples stood by the cross. Priscilla with her husband Aquila was a valued teacher in the early Church, a teacher who led Apollos to a knowledge of the truth (Acts 18:26). Euodia and Syntyche, in spite of their quarrel, were women who laboured in the gospel (Philippians 4:2–3). Philip, the evangelist, had four daughters who were prophetesses (Acts 21:9). The older women were to teach (Titus 2:3). Paul held Lois and Eunice in the highest honour (2 Timothy 1:5), and there are many women's names held in honour in Romans 16.

All the things in this chapter are mere temporary regulations to meet a given situation. If we want Paul's permanent view on this matter, we get it in Galatians 3:28: 'There is no longer Jew or Greek, there is no longer slave or free, there is no longer male or female; for all of you are one in Christ Jesus.' In Christ, the differences of place and honour and function within the Church are all wiped out.

And yet this passage ends with a real truth. Women, it says, will be saved in childbearing. There are two possible meanings here. It is just possible that this is a reference to the fact that Mary, a woman, was the mother of Jesus and that it means that women will be saved – as all others will – by that supreme act of childbearing. But it is much more likely that the meaning is much simpler, and that Paul means that women will find salvation not in addressing meetings but in motherhood, which is their crowning glory.

We must read this passage not as a barrier to all women's service within the Church, but in the light of its Jewish and its Greek background. And we must look for Paul's permanent views in the passage where he tells us that the differences are wiped out, and that men and women, slaves and free, Jews and Gentiles, are all eligible to serve Christ.

THE LEADERS OF THE CHURCH

1 Timothy 3:1–7

There is a saying which everyone must believe – if a man aspires to the office of overseer in the Church, it is a fine work on which his heart is set. An overseer must be a man against whom no criticism can be made; he must have been married only once; he must be sober, prudent, well-behaved, hospitable and possessed of an aptitude for teaching. He must not overindulge in wine, nor must he be the kind of man who assaults others, but he must be gentle and peaceable, and free from the love of money. He must manage his own house well, keeping his children under control with complete dignity. (If a man does not know how to manage his own house, how can he take charge of the congregation of God?) He must not be a recent convert, in case he becomes inflated with a sense of his own importance, and so fall into the same condemnation as the devil did. He must have earned the respect of those outside the Church, that he may not fall into reproach and into the snare of the devil.

THIS is a very important passage from the point of view of church government. It deals with the man whom the Authorized and Revised Standard Versions call the *bishop*, and whom we have translated as *overseer*.

In the New Testament, there are two words which describe the principal office-bearers of the Church, the office-bearers who were to be found in every congregation, and on whose conduct and administration its welfare depended.

(1) There was the man who was called the *elder* (*presbuteros*). The eldership is the most ancient of all offices within the Church. The Jews had their elders, and they traced their origin to the occasion when Moses, in the desert wanderings, appointed seventy men to help him in the task of controlling and caring for the people (Numbers 11:16). Every synagogue had its elders, and they were the real leaders of the Jewish community. They presided over the worship of the synagogue; they administered rebuke and discipline where these were necessary; they settled the disputes which other nations would have taken to the law courts. Among the Jews, the elders were the respected men who exercised a fatherly oversight over the spiritual and material affairs of every Jewish community. But more nations than the Jews had an eldership. The presiding body of the Spartans was called the *gerousia*, which means *the board of the elder men*. The Parliament of Rome was called the *senate*, which comes from *senex*, which means *an old man*. In England, the men who looked after the affairs of the community were called the *aldermen*, which means the *elder men*. In New Testament times, every Egyptian village had its village elders who looked after the affairs of the community. The elders had a long history, and they had a place in the life of almost every community.

(2) But sometimes the New Testament uses another word, *episkopos*, which the Authorized and Revised Standard

Versions translate as *bishop*, and which literally means *overseer* or *superintendent*. This word, too, has a long and honourable history. The Septuagint, the Greek version of the Hebrew Scriptures, uses it to describe those who were the *taskmasters*, who were overseers for the public works and public building schemes (2 Chronicles 34:17). The Greeks use it to describe the men appointed to go out from the founding city to regulate the affairs of a newly established colony in some distant place. They use it to describe what we might call *commissioners* appointed to regulate the affairs of a city. The Romans use it to describe the magistrates appointed to oversee the sale of food within the city of Rome. It is used of the special delegates appointed by a king to see that the laws he had laid down were carried out. *Episkopos* always implies two things: *oversight* over some area or sphere of work, and *responsibility* to some higher power and authority.

The great question is: what was the relationship in the early Church between the elder, the *presbuteros*, and the overseer, the *episkopos*?

Modern scholarship is practically unanimous in holding that in the early Church the *presbuteros* and the *episkopos* were one and the same. The grounds for that identification are fivefold. (1) Elders were appointed everywhere. After the first missionary journey, Paul and Barnabas appointed elders in all the churches they had founded (Acts 14:23). Titus is instructed to appoint and ordain elders in all the cities of Crete (Titus 1:5). (2) The qualifications of a *presbuteros* and of an *episkopos* are to all intents and purposes identical (1 Timothy 3:2-7; Titus 1:6-9). (3) At the beginning of Philippians, Paul's greetings are to the *bishops and the deacons* (Philippians 1:1). It is quite impossible that Paul would have sent no greetings at all to the *elders*, who, as we have already seen, were in every church; and therefore the *bishops* and the *elders* must be one and the same body of people. (4) When Paul was on his last journey to Jerusalem, he sent for the *elders* of Ephesus to meet him at Miletus (Acts 20:17), and in the course of his talk to them he says that God has made them *episkopoi* to feed the Church of God (Acts 20:28). That is to say, he addresses precisely the same body of men first as *elders* and second as bishops or overseers. (5) When Peter is writing to his people, he talks to them as an *elder* to *elders* (1 Peter 5:1), and then he goes on to say that their function is *oversight* of the flock of God (1 Peter 5:2) – and the word he uses for *oversight* is the verb *episkopein*, from which *episkopos* comes. All the evidence from the New Testament goes to prove that the *presbuteros* and the *episkopos*, the elder and the bishop or overseer, were one and the same person.

Two questions arise. First, if they were the same, why were there two names for them? The answer is that *presbuteros* described these leaders of the Church literally as they were personally. They were the elder men, the older and respected members of the community. *Episkopos*, on the other hand, described *their function*, which was to oversee the life and the work of the Church. The one word described the individual; the other described the task.

The second question is: if the elder and the bishop were originally the same, how did the bishop become what he did? The answer is simple. Inevitably, the body of the elders would acquire a leader. Someone to lead would be essential and would inevitably emerge. The more organized the Church became, the more such a figure would be bound to arise. And the elder who stood out as leader came to be called the *episkopos*, the *superintendent* of the church. But it is to be noted that he was simply a leader among equals. He was in fact the elder whom circumstances and personal qualities had combined to make a leader for the work of the church.

It will be seen that to translate *episkopos* by the word *bishop* in the New Testament now gives the word a misleading meaning. It is better to translate it as *overseer* or *superintendent*.

THE APPOINTMENT AND THE DUTIES OF THE LEADERS OF THE CHURCH

1 Timothy 3:1–7 (*contd*)

THIS passage is also interesting in that it tells us something of the appointment and the duties of the leaders of the Church.

(1) They were formally set apart for their office. Titus was to ordain elders in every church (Titus 1:5). The office-bearer of the church is not made an office-bearer in secret but is publicly set apart; the honour of the church is delivered into his hands in public.

(2) They had to undergo a period of testing. They had first to be proved (1 Timothy 3:10). No one builds a bridge or a piece of machinery with metal which has not been tested. The Church might do well to be stricter than it is in the testing of those chosen for leadership.

(3) They were paid for the work which they had to do. The labourer deserved to be paid (1 Timothy 5:18). The Christian leader does not work for pay; but, on the other hand, the duty of the church which chose him for the work is to supply him with the means to live.

(4) They could be reprimanded (1 Timothy 5:19–22). In the early Church, the office-bearer had a double function. He was a leader of the church, but he was also the servant of the church. He had to answer for his stewardship. Christian

office-bearers must never think themselves answerable to no one; they are answerable to God and to the people over whom God gave them the task of presiding.

(5) They had the duty of *presiding* over the Christian assembly and of *teaching* the Christian congregation (1 Timothy 5:17). The Christian office-bearer has the double duty of *administration* and *instruction*. It may well be that one of the tragedies of the modern Church is that the administrative function of the office-bearer has almost entirely taken the place of the teaching function. It is, for instance, sad to see how few elders of the Church are actively engaged in the teaching work of Sunday Schools.

(6) The office-bearer was not to be *a recent convert*. Two reasons are given for this advice. The first is quite clear. It is 'in case he becomes inflated with a sense of his own importance'. The second is not so clear. It is, as the Revised Standard Version has it, 'lest he fall into the condemnation of the devil'. There are three possible explanations of that strange phrase. (a) It was through his pride that Lucifer rebelled against God and was expelled from heaven. And this may simply be a second warning against the danger of pride. (b) It may mean that, if the convert who makes progress too rapidly becomes guilty of pride, he gives the devil a chance to level his charges against him. A conceited church office-bearer gives the devil a chance to say to critics of the Church: 'Look! There's your Christian! There's your church member! That's what an office-bearer is like!' (c) The word *diabolos* has two meanings. It means *devil*, and that is the way in which the Revised Standard Version has taken it here; but it also means *slanderer*. It is in fact the word used for *slanderer* in verse 11, where the women are forbidden to be slanderers. So, this phrase may mean that the recent convert, who has been appointed to office and has become, as we say, big-

headed, gives opportunity to the slanderers. His unworthy conduct is ammunition for those who are ill-disposed to the Church. No matter how we take it, the point is that the conceited church official is a liability to the Church.

But, as the early Church saw it, the responsibility of the office-bearer did not begin and end in the church. He had two other spheres of responsibility, and if he failed in them he was bound also to fail in the church.

(1) His first sphere of duty was his own home. If a man did not know how to rule his own household, how could he engage upon the task of ruling the congregation of the church (1 Timothy 3:5)? A man who had not succeeded in making a Christian home could hardly be expected to succeed in making a Christian congregation. A man who had not instructed his own family could hardly be the right man to instruct the family of the church.

(2) The second sphere of responsibility was the world. He must be 'well thought of by outsiders' (1 Timothy 3:7). He must be a man who has gained the respect of others in the day-to-day business of life. Nothing has hurt the Church more than the sight of people who are active in it but whose business and social life contradicts the faith which they claim and the principles which they teach. The Christian office-bearer must first of all be a good person.

THE CHARACTER OF THE CHRISTIAN LEADER

1 Timothy 3:1–7 (contd)

WE have just seen that the Christian leader must be someone who has won the respect of all. In this passage, there is a great series of words and phrases describing the character of the Christian leader; and it will be worth while to look at

each in turn. Before we do that, it will be interesting to set
beside them two famous descriptions by great Greek thinkers
of the good leader's character. Diogenes Laertius (7:116–26)
hands down to us the Stoic description. He must be married;
he must be without pride; he must be abstemious; and he
must combine prudence of mind with excellence of outward
behaviour. A writer called Onosander gives us the other. He
must be prudent, self-controlled, sober, frugal, hard-working,
intelligent, without love of money, neither young nor old, if
possible the father of a family, able to speak competently,
and of good reputation. It is interesting to see how these
descriptions and the Christian descriptions coincide.

The Christian leader must be *a man against whom no
criticism can be made* (*anepilēptos*). *Anepilēptos* is used of a
position which is not open to attack, of a life which is not
open to censure, of an art or technique which is so perfect
that no fault can be found with it, of an agreement which
cannot be broken. The Christian leader must not only be free
from such faults as can be attacked by definite charges; he
must be of such fine character as to be even beyond criticism.
The Douai–Rheims version of the New Testament produced
in 1582 translates this Greek word by the very unusual English
word *irreprehensible*, unable to be found fault with. The
Greeks themselves defined the word as meaning 'affording
nothing of which an adversary can take hold'. Here is the
ideal of perfection. We will not be able fully to achieve it;
but the fact remains that the Christian leader must seek to
offer to the world a life of such purity that he leaves no
loophole even for criticism of himself.

The Christian leader must have been married only once.
The Greek literally means that he must be 'the husband of
one wife'. Some take this to mean that the Christian leader
must be a married man – and it is possible that the phrase

could mean that. It is certainly true that a married man can be a recipient of confidences and a bringer of help in a way that a single man cannot be, and that he can bring a special understanding and sympathy to many situations. A few scholars take it to mean that the Christian leader cannot marry a second time, even after his wife's death. In support, they quote Paul's teaching in 1 Corinthians 7. But, in its context here, we can be quite certain that the phrase means that the Christian leader must be a loyal husband, preserving marriage in all its purity. In later days, the *Apostolic Canons* laid it down: 'He who is involved in two marriages, after his baptism, or he who has taken a concubine, cannot be an *episkopos*, a bishop.'

We may well ask why it should be necessary to lay down what seems obvious – but we must understand the state of the world in which this was written. It has been said, and with much truth, that the only totally new virtue which Christianity brought into this world was chastity. In many ways, the ancient world was in a state of moral chaos. That was true even of the Jewish world. Astonishing as it may seem, certain Jews still practised polygamy. In the *Dialogue with Trypho*, in which Justin Martyr discusses Christianity with a Jew, it is said that 'it is possible for a Jew even now to have four or five wives' (*Dialogue with Trypho*, 134). The Jewish historian Josephus can write: 'By ancestral custom a man can live with more than one wife' (*Antiquities of the Jews*, 17:1:2).

Quite apart from these unusual cases, divorce was tragically easy in the Jewish world. The Jews had the highest ideals of marriage. They said that a man must surrender his life rather than commit murder, idolatry or adultery. They had the belief that marriages are made in heaven. In the story of the marriage of Isaac and Rebecca, it is said: 'The thing comes from the Lord' (Genesis 24:50). This was taken to mean that the marriage was arranged by God. So it is said in Proverbs 19:14: 'A prudent wife is from the Lord.' In the story of Tobit, the angel says to Tobit: 'Do not be afraid, for she was set apart for you before the world was made' (Tobit 6:17). The Rabbis said: 'God sits in heaven arranging marriages.' 'Forty days before the child is formed, a heavenly voice proclaims its mate.'

For all that, the Jewish law allowed divorce. Marriage was indeed the ideal; but divorce was permitted. Marriage was 'inviolable but not indissoluble'. The Jews held that once the marriage ideal had been shattered by cruelty or infidelity or incompatibility, it was far better to allow a divorce and to permit the two to make a fresh start. The great tragedy was that the wife had no rights whatsoever. The Jewish historian Josephus says: 'With us it is lawful for a husband to dissolve a marriage, but a wife, if she departs from her husband, cannot marry another, unless her former husband put her away' (*Antiquities of the Jews*, 15:8:7). In a case of divorce by consent, in the time of the New Testament, all that was required was two witnesses and no court case at all. A husband could send his wife away for any reason; at the most, a wife could petition the court to urge her husband to write her a bill of divorce, but it could not force him even to do that.

Faced with that situation, things reached a point where 'women refused to contract marriages, and men grew grey and celibate'. A brake was put upon this process by legislation introduced by Simon ben Shetah. A Jewish wife always brought her husband a dowry which was called *Kethubah*. Simon decreed that a man had unrestricted use of the *Kethubah*, as long as he remained married to his wife, but on divorce he was absolutely liable to repay it, even if he had 'to sell his hair' to do so. This slowed down the rate of divorce;

but the Jewish system was always impaired by the fact that a wife had no rights.

In the Gentile world, things were infinitely worse. There, too, according to Roman law, a wife had no rights. Cato, the Roman statesman, said: 'If you were to take your wife in adultery, you could kill her with impunity, without any court judgment; but if you were involved in adultery, she would not dare to lift a finger against you, for it is unlawful.' Things grew so bad, and marriage became so unattractive, that in 131 BC a well-known Roman called Metellus Macedonicus made a statement which the Emperor Augustus was after-wards to quote: 'If we could do without wives, we would be rid of that nuisance. But since nature has decreed that we can neither live comfortably with them, nor live at all without them, we must look rather to our permanent interests than to passing pleasure.'

Even the Roman poets saw the dreadfulness of the situation. 'Ages rich in sin', wrote Horace, 'were the first to taint marriage and family life. From this source the evil has over-flowed.' 'Sooner will the seas be dried up,' said Propertius, 'and the stars be reft from heaven, than our women reformed.' Ovid wrote his famous, or infamous, book *The Art of Love*, and never from beginning to end mentions married love. He wrote cynically: 'These women alone are pure who are unsolicited, and a man who is angry at his wife's love affair is nothing but a rustic boor.' Seneca declared: 'Anyone whose affairs have not become notorious, and who does not pay a married woman a yearly fee, is despised by women as a mere lover of girls; in fact husbands are got as a mere decoy for lovers.' 'Only the ugly', he said, 'are loyal.' 'A woman who is content to have only two followers is a paragon of virtue.' Tacitus commended the supposedly barbarian German tribes for 'not laughing at evil, and not making seduction the spirit of the age'. When a marriage took place, the home to which the couple were going was decorated with green bay leaves. Juvenal said that there were those who entered on divorce before the bays of welcome had faded. In 19 BC, a man named Quintus Lucretius Vespillo erected a tablet to his wife which said: 'Seldom do marriages last until death undivorced, but ours continued happily for forty-one years.' The happy marriage was the astonishing exception.

Ovid and Pliny each had three wives; Caesar and Antony had four; Sulla and Pompey had five; Herod had nine; Cicero's daughter Tullia had three husbands. The Emperor Nero was the third husband of Poppaea and the fifth husband of Statilla Messalina.

It was not for nothing that the Pastorals laid it down that a Christian leader must be the husband of one wife. In a world where even the highest positions and places in society were awash with immorality, the Christian Church had to demonstrate the chastity, the stability and the sanctity of the Christian home.

THE CHARACTER OF THE CHRISTIAN LEADER

1 Timothy 3:1–7 (contd)

THE Christian leader must be *sober* (*nēphalios*) and must not *overindulge in wine* (*paroinos*). In the ancient world, wine was used all the time. Where the water supply was very inadequate and sometimes dangerous, wine was the most natural drink of all. It is wine which cheers the hearts of gods and mortals (Judges 9:13). In the restoration of Israel, the people will plant vineyards and drink wine (Amos 9:14). Strong drink is given to those who are ready to perish, and wine to those whose hearts are heavy (Proverbs 31:6).

This is not to say that the ancient world was not fully alive to the dangers of strong drink. Proverbs speaks of the disaster which comes to those who look on the wine when it is red (Proverbs 23:29–35). Wine is a mocker, strong drink a brawler (Proverbs 20:1). There are terrible stories of what happened to people through overindulgence in wine. There is the case of Noah (Genesis 9:18–27), of Lot (Genesis 19:30–8) and of Amnon (2 Samuel 13:28–9). Although the ancient world used wine as the most common of all drinks, it used it abstemiously. When wine was drunk, it was drunk in the proportion of two parts of wine to three parts of water. Anyone who got drunk would be disgraced in ordinary Roman society, let alone in the Church.

The interesting thing is the double meaning that both words in this section possess. *Nēphalios* means *sober*, but it also means *watchful* and *vigilant*; *paroinos* means *addicted to wine*, but it also means *quarrelsome* and *violent*. The point that the Pastorals make here is that Christians must allow themselves no indulgence which would lessen their Christian vigilance or tarnish their Christian conduct.

There follow two Greek words which describe two great qualities which must characterize the Christian leader. He must be *prudent* (*sōphrōn*) and *well-behaved* (*kosmios*).

We have translated *sōphrōn* as *prudent*, but it is virtually untranslatable. It is variously translated as *of sound mind*, *discreet*, *prudent*, *self-controlled*, *chaste* or *having complete control over sensual desires*. The Greeks derived it from two words which mean *to keep one's mind safe and sound*. The corresponding noun is *sōphrosunē*, and the Greeks wrote and thought much about it. It is the opposite of extreme behaviour and lack of self-control. Plato defined it as 'the mastery of pleasure and desire'. Aristotle defined it as 'that power by which the pleasures of the body are used as law commands'.

The Jewish writer Philo defined it as 'a certain limiting and ordering of the desires, which eliminates those which are external and excessive, and which adorns those which are necessary with timeliness and moderation'. Pythagoras said that it was 'the foundation on which the soul rests'. The second-century Syrian-Greek author, Iamblichus, said that 'it is the safeguard of the most excellent habits in life'. Euripides, the Greek dramatist, said that it was 'the fairest gift of God'. The seventeenth-century churchman Jeremy Taylor called it 'reason's girdle and passion's bridle'. R. C. Trench describes *sōphrosunē* as 'the condition of entire command over the passions and desires, so that they receive no further allowance than that which law and right reason admit and approve'. Gilbert Murray, the classical scholar, wrote of *sōphrōn*: 'There is a way of thinking which destroys and a way which saves. The man or woman who is *sōphrōn* walks among the beauties and perils of the world, feeling love, joy, anger and the rest; and through all he has that in his mind which saves. Whom does it save? Not him only, but, as we should say, the whole situation. It saves the imminent evil from coming to be.' E. F. Brown, who was a missionary in India, quotes in illustration of *sōphrosunē* a prayer of the thirteenth-century theologian Thomas Aquinas which asks for 'a quieting of all our impulses, fleshly and spiritual'.

The one who is *sōphrōn* is in perfect control of every emotion and instinct, which is to say that the person who is *sōphrōn* is the one in whose heart Christ reigns supreme.

The companion word is *kosmios*, which we have translated as *well-behaved*. If someone is *kosmios* in all outward behaviour, it is because that person is *sōphrōn* in the inner life. *Kosmios* means *orderly*, *honest*, *respectful*. In Greek, it has two special usages. It is common in tributes and in inscriptions to the dead. And it is commonly used to describe the person who is a good citizen. Plato defines the man who is *kosmios* as 'the citizen who is quiet in the land, who duly fulfils in his place and order the duties which are incumbent upon him as such'. This word has more in it than simply good behaviour. It describes the person whose life is beautiful and in whose character all things are harmoniously integrated.

The leader of the Church must be a man who is *sōphrōn*, his every instinct and desire under perfect control; he must be a man who is *kosmios*, his inner control being reflected in outward beauty. The leader must be one in whose heart Christ's power reigns and on whose life Christ's beauty shines.

THE CHARACTER OF THE CHRISTIAN LEADER

1 Timothy 3:1–7 (*contd*)

THE Christian leader must be *hospitable* (*philoxenos*). This is a quality on which the New Testament lays much stress. Paul bids the Roman church to 'extend hospitality' (Romans 12:13). 'Be hospitable to one another without complaining', says Peter (1 Peter 4:9). In the *Shepherd of Hermas*, one of the very early Christian writings, it is laid down: 'The *episkopos* must be hospitable, a man who gladly and at all times welcomes into his house the servants of God.' The Christian leader must be a man with an open heart and an open house.

The ancient world was very careful of the rights of guests. Strangers were under the protection of Zeus Xenios, whose title was Protector of Strangers. In the ancient world, inns were notoriously bad. In one of Aristophanes' plays, Heracles asks his companion where they will stay for the night; and the answer is: 'Where the fleas are fewest.' Plato speaks of the innkeeper being like a pirate who holds his guests to ransom. Inns tended to be dirty and expensive and, above all, immoral. The ancient world had a system of what were called *guest friendships*. Over generations, families had arrangements to give each other accommodation and hospitality. Often, the members of the families came eventually to be unknown to each other by sight and identified themselves by means of what were called *tallies*. A stranger seeking accommodation would produce one half of some object; the host would possess the other half of the tally; and when the two halves fitted each other the host knew that he had found his guest, and the guest knew that the host was indeed the long-standing family friend.

In the Christian Church, there were wandering teachers and preachers who needed hospitality. There were also many slaves with no homes of their own to whom it was a great privilege to have the right of entry to a Christian home. It was of the greatest blessing that Christians should have open to them at all times Christian homes in which they could meet like-minded people. We live in a world where there are still many who are far from home, many who are strangers in a strange place, many who live in conditions where it is hard to be a Christian. The door of the Christian home and the welcome of the Christian heart should be open to all who find themselves in such situations.

The Christian leader must be *didaktikos*, that is, must possess an *aptitude for teaching*. It has been said that his duty is 'to preach to the unconverted and to teach the converted'. There are two things to be said about this. First, it is one of the disasters of modern times that the teaching ministry of the Church is not being carried out as it should be. There is any amount of topical preaching and any amount of encouragement; but there is little use in urging people to be

Christians when they do not know what being a Christian means. Instruction is a primary duty of the Christian preacher and leader. The second thing is this. The finest and the most effective teaching is done not by *speaking* but by *being*. Even those with no gift of words can teach, by living in such a way that in them others see the reflection of the Master. A saint has been defined as someone 'in whom Christ lives again'.

The Christian leader *must not be a man who assaults others* (*plēktēs*, a *striker*). That this instruction was not unnecessary is seen in one of the very early regulations of the *Apostolic Canons*: 'A bishop, priest or deacon who smites the faithful when they err, or the unbelievers when they commit injury, and desires by such means as this to terrify them, we command to be deposed; for nowhere hath the Lord taught us this. When he was reviled, he reviled not again, but the contrary. When he was smitten, he smote not again; when he suffered, he threatened not.' It would be most unlikely that any Christian leader today would strike another Christian, but the fact remains that blustering, bullying, irritable, bad-tempered speech or action is forbidden to Christians.

The Christian leader must be *gentle*. The Greek is *epieikēs*, another of these completely untranslatable words. The noun is *epieikeia*, and Aristotle describes it as 'that which corrects justice' and as that which 'is just and better than justice'. He said that it was that quality which corrects the law when the law errs because of its generality. What he means is that sometimes it may actually be unjust to apply the strict letter of the law. R. C. Trench said that *epieikeia* means 'retreating from the letter of right better to preserve the spirit of right' and is 'the spirit which recognizes the impossibility of cleaving to all formal law . . . that recognizes the danger that ever waits upon the assertion of legal rights, lest they should be pushed into moral wrongs ... the spirit which rectifies and redresses the injustice of justice'. Aristotle describes in full the action of *epieikeia*: 'To pardon human failings; to look to the law-giver, not to the law; to the intention, not to the action; to the whole, not to the part; to the character of the actor in the long run and not in the present moment; to remember good rather than evil, and the good that one has received rather than the good that one has done; to bear being injured; to wish to settle a matter by words rather than deeds.' If there is a matter under dispute, it can be settled by consulting a book of practice and procedure, or it can be settled by consulting Jesus Christ. If there is a matter of debate, it can be settled in law, or it can be settled in love. The atmosphere of many churches would be radically changed if there was more *epieikeia* within them.

The Christian leader must be *peaceable* (*amachos*). The Greek word means *disinclined to fight*. There are people who, as we might put it, are 'trigger-happy' in their relationships with other people. But real Christian leaders want nothing so much as they want peace with other people.

The Christian leader must be *free from the love of money*. He will never do anything simply for profit's sake. He will know that there are values which are beyond all monetary value.

IN CHRISTIAN SERVICE

1 Timothy 3:8–10, 12–13

> In the same way, the deacons must be men of dignity. They must not be the kind of men who say one thing to one person and another to another. They must not be given to overindulgence in wine or prepared to stoop to disgraceful ways of making money; they must hold the

secret of the faith which has been revealed to them with a clear conscience. The deacons too must first of all be put upon probation, and, if they emerge blameless from the test, let them become deacons . . . Deacons must be married only once; they must manage their own children and their own homes well. For those who make a fine job of the office of deacon win for themselves a fine degree of honour, and they gain much boldness in their faith in Christ Jesus.

IN the early Church, the function of the deacons lay much more in the sphere of practical service. The Christian Church inherited a magnificent organization of charitable help from the Jews. No nation has ever had such a sense of responsibility for the poorer brother and sister as the Jews had. The synagogue had a regular organization for helping such people. The Jews rather discouraged the giving of individual help to individual people. They preferred that help should be given through the community and especially through the synagogue.

Each Friday in every community, two official collectors went round the markets and called on each house, collecting donations for the poor in money and in goods. The material collected in this way was distributed to those in need by a committee of two, or more if necessary. The poor of the community were given enough food for fourteen meals, that is for two meals a day for the week; but no one who already possessed a week's food in the house could receive from this fund. The fund for the poor was called the *Kuppah*, or the *basket*. In addition, to cover emergencies, there was a daily collection of food from house to house for those who were actually in dire need that day. This fund was called the *Tamhui*, or the *tray*. The Christian Church inherited this charitable organization, and no doubt it was the task of the deacons to attend to it.

Many of the qualifications of the deacon are the same as for the *episkopos*. They are to be of dignified character; they are to be abstemious; they are not to soil their hands with disreputable ways of making money; they have to undergo a test and a time of probation; they must practise what they preach, so that they can hold the Christian faith with a clear conscience.

One new qualification is added. They are to be people who are consistent in what they say. The Greek says that they must not be *dilogos* – and *dilogos* means *speaking with two voices*, saying one thing to one and another to another. In *The Pilgrim's Progress*, John Bunyan puts into By-end's mouth a description of the people who live in the town of Fair-speech. There is my Lord Turn-about, my Lord Time-server, my Lord Fair-speech, after whose ancestors the town was named, Mr Smooth-man, Mr Facing-both-ways, Mr Any-thing; and there is the parson of the parish, Mr Two-tongues. In going from house to house, and in dealing with those who needed charity, deacons had to be completely straight. Again and again, they would be tempted to evade issues by a little timely hypocrisy and smooth speaking. But those who would do the work of the Christian Church must be honest and direct.

It is clear that those who perform the office of deacon well can look for promotion to the high office of elder and will gain such a confidence in the faith that they can look anyone in the face.

WOMEN WHO SERVE THE CHURCH

1 Timothy 3:11

> In the same way, the women must be dignified; they must not be given to slanderous gossip; they must be sober; they must be in all things reliable.

As far as the Greek goes, this could refer to the wives of the deacons, or to women engaged in a similar service. It seems far more likely that it refers to women who are also engaged upon this work of charity. There must have been acts of kindness and of help which only a woman could properly do for another woman. Certainly, in the early Church there were deaconesses. They had the duty of instructing female converts and in particular of presiding and attending at their baptism, which was by total immersion.

It was necessary that such female workers should be warned against slanderous gossip and told to be absolutely reliable. When young doctors graduate and before they begin to practise, they take the Hippocratic oath, and part of that oath is a pledge never to repeat anything that they have heard in the house of a patient, or anything that they have heard about a patient, even if they have heard it on the street. In the work of helping the poor, things might easily be heard and be repeated, and infinite damage might be done.

There is always the danger of talking about the personal relationships from which slanderous gossip arises. It is a shocking and terrible thought that Christians might be responsible for repeating a confidence or passing on malicious gossip.

In Greek civilization, it was essential that the female workers of the Church should preserve their dignity. Respectable Greek women lived in the greatest seclusion; they never went out alone; they never even shared meals with the men of the family. Pericles said that the duty of an Athenian mother was to live a life so sheltered that her name should never be mentioned among men for praise or blame. The Greek historian, Xenophon, tells how a country gentleman who was a friend of his said about the young wife whom he had just married and whom he dearly loved: 'What was she

97

likely to know when I married her? Why, she was not yet fifteen when I introduced her to my house, and she had been brought up always under the strictest supervision; as far as could be managed, she had not been allowed to see anything, hear anything or ask any questions.' That is the way in which respectable Greek girls were brought up. Xenophon gives a vivid picture of one of these girl-wives gradually 'growing accustomed to her husband and becoming sufficiently tame to hold conversation with him'.

Christianity liberated women; it freed them from a kind of slavery. But there were dangers. Liberated women might misuse their new-found freedom; the respectable world might be shocked by such freedom; and so the Church had to lay down its regulations. It was by wisely using freedom, and not misusing it, that women came to hold the proud position in the Church which they hold today.

THE PRIVILEGE AND THE RESPONSIBILITY OF LIFE WITHIN THE CHURCH

1 Timothy 3:14–15

> I am writing these things to you, hoping, as I write, to come to you soon. But I am writing so that, if I am delayed, you may know how to behave yourselves in the household of God, which is the assembly of the living God, and the pillar and buttress of the truth.

HERE in one phrase is the reason why the Pastoral Epistles were written: they were written to tell people how to behave within the Church. The word for *to behave* is *anastrephesthai*; it describes what we might call a person's *way of life and conversation*. It describes an individual's whole life and character, but it especially describes people in their relationships with others. As it has been said, the word in itself lays it down that a church member's personal character must be excellent and that an individual's personal relationships with other people should be a true fellowship. A church congregation is a body of people who are friends with God and friends with each other. Paul goes on to use four words which describe four great functions of the Church.

(1) The Church is the *household* (*oikos*) of God. First and foremost, it must be a family. In a despatch written after one of his great naval victories, Admiral Nelson ascribed his victory to the fact that he 'had the happiness to command a band of brothers'. Unless a church is a band of brothers and sisters, it is not a true church at all. Love of God can exist only where mutual love exists.

(2) The Church is the assembly (*ekklēsia*) of the living God. The word *ekklēsia* literally means a company of people who have been called out. It does not mean that they have been *selected* or *picked out*. In Athens, the *ekklēsia* was the governing body of the city; and its membership consisted of *all* the citizens gathered together in an assembly. But, very naturally, at no time did everyone attend. The summons went out to come to the Assembly of the City, but only some citizens answered it and came. God's call has gone out to everyone; but only some have accepted it; and they are the *ekklēsia*, the Church. It is not that God has been selective. The invitation comes to all; but to an invitation there must be a response.

(3) The Church is the *pillar* of the truth (*stulos*). In Ephesus, to which these letters were written, the word *pillar* would have a special significance. The greatest glory of Ephesus was the Temple of Diana, or Artemis. 'Great is Artemis of the Ephesians' (Acts 19:28). It was one of the seven wonders of the world. One of its features was its pillars.

It contained 127 pillars, every one of them the gift of a king. All were made of marble, and some were studded with jewels and overlaid with gold. The people of Ephesus knew very well how beautiful a thing a pillar could be. It may well be that the idea of the word *pillar* here is not so much *support* – that is contained in the word *buttress* – as *display*. Often, the statue of a famous person is set on the top of a pillar so that it may stand out above all ordinary things and so be clearly seen, even from a distance. The idea here is that the Church's duty is to hold up the truth in such a way that all may see it.

(4) The Church is the *buttress* (*hedraiōma*) of the truth. The buttress is the support of the building. It keeps it standing intact. In a world which does not wish to face the truth, the Church holds it up for all to see. In a world which would often gladly eliminate unwelcome truth, the Church supports it against all who would seek to destroy it.

A HYMN OF THE CHURCH

1 Timothy 3:16

> As everyone must confess, great is the secret which God
> has revealed to us in our religion:
> 　He who was manifested in the flesh:
> 　He who was vindicated by the Spirit:
> 　He who was seen by angels:
> 　He who has been preached among the nations:
> 　He in whom men have believed all over the world:
> 　He who was taken up into glory.

THE great interest of this passage is that here we have a fragment of one of the hymns of the early Church. It is a setting of belief in Christ to poetry and to music, a hymn in which men and women sang their creed. We cannot expect from poetry the precision of statement for which we would look in a creed; but we must try to see what each line in this hymn is saying to us.

(1) *He who was manifested in the flesh.* Right at the beginning, it stresses the real humanity of Jesus. It says: 'Look at Jesus, and you will see the mind and the heart and the action of God, in a form that everyone can understand.'

(2) *He who was vindicated by the Spirit.* This is a difficult line. There are three things it may mean.

(a) It may mean that all through his earthly days Jesus was kept sinless by the power of the Spirit. It is the Spirit who gives us guidance; our error is that we so often refuse the Spirit's guidance. It was Jesus' perfect submission to the Spirit of God which kept him without sin.

(b) It may mean that Jesus' claims were justified by the action of the Spirit who dwelt in him. When Jesus was accused by the scribes and Pharisees of bringing about cures by the power of the devil, his answer was: 'If it is *by the Spirit of God* that I cast out demons, then the kingdom of God has come to you' (Matthew 12:28). The power that was in Jesus was the power of the Spirit, and the mighty acts which he performed were the evidence of the tremendous claims which he made.

(c) It may be that this is a reference to the resurrection. Jesus was taken and crucified as a criminal upon a cross, but through the power of the Spirit he rose again; the verdict of those who killed him was demonstrated to be false, and he was vindicated. No matter how we take this line, its meaning is that the Spirit is the power who proved Jesus to be what he claimed to be.

(3) *He who was seen by angels.* Again, there are three possible meanings.

(a) It may be a reference to Jesus' life before he came to earth.

(b) It may be a reference to his life on earth. Even on earth, the hosts of heaven were looking on at his tremendous contest with evil.

(c) It may connect with the belief of everyone in the time of Jesus that the air was full of demonic and angelic powers. Many of these powers were hostile to God and to human beings, and set on the destruction of Jesus. Paul at least once argued that they were intent on the destruction of Jesus through ignorance, and that Jesus brought to them and to men and women the wisdom which had been hidden since the world began (1 Corinthians 2:7–8). This phrase may mean that Jesus brought the truth even to the angelic and demonic powers who had never known it. However we take it, it means that the work of Jesus is so tremendous that it includes both heaven and earth.

(4) *He who has been preached among the nations.* Here we have the great truth that Jesus was not the exclusive possession of a particular race or nation. He was not the Messiah who had come to raise the Jews to earthly greatness, but the Saviour of the whole wide world.

(5) *He in whom men have believed all over the world.* Here is an almost miraculous truth stated with utter simplicity. After Jesus had died and risen again and ascended to his glory, the number of his followers was 120 (Acts 1:15). All that his followers had to offer was the story of a Galilaean carpenter who had been crucified on a hilltop in Palestine as a criminal. And yet, before seventy years had passed, that story had gone out to the ends of the earth, and men and women of every nation accepted this crucified Jesus as Saviour and Lord. In this simple phrase, there is the whole wonder of the expansion of the Church, an expansion which by any human standards is incredible.

(6) *He who was taken up into glory*. This is a reference to the ascension. The story of Jesus begins in heaven and ends in heaven. He lived as a servant; he was branded as a criminal; he was crucified on a cross; he rose with the nailprints still upon him; but the end is glory.

THE SERVICE OF GOD OR
THE SERVICE OF SATAN

I Timothy 4:1–5

> The Spirit clearly says that in the later times some will desert from the faith, through paying attention to spirits who can do nothing but lead them astray, and to teachings which come from the demons, teachings of false men whose characteristic is insincerity, teachings of men whose conscience has been branded with the mark of Satan, teachings of those who forbid marriage, and who order men to abstain from foods which God created in order that men might gratefully take their share of them in the company of those who believe and who really know the truth; for everything that God has made is good, and nothing is to be rejected, but it is to be gratefully received; for it is hallowed by the word of God and by prayer.

THE Christian Church had inherited from the Jews the belief that in this world things would be a great deal worse before they got better. The Jews always thought of time in terms of two ages. There was *this present age*, which was altogether bad and in the grip of the evil powers; and there was *the age to come*, which was to be the perfect age of God and of goodness. But the one age would not pass into the other without a last convulsive struggle. In between the two ages would come *the day of the Lord*. On that day, the world would be shaken to its foundations; there would be a last supreme battle with evil, a last universal judgment, and then the new day would dawn.

The New Testament writers took over that picture. Being Jews, they had been brought up with it. One of the expected features of the last age was heresies and false teachers. 'Many false prophets will arise and lead many astray' (Matthew 24:11). 'False messiahs and false prophets will appear and produce signs and omens, to lead astray, if possible, the elect' (Mark 13:22). In these last days, Paul looks for the emergence of 'the lawless one . . . the one destined for destruction', who would set himself up against God (2 Thessalonians 2:3).

Into the church at Ephesus such false teachers had come. The way in which their false teaching is viewed in this passage should make us think very seriously. At that time, people believed in evil spirits which haunted the air and were out to ruin men and women. It was from them that this false teaching came. But though it came *from* the demons, it came *through* human beings. It came through people whose characteristic was a smooth hypocrisy and whose consciences had been branded by Satan. It sometimes happened that slaves were branded with a mark identifying them as belonging to a certain owner. These false teachers bear upon their consciences the very brand of Satan, marking them out as his property.

Here is the threatening and the terrible thing. God is always searching for men and women who will be his instruments in the world, but the terrible fact is that the forces of evil are also looking for people to use. Here is the terrible responsibility placed upon every individual. We may accept the service of God or the service of the devil. Whose service are we to choose?

INSULTING GOD

1 Timothy 4:1–5 (*contd*)

THE heretics of Ephesus were teaching a heresy with very definite consequences for life. As we have already seen, these heretics were Gnostics; and the essence of Gnosticism was that spirit is altogether good and matter altogether evil. One of the consequences was that there were some who preached that everything to do with the body was evil and that everything in the world was evil. In Ephesus, this resulted in two definite errors. The heretics insisted that people must, as far as possible, abstain from food, for food was material and therefore evil; food ministered to the body, and the body was evil. They also insisted that people must abstain from marriage, for the instincts of the body were evil and must be entirely suppressed.

This was a constantly recurring heresy in the Church; in every generation, there were some who tried to be stricter than God. When the *Apostolic Canons* came to be written, it was necessary to set it down in black and white: 'If any overseer, priest or deacon, or anyone on the priestly list, abstains from marriage and flesh and wine, not on the ground of asceticism (that is, for the sake of discipline), but through abhorrence of them as evil in themselves, forgetting that all things are very good, and that God made man male and female, but blaspheming and slandering the workmanship of God, either let him amend, or be deposed and cast out of the Church. Likewise a layman also' (*Apostolic Canons*, 51). Irenaeus, the Bishop of Lyons, writing towards the end of the second century, tells how certain followers of Saturninus 'declare that marriage and generation are from Satan. Many likewise abstain from animal food, and draw away multitudes by a feigned temperance of this kind' (*Against Heresies*,

1:24:2). This kind of thing reached its peak in the fourth century. At that time, monks went away and lived in the Egyptian desert, entirely cut off from other people. They spent their lives in self-denial and physical deprivation. One never ate cooked food and was famous for his 'fleshlessness'. Another stood all night by a jutting crag so that it was impossible for him to sleep. Another was famous because he allowed his body to become so dirty and neglected that vermin dropped from him as he walked. Another deliberately ate salt in midsummer and then abstained from drinking water. 'A clean body', they said, 'necessarily means an unclean soul.'

The answer to those who lived in this way was that, by doing things like that, they were insulting God – for he is the creator of the world, and repeatedly his creation is said to be good. 'God saw everything that he had made, and indeed it was very good' (Genesis 1:31). 'Every moving thing that lives shall be food for you' (Genesis 9:3). 'God created humankind in his image . . . male and female he created them. God blessed them, and God said to them, "Be fruitful and multiply, and fill the earth"' (Genesis 1:27–8).

But all God's gifts have to be used in a certain way.

(1) They have to be used *in the memory that they are gifts of God*. There are things which come to us so unfailingly that we begin to forget that they are gifts and begin to take them as rights. We are to remember that all that we have is a gift from God and that there is not a living thing which could have life without him.

(2) They have to be used *in sharing*. All selfish use is forbidden. No one can monopolize God's gifts; everyone must share them.

(3) They are to be used *with gratitude*. Grace is always to be said before a meal. The Jews always said grace. They had a grace for different things. When they ate fruit, they said:

'Blessed art thou, King of the Universe, who createst the fruit of the tree.' When they drank wine, they said: 'Blessed art thou, King of the Universe, who createst the fruit of the vine.' When they ate vegetables, they said: 'Blessed art thou, King of the Universe, who createst the fruit of the earth.' When they ate bread, they said: 'Blessed art thou, King of the Universe, who bringest forth bread from the ground.' The very fact that we thank God for it makes a thing sacred. Not even the demons can touch it when it has been touched by the Spirit of God.

True Christians do not serve God by enslaving themselves with rules and regulations and insulting his creation; they serve him by gratefully accepting his good gifts and remembering that this is a world where God made all things well, and by never forgetting to share God's gifts with others.

ADVICE TO A SERVANT OF CHRIST

I Timothy 4:6–10

> If you lay these things before the brothers, you will be a fine servant of Jesus Christ, if you feed your life on the words of faith, and the fine teaching of which you have been a student and a follower. Refuse to have anything to do with irreligious stories like the tales old women tell to children. Train yourself towards the goal of true godliness. The training of the body has only a limited value; but training in godliness has a universal value for mankind, because it has the promise of life in this present age, and life in the age to come. This is a saying which deserves to be accepted by all. The reason why we toil and struggle so hard is that we have set our hopes on the living God, who is the Saviour of all men, and especially of those who believe.

THIS passage is closely packed with practical advice, not only for Timothy but for any servant of the Church who is charged with the duty of work and leadership.

(1) It tells us *how to instruct others*. The word used for *laying these things (hupotithesthai) before the brothers* is significant. It does not mean *to issue orders* but rather *to advise*, *to suggest*. It is a gentle, humble and modest word. It means that teachers must never dogmatically and belligerently lay down the law. It means that they must act rather as if they were reminding people of what they already knew or suggesting to them, not that they should learn from them, but that they should discover from their own hearts what is right. Guidance given in gentleness will always be more effective than bullying instructions laid down with force. It is possible to lead people when they will refuse to be driven.

(2) It tells us *how to face the task of teaching*. Timothy is told that he must feed his life on the words of faith. No one can give out without taking in. Those who teach must be continually learning. It is the reverse of the truth that when people become teachers they cease to be learners; each day they must come to know Jesus Christ better before they can bring him to others.

(3) It tells us *what to avoid*. Timothy is to avoid pointless tales like those which old women tell to children. It is easy to get lost in side issues and to get entangled in things which are at best embellishments. It is on the great central truths that people must constantly feed their minds and nourish their faith.

(4) It tells us *what to seek*. Timothy is told that, as athletes train their bodies, so Christians must train their souls. It is not that bodily fitness is despised; the Christian faith believes that the body is the temple of the Holy Spirit. But Paul is pleading for a sense of proportion. Physical training is good,

and even essential; but its use is limited. It develops only part of an individual, and it produces only results which last for a short time, for the body passes away. Training in godliness develops the whole person in body, mind and spirit, and its results affect not only time but eternity as well. Christians are not athletes of the gymnasium, they are the athletes of God. The greatest of the Greeks recognized this. The Athenian orator Isocrates wrote: 'No ascetic ought to train his body as a king ought to train his soul.' 'Train yourself by submitting willingly to toils, so that when they come on you unwillingly you will be able to endure them.'

(5) It shows us *the basis of the whole matter*. No one has ever claimed that the Christian life is an easy way; *but its goal is God*. It is because life is lived in the presence of God and ends in his still nearer presence that Christians are willing to struggle so hard. The greatness of the goal makes the toil worth while.

THE ONLY WAY TO SILENCE CRITICISM

1 Timothy 4:11–16

> Make it your business to hand on and to teach these commandments. Do not give anyone a chance to despise you because you are young; but in your words and in your conduct, in love, in loyalty and in purity, show yourself an example of what believing people should be. Until I come, devote your attention to the public reading of the Scriptures, to exhortation and to teaching. Do not neglect the special gift which was given to you, when the voices of the prophets picked you out for the charge which has been given to you, when the body of the elders laid their hands upon you. Think about these things; find your whole life in them, that your progress

> may be evident to all. Take heed to yourself and to your
> teaching; stick to them; for if you do, you will save
> yourself and those who hear you.

ONE of the difficulties Timothy had to overcome concerned his age. We are not to think of him as a mere youth. After all, it was fifteen years since he had first become Paul's helper. The word used for *youth* (*neotēs*) can in Greek describe anyone of military age, that is up to the age of forty. But the Church generally liked its office-bearers to be people of maturity. The *Apostolic Canons* laid it down that a man was not to become a bishop until he was over fifty, for by then 'he will be past youthful disorders'. Timothy was young in comparison with Paul, and there would be many who would watch him with a critical eye. When the British politician the elder William Pitt was making a speech in the House of Commons at the age of thirty-three, he said: 'The atrocious crime of being a young man . . . I will neither attempt to palliate or deny.' The Church has always regarded youth with a certain suspicion, and under that suspicion Timothy inevitably fell.

The advice given to Timothy is the hardest of all to follow, and yet it was the only possible advice. It was that he must silence criticism by conduct. Plato was once falsely accused of dishonourable conduct. 'Well,' he said, 'we must live in such a way that all men will see that the charge is false.' Verbal defences may not silence criticism; conduct will. What then were to be the characteristics of Timothy's conduct?

(1) First, there was to be *love*. Agape, the Greek word for the greatest of the Christian virtues, is largely untranslatable. Its real meaning is unconquerable benevolence. If we have *agape*, no matter what other people do to us or say about us, we will seek nothing but their good. We will never be bitter, never resentful, never vengeful; we will never allow ourselves

to hate; we will never refuse to forgive. Clearly, this is the kind of love which requires the whole of our nature and strength of character to achieve. Ordinarily, love is something which we cannot help. Love of our nearest and dearest is an instinctive thing. The love between the sexes is an experience which comes naturally. Ordinarily, love comes from the *heart*; but clearly this Christian love comes from the *will*. It is that conquest of self whereby we develop an unconquerable caring for other people. So, the first authenticating mark of Christian leaders is that they care for others, no matter what others do to them. That is something which any Christian leader quick to take offence and prone to bear grudges should constantly bear in mind.

(2) Second, there was to be *loyalty*. Loyalty is an unconquerable faithfulness to Christ, no matter what it may cost. It is not difficult to be a good soldier when things are going well. But the really valuable soldier is the one who can fight well with a weary body and an empty stomach, when the situation seems hopeless and the campaign seems pointless and beyond understanding. The second authenticating mark of Christian leaders is a loyalty to Christ which defies circumstances.

(3) Third, there was to be *purity*. Purity is unconquerable allegiance to the standards of Christ. When Pliny was reporting back to Trajan about the Christians in Bithynia, where he was governor, he wrote: 'They are accustomed to bind themselves by an oath to commit neither theft, nor robbery, nor adultery; never to break their word; never to deny a pledge that has been made when summoned to answer for it.' The Christian pledge is to a life of purity. Christians ought to have a standard of honour and honesty, of self-control and chastity, of discipline and consideration, far above the standards of the world. The simple fact is that the world will

never have any use for Christianity unless it can prove that it produces the best men and women. The third authenticating mark of Christian leaders is a life lived according to the standards of Jesus Christ.

THE DUTIES OF THE CHRISTIAN LEADER WITHIN THE CHURCH

1 Timothy 4:11–16 (*contd*)

CERTAIN duties are laid upon Timothy, the young leader designate of the Church. He is to devote himself to the public reading of Scripture, to exhortation and to teaching. Here we have the pattern of the Christian church service.

We possess a description of a church service in the works of Justin Martyr. About the year AD 170, he wrote a defence of Christianity to the Roman government, and in it (*First Apology*, 1:67) he says: 'On the day called the day of the Sun, a gathering takes place of all who live in the towns or in the country in one place. The Memoirs of the Apostles or the writings of the prophets are read as long as time permits. Then the reader stops, and the leader by word of mouth impresses and urges to the imitation of these good things. Then we all stand together and send forth prayers.' So, in the pattern of any Christian service, there should be four things.

(1) There should be *the reading and exposition of Scripture*. People ultimately do not gather together to hear the opinions of a preacher; they gather together to hear the word of God. The Christian service is Bible-centred.

(2) There should be *teaching*. The Bible is a difficult book, and therefore it has to be explained. Christian doctrine is not easy to understand, but Christians must be able to give a reason for the hope that is in them. There is little use in

exhorting people to be Christians if they do not know what being a Christian is. Christian preachers have given many years of their lives to gain the necessary equipment to explain the faith to others. They have been released from the ordinary duties of life in order to think, to study and to pray so that they may better expound the word of God. There can be no lasting Christian faith in any church without a teaching ministry.

(3) There should be *exhortation*. The Christian message must always end in Christian action. Someone has said that every sermon should end with the challenge: 'What about it, then?' It is not enough to present the Christian message as something to be studied and understood; it has to be presented as something to be done. Christianity is truth, but it is truth in action.

(4) There should be *prayer*. The gathering meets in the presence of God; it thinks in the Spirit of God; it goes out in the strength of God. Neither the preaching nor the listening during the service, nor the consequent action in the world, is possible without the help of the Spirit of God.

It would do us no harm sometimes to test our modern services against the pattern of the first services of the Christian Church.

THE PERSONAL DUTY OF
THE CHRISTIAN LEADER

1 Timothy 4:11–16 (*contd*)

HERE in this passage is set out in the most vivid way the personal duty of every Christian leader.

(1) Christian leaders must remember that they have been *set apart for a special task by the Church*. Their position

does not make sense apart from the Church. Their commission came from it; their work is within its fellowship; their duty is to build others into it. That is why the really important work of the Christian Church is never done by any travelling evangelist but always by its settled ministry.

(2) Christian leaders must remember *the duty to think about these things*. Their great danger is intellectual laziness and the closed mind, neglecting to study and allowing their thoughts to continue in well-worn grooves. The danger is that new truths, new methods and the attempt to restate the faith in contemporary terms may merely annoy them. Christian leaders must be Christian thinkers or they fail in their task; and to be a Christian thinker is to be an adventurous thinker as long as life lasts.

(3) Christian leaders must remember *the duty of concentration*. The danger is that they may waste their energies on many things which are not central to the Christian faith. They are presented with the invitation to many duties and confronted with the claims of many spheres of service. There was a prophet who confronted Ahab with a kind of parable. He said that in a battle a man brought him a prisoner to guard, telling him that if the prisoner escaped his own life would be forfeit; but he allowed his attention to wander, and 'while your servant was busy here and there, he was gone' (1 Kings 20:35–43). It is easy for a Christian leader to be busy here and there, and to let the central things go. Concentration is a prime duty of all Christian leaders.

(4) Christian leaders must remember *the duty of progress*. Their progress must be evident to all. It is all too true of most of us that the same things get the better of us year in and year out; that as year succeeds year, we are no further on. Christian leaders plead with others to become more like Christ. How can they do so with honesty unless daily they become more

like the Master to whom they belong and whom they seek to serve? When Toyohiko Kagawa decided to become a Christian, his first prayer was: 'God, make me like Christ.' The first prayer of Christian leaders must be that they may grow more like Christ, for only in this way will they be able to lead others to him.

THE DUTY TO REPRIMAND

1 Timothy 5:1-2

> If you have occasion to reprimand an older man, do not do so sharply, but appeal to him as you would to a father. Treat the younger men like brothers; the older women as mothers; the younger women as sisters, in complete purity.

IT is always difficult to reprimand anyone with graciousness; and to Timothy there would sometimes fall a duty that was doubly difficult – that of reprimanding someone older than himself. The fourth-century Church father John Chrysostom writes: 'Rebuke is in its own nature offensive particularly when it is addressed to an old man; and when it proceeds from a young man too, there is a threefold show of forwardness. By the manner and mildness of it, therefore, he would soften it. For it is possible to reprove without offence, if one will only make a point of this; it requires great discretion, but it may be done.'

Rebuke is always a problem. We may so dislike the task of speaking a warning word that we may avoid it altogether. Many people would have been saved from sorrow and disaster if someone had only spoken a word of warning in time. There can be no more poignant tragedy than to hear someone say: 'I would never have come to this, if you had only spoken in time.' It is always wrong to hold back from speaking the word that needs to be heard.

We may reprimand a person in such a way that there is clearly nothing but anger in our voice and nothing but bitterness in our minds and hearts. A rebuke given solely in anger may produce fear, and may cause pain, but it will almost inevitably arouse resentment; and its ultimate effect may well be to drive those who are rebuked even more firmly into their mistaken ways. The rebuke of anger and the reprimand of contemptuous dislike are seldom effective and are far more likely to do harm than good.

It was said of Florence Allshorn, the great missionary teacher, that, when she was principal of a women's college, she always rebuked her students, when the need arose, as it were with her arm around them. The rebuke which clearly comes from love is the only effective one. If we ever have cause to reprimand anyone, we must do so in such a way as to make it clear that we do this not because we find a cruel pleasure in it, not because we want to do it, but because we are under the compulsion of love and seek to help, not to hurt.

THE RELATIONSHIPS OF LIFE

1 Timothy 5:1-2 (contd)

THESE two verses lay down the spirit which the relationships between different age groups should display.

(1) To older people, we must show *affection and respect*. An older man is to be treated like a father and an older woman like a mother. The ancient world knew very well the deference and respect which were appropriate to age. The Roman orator and statesman Cicero writes: 'It is, then, the duty of a young

man to show deference to his elders, and to attach himself to the best and most approved of them, so as to receive the benefit of their counsel and influence. For the inexperience of youth requires the practical wisdom of age to strengthen and direct it. And this time of life is above all to be protected against sensuality and trained to toil and endurance of both mind and body, so as to be strong for active duty in military and civil service. And even when they wish to relax their minds and give themselves up to enjoyment, they should beware of excesses and bear in mind the rules of modesty. And this will be easier, if the young are not unwilling to have their elders join them, even in their pleasures' (*De Officiis*, 1:34). Aristotle writes: 'To all older persons too one should give honour appropriate to their age, by rising to receive them and finding seats for them and so on' (*Nicomachean Ethics*, 9:2). It is one of the tragedies of life that youth is so often apt to find age a nuisance. A famous French phrase says with a sigh: 'If youth but had the knowledge, if age but had the power.' But when there is mutual respect and affection, then the wisdom and experience of age can co-operate with the strength and enthusiasm of youth, to the great profit of both.

(2) To our contemporaries, we must show *brotherliness*. The younger men are to be treated like brothers. Aristotle has it: 'To comrades and brothers, one should allow freedom of speech and common use of all things' (*Nicomachean Ethics*, 9:2). With our contemporaries, there should be tolerance and sharing.

(3) To those of the opposite sex, our relationships must always be marked with *purity*. The Arabs have a phrase for a man of honour; they call him 'a brother of girls'. There is a famous phrase which speaks of 'Platonic friendship'. Love must be kept for one; it is a fearful thing when physical matters dominate the relationship between the sexes, and a

man cannot see a woman without thinking in terms of her body.

CHURCH AND FAMILY DUTY

I Timothy 5:3–8

> Honour widows who are genuinely in a widow's desti-
> tute position. But if any widow has children or grand-
> children, let such children learn to begin by discharging
> the duties of religion in their own homes; and let them
> learn to give a return for all that their parents have done
> for them; for this is the kind of conduct that meets with
> God's approval. Now she who is genuinely in the
> position of a widow, and who is left all alone, has set
> her hope on God, and night and day she devotes herself
> to petitions and prayers. But she who lives with
> voluptuous wantonness is dead even though she is still
> alive. Pass on these instructions that they may be
> irreproachable. If anyone fails to provide for his own
> people, and especially for the members of his own
> family, he has denied the faith and is worse than an
> unbeliever.

THE Christian Church inherited a fine tradition of charity to those in need. No nation has ever cared more for the needy and the elderly than the Jews. Advice is now given for the care of widows. There may well have been two classes of women here. There were certainly widows who had become widows in the normal way by the death of their husbands. But it was not uncommon in the Gentile world, in certain places, for a man to have more than one wife. When a man became a Christian, he could not go on being a polygamist, and therefore he had to choose which wife he was going to live with. That meant that some wives had to be sent away, and they were clearly in a very unfortunate position. It may be that such women as these were also considered to be widows and were given the support of the Church.

Jewish law laid it down that at the time of his marriage a man ought to make provision for his wife, should she become a widow. The very first office-bearers whom the Christian Church appointed had this duty of caring fairly for the widows (Acts 6:1). Ignatius lays it down: 'Let not widows be neglected. After the Lord be thou their guardian.' The *Apostolic Constitutions* direct the bishop: 'O bishop, be mindful of the needy, both reaching out thy helping hand and making provision for them as the steward of God, distributing the offerings seasonably to every one of them, to the widows, the orphans, the friendless, and those tried with affliction.' The same book has an interesting and kindly instruction: 'If anyone receives any service to carry to a widow or poor woman . . . let him give it the same day.' As the proverb has it, 'He gives twice who gives quickly' – and the Church was concerned that those in poverty should not have to remain in need while one of its servants delayed.

It is to be noted that the Church did not propose to assume responsibility for older people whose children were alive and well able to support them. The ancient world was very definite that it was the duty of children to support elderly parents; and, as E. K. Simpson has pointed out in his commentary, 'A religious profession which falls below the standard of duty recognized by the world is a wretched fraud.' The Church would never have agreed that its charity should become an excuse for children to evade their responsibility.

It was Greek law from the time of the Athenian law-giver Solon that sons and daughters were not only morally but also legally bound to support their parents. Those who refused that duty lost their civil rights. Aeschines, the Athenian orator, says in one of his speeches: 'And whom did our law-giver [Solon] condemn to silence in the Assembly of the people? And where does he make this clear? "Let there be", he says, "a scrutiny of public speakers, in case there be any speaker in the Assembly of the people who is a striker of his father or mother, or who neglects to maintain them or to give them a home."' Demosthenes, the orator and statesman, says: 'I regard the man who neglects his parents as unbelieving in and hateful to the gods, as well as to men.' The Jewish writer Philo, writing of the commandment to honour parents, says: 'When old storks become unable to fly, they remain in their nests and are fed by their children, who go to endless exertions to provide their food because of their piety.' To Philo, it was clear that even the animals acknowledged the obligation to elderly parents – and how much more must human offspring? In the *Nicomachean Ethics*, Aristotle lays it down: 'It would be thought in the matter of food we should help our parents before all others, since we owe our nourishment to them, and it is more honourable to help in this respect the authors of our being, even before ourselves.' As Aristotle saw it, adult children themselves must starve before they would see their parents starve. In *The Laws*, Plato has the same conviction of the debt that is owed to parents: 'Next comes the honour of loving parents, to whom, as is meet, we have to pay the first and greatest and oldest of debts, considering that all which a man has belongs to those who gave him birth and brought him up, and that he must do all that he can to minister to them; first, in his property; secondly, in his person; and thirdly, in his soul; paying the debts due to them for their care and travail which they bestowed upon him of old in the days of his infancy, and which he is now able to pay back to them, when they are old and in the extremity of their need.'

It is the same with the Greek poets. When Iphigenia is speaking to her father Agamemnon, in Euripides' *Iphigenia at Aulis*, she says (the translation is that of A. S. Way):

> 'Twas I first called thee father, thou me child.
> 'Twas I first throned my body on thy knees,
> And gave thee sweet caresses and received.
> And this thy word was: 'Ah, my little maid,
> Blest shall I see thee in a husband's halls
> Living and blooming worthily of me?'
> And as I twined my fingers in thy beard,
> Whereto I now cling, thus I answered thee:
> 'And what of thee? Shall I greet thy grey hairs,
> Father, with loving welcome in mine halls,
> Repaying all thy fostering toil for me?'

The child's joy was to look forward to the day when she could repay all that her father had done for her.

When Euripides tells how Orestes discovered that an unkind fate had made him unwittingly kill his own father, he makes him say:

> He fostered me a babe, and many a kiss
> Lavished upon me . . .
> O wretched heart and soul of mine!
> I have rendered foul return! What veil of gloom
> Can I take for my face? Before me spread
> What cloud, to shun the old man's searching eye?

To Euripides, the most haunting sin on earth was failure in duty to a parent.

The New Testament ethical writers were certain that support of parents was an essential part of Christian duty. It is something to be remembered. We live in a time when even the most sacred duties are pushed on to the state and when we expect, in so many cases, public charity to do what private piety ought to do. As the Pastorals see it, help given to a parent is two things. First, it is an honouring of the recipient. It is the only way in which children can demonstrate the esteem that they feel. Second, it is an admission of the claims of love. It is repaying love received in time of need with love given in time of need; and only with love can love be repaid.

There remains one thing left to say, and to leave it unsaid would be unfair. This passage goes on to lay down certain of the qualities of the people whom the Church is called upon to support. What is true of the Church is true within the family. If a person is to be supported, that person must be supportable. If a parent is taken into the home of a son or daughter and then by inconsiderate conduct causes nothing but trouble, another situation arises. There is a double duty here – the duty of the child to support the parent, and the duty of the parent to behave in such a way that that support is possible within the structure of the home.

AN HONOURED AND A USEFUL OLD AGE

1 Timothy 5:9–10

> Let a woman be enrolled as a widow only if she is more than sixty years of age; if she has been the wife of one husband; if she has earned an attested reputation for good works; if she has nourished children; if she has been hospitable to strangers; if she has helped those in trouble; if she has washed the feet of the saints; if she has devoted herself to every good work.

FROM this passage, it is clear that the Church had an official register of widows; and it seems that the word *widow* is being used in a double sense. Women who were elderly and whose husbands had died and whose lives were lovely and filled with good works were the responsibility of the Church; but it is also true that, perhaps as early as this, and certainly later in the early Church, there was an official order of widows, an order of elderly women who were set apart for special duties.

In the regulations of the *Apostolic Constitutions*, which tell us what the life and organization of the Church were like in the third century, it is laid down: 'Three widows shall be appointed, two to persevere in prayer for those who are in temptation, and for the reception of revelations, when such are necessary, but one to assist women who are visited with sickness; she must be ready for service, discreet, telling the elders what is necessary, not avaricious, not given to much love of wine, so that she may be sober and able to perform the night services, and other loving duties.'

Such widows were not ordained as the elders and the bishops were; they were set apart by prayer for the work which they had to do. They were not to be set apart until they were over sixty years of age. That was an age which the ancient world also considered to be specially suited for concentration on the spiritual life. Plato, in his plan for the ideal state, held that sixty was the right age for men and women to become priests and priestesses.

The Pastoral Epistles are always intensely practical; and in this passage we find seven qualifications which the Church's widows must satisfy.

They must have been the wife of one husband. In an age when the marriage bond was taken lightly and almost universally dishonoured, they must be examples of purity and fidelity.

They must have earned an attested reputation for good works. The office-bearers of the Church, male or female, have within their keeping not only their personal reputation but also the good name of the Church. Nothing discredits a church like unworthy office-bearers; and nothing is so good an advertisement for it as an office-bearer who has taken his or her Christianity into the activity of daily living.

They must have nourished children. This may well mean more than one thing. It may mean that widows must have given proof of their Christian piety by bringing up their own families in the Christian way. But it can mean more than that. In an age when the marriage bond was very lax, and men and women changed their partners with bewildering rapidity, children were regarded as a misfortune. When a child was born, it was brought and laid before the father's feet. If the father stooped and lifted the child, that meant that he acknowledged it and was prepared to accept responsibility for its upbringing. If the father turned and walked away, the child was quite literally thrown out, like an unwanted piece of rubbish. It often happened that such unwanted children were collected by unscrupulous people and, if they were girls, brought up to stock the public brothels. If they were boys, they were trained to be slaves or gladiators for the public games. It would be a Christian duty to rescue such children from death and worse than death, and to bring them up in a Christian home. So, this may mean that widows must be women who had been prepared to give a home to abandoned children.

They must have been hospitable to strangers. Inns in the ancient world were notoriously dirty, expensive and immoral. Those who opened their homes to travellers, or to strangers in an unfamiliar place, or to young people whose work and study took them far from home, were doing a most valuable service to the community. The open door of the Christian home is always a precious thing.

They must have washed the feet of the saints. That need not be taken literally, although the literal sense is included.

To wash a person's feet was the task of a slave, the lowest of all duties. This means that Christian widows must have been willing to accept the humblest tasks in the service of Christ and of his people. The Church needs its leaders who will be prominent in its work, but no less it needs those who are prepared to do the tasks which receive no prominence and little thanks.

They must have helped those in trouble. In times of persecution, it was no small thing to help Christians who were suffering for their faith. This was to identify oneself with them and to accept the risk of coming to a similar punishment. Christians must stand by those in trouble for their faith, even if, in so doing, they bring trouble on themselves.

They must have devoted themselves to all good works. We all concentrate on something; Christians concentrate their lives on obeying Christ and helping others.

When we study these qualifications for those who were to be enrolled as widows, we see that they are the qualifications of every true Christian.

THE PRIVILEGE AND THE DANGERS OF SERVICE

1 Timothy 5:9–10 (*contd*)

As we have already said, the widows became an accepted order in the Christian Church, if not as early as the time of the Pastoral Epistles then certainly in later days. Their place and work are dealt with in the first eight chapters of the third book of the *Apostolic Constitutions*, and these chapters reveal the use that such an order could be and the dangers into which it almost inevitably ran.

(1) It is laid down that women who would serve the Church must be women of discretion. Particularly, they must

be discreet in speech: 'Let every widow be meek, quiet, gentle, sincere, free from anger, not talkative, not clamorous, not hasty of speech, not given to evil-speaking, not given to finding fault, not double-tongued, not a busybody. If she sees or hears anything that is not right, let her be as one that does not see, and as one that does not hear.' Such officers of the church must be very careful when they discuss the faith with outsiders: 'For unbelievers when they hear the doctrine concerning Christ, not explained as it ought to be, but defectively, especially that concerning his incarnation or his passion, will rather reject it with scorn, and laugh at it as false, than praise God for it.'

There is nothing more dangerous than an officer of the church who talks about things which ought to be kept secret; and a church office-bearer must be equipped to communicate the gospel in a way that will make people think more and not less of Christian truth.

(2) It is laid down that women who serve the Church must not be gadabouts, always popping into and out of the houses of neighbours: 'Let the widow therefore own herself to be the "altar of God", and let her sit in her own house, and not enter into the houses of the unfaithful, under any pretence to receive anything; for the altar of God never runs about, but is fixed in one place. Let therefore the virgin and the widow be such as do not run about, or visit the houses of those who are alien from the faith. For such as these are gadabouts and impudent.' The restless gossip is ill-equipped to serve the Church.

(3) It is laid down that widows who accept the charity of the Church are not to be greedy. 'There are some widows who esteem gain their business; and since they ask without shame, and receive without being satisfied, render other people more backward in giving . . . Such a woman is thinking

in her mind of where she can go to get, or that a certain woman who is her friend has forgotten her, and she has something to say to her . . . She murmurs at the deaconess who distributed the charity, saying, "Do you not see that I am in more distress and need of your charity? Why therefore have you preferred her before me?"' It is not an attractive act to seek to live off the Church rather than for the Church.

(4) It is laid down that such women must do all they can to help themselves: 'Let her take wool and assist others rather than herself want from them.' The charity of the Church does not exist to make people lazy and dependent.

(5) Such women are not to be envious and jealous: 'We hear that some widows are jealous, envious slanderers, and envious of the quiet of others . . . It becomes them when one of their fellow-widows is clothed by anyone, or receives money, or meat, or drink, or shoes, at the refreshment of their sister, to thank God.'

There we have at one and the same time a picture of the faults of which the Church is all too full, and of the virtues which should be the marks of the true Christian life.

THE PERILS OF IDLENESS

I Timothy 5:11–16

> Refuse to enrol the younger women as widows, for when they grow impatient with the restrictions of Christian widowhood, they wish to marry, and so deserve condemnation, because they have broken the pledge of their first faith; and, at the same time, they learn to be idle and to run from house to house. Yes, they can become more than idle; they can become gossips and busybodies, saying things which should not be repeated. It is my wish that the younger widows should marry,

and bear children, and run a house and home, and give our opponents no chance of abuse. For, even as things are, some of them have turned aside from the way to follow Satan. If any believing person has widowed relations, let such a person help them, and let not the Church be burdened with the responsibility, so that it may care for those who are genuinely in the position of widows.

A PASSAGE like this reflects the situation in society in which the early Church found itself.

It is not that younger widows are condemned for marrying again. What is condemned is this. A young husband dies; and the widow, in the first bitterness of sorrow and on the impulse of the moment, decides to remain a widow all her life and to dedicate her life to the Church, but later she changes her mind and remarries. That woman is regarded as having taken Christ as her bridegroom. So, by marrying again, she is regarded as breaking her marriage vow to Christ. She would have been better never to have taken the vow.

What complicated this matter very much was the social background of the times. It was next to impossible for a single or a widowed woman to earn her living honestly. There was practically no trade or profession open to her. The result was inevitable; she was almost driven to prostitution in order to live. The Christian woman, therefore, had either to marry or to dedicate her life completely to the service of the Church; there was no half-way house.

In any event, the perils of idleness remain the same in any age. There was the danger of becoming *restless*: because a woman did not have enough to do, she might become one of those individuals who drift from house to house in an empty social round. It was almost inevitable that such a woman would become a *gossip*: because she had nothing important to talk about, she would tend to talk scandal, repeating tales from house to house, each time with a little more embellishment and a little more malice. Such a woman ran the risk of becoming a *busybody*: because she had nothing of her own to hold her attention, she would be very apt to be over-interested and over-interfering in the affairs of others.

It was true then, as it is true now, that, as the hymn-writer Isaac Watts had it, 'Satan finds some mischief still for idle hands to do.' The full life is always the safe life, and the empty life is always the life in peril.

So, the advice is that these younger women should marry and engage upon the greatest task of all, rearing a family and making a home. Here we have another example of one of the main thoughts of the Pastoral Epistles. They are always concerned with how Christians appear to the outside world. Do they give any opportunity to criticize the Church or reason to admire it? It is always true that 'the greatest handicap the Church has is the unsatisfactory lives of professing Christians' and equally true that the greatest argument for Christianity is a genuinely Christian life.

RULES FOR PRACTICAL ADMINISTRATION

1 Timothy 5:17–22

> Let elders who discharge their duties well be judged worthy of double honour, especially those who toil in preaching and in teaching; for Scripture says: 'You must not muzzle the ox when he is treading the corn', and 'The workman deserves his pay.'
>
> Do not accept an accusation against an elder unless on the evidence of two or three witnesses.
>
> Rebuke those who persist in sin in the presence of all, so that the others may develop a healthy fear of sinning.

> I adjure you before God and Christ Jesus and the chosen angels that you keep these regulations impartially, and that you do nothing because of your own prejudices or predilection.
>
> Do not be too quick to lay your hands on any man, and do not share the sins of others. Keep yourself pure.

HERE is a series of the most practical regulations for the life and administration of the Church.

(1) Elders are to be properly honoured and properly paid. When threshing was done in the middle east, the sheaves of corn were laid on the threshing-floor; then oxen in pairs were driven repeatedly across them; or they were tethered to a post in the middle and made to march round and round on the grain; or a threshing sledge was harnessed to them and the sledge was drawn to and fro across the corn. In all cases, the oxen were left unmuzzled and were free to eat as much of the grain as they wanted, as a reward for the work they were doing. The actual law that the ox must not be muzzled is in Deuteronomy 25:4.

The saying that the labourer deserves to be paid is a saying of Jesus (Luke 10:7). It is most likely a proverbial saying which he quoted. Everyone who works deserves financial support; and the harder people work, the more they deserve. Christianity has never had anything to do with the sentimental ethic which clamours for equal shares for all. The reward must always be proportionate to the level of toil.

It is to be noted what kind of elders are to be especially honoured and rewarded. It is those who toil in *preaching* and *teaching*. The elder whose service consisted only in words and discussion and argument is not in question here. Those whom the Church really honoured were the ones who worked to edify and build it up by preaching the truth and by educating the young and the new converts in the Christian way.

(2) It was Jewish law that no one should be condemned on the evidence of a single witness: 'A single witness shall not suffice to convict a person of any crime or wrongdoing in connection with any offence that may be committed. Only on the evidence of two or three witnesses shall a charge be sustained' (Deuteronomy 19:15). The *Mishnah*, the codified Rabbinic law, in describing the process of trial, says: 'The second witness was likewise brought in and examined. If the testimony of the two was found to agree, the case for the defence was opened.' If a charge was supported by the evidence of only one witness, it was held that there was no case to answer.

In later times, church regulations laid it down that the two witnesses must be Christian, for it would have been easy for a malicious non-Christian to make up a false charge against a Christian elder in order to discredit him, and through him to discredit the Church. In the early days, the Church authorities did not hesitate to apply discipline; and Theodore of Mopseuestia, one of the early fathers who lived in the late fourth and early fifth centuries, points out how necessary this regulation was, because the elders were always liable to be disliked and were especially open to malicious attack 'due to the retaliation by some who had been rebuked by them for sin'. Those who had been disciplined might well seek to get their own back by maliciously charging an elder with some irregularity or some sin.

The fact remains that this would be a happier world – and the Church, too, would be happier – if people would realize that it is nothing less than sin to spread stories of whose truth they are not sure. Irresponsible, slanderous and malicious talk does infinite damage and causes infinite heartbreak, and such talk will not go unpunished by God.

RULES FOR PRACTICAL ADMINISTRATION

I Timothy 5:17-22 (*contd*)

(3) Those who persist in sin are to be publicly rebuked. That public rebuke had a double value. It sobered sinners into a consideration of their ways, and it made others take care that they did not involve themselves in a similar humiliation. The threat of publicity is no bad thing if it keeps people on the right path, even through fear. A wise leader will know the time to keep things quiet and the time for public rebuke. But, whatever happens, the Church must never give the impression that it is condoning sin.

(4) Timothy is urged to administer his office without favouritism or prejudice. The biblical scholar B. S. Easton writes: 'The well-being of every community depends on impartial discipline.' Nothing does more harm than when some people are treated as if they could do no wrong and others as if they could do no right. Justice is a universal virtue, and the Church must surely never fall below the impartial standards which even the world demands.

(5) Timothy is warned not to be too hasty 'in laying hands on any man'. That may mean one of two things.

(a) It may mean that he is not to be too quick in laying hands on any man to ordain him to office in the Church. Before people gain promotion in business, or in teaching, or in the army or the navy or the air force, they must prove that they deserve it. No one should ever start at the top. This is doubly important in the Church, for those who are raised to high office and then fail in it bring dishonour, not only on themselves, but also on the Church. In a critical world, the Church cannot be too careful in regard to the kind of men and women whom it chooses as its leaders.

(b) In the early Church, it was the custom to lay hands on a sinner who repented, who had given proof of repentance and who had returned to the fold of the Church. It is laid down: 'As each sinner repents, and shows the fruits of repentance, lay hands on him, while all pray for him.' The early Church historian Eusebius tells us that it was the ancient custom that repentant sinners should be received back with the laying on of hands and with prayer. If that is the meaning here, it will be a warning to Timothy not to be too quick to receive back anyone who has brought disgrace on the Church, to wait until the individual has shown genuine penitence and a true determination to live according to that declaration of repentance. That is not for a moment to say that such a person is to be held at arm's length and treated with suspicion, but rather to be treated with all sympathy and with all help and guidance in the period of probation. But it is to say that membership of the Church is never to be treated lightly, and that people must show their penitence for the past and their determination for the future before they are received not into the *fellowship* of the Church but into its *membership*. The fellowship of the Church exists to help such people redeem themselves, but its membership is for those who have truly pledged their lives to Christ.

ADVICE FOR TIMOTHY

I Timothy 5:23

> Stop drinking only water, and use a little wine for the
> sake of your stomach, to help your frequent illnesses.

THIS sentence shows the real intimacy of these letters. Amid the affairs of the Church and the problems of administration,

Paul finds time to slip in a little bit of loving advice to Timothy about his health.

There had always been a strain of self-denial in Jewish religion. When a man took the Nazirite vow (Numbers 6:1–21), he was pledged never to taste any of the product of the vine: 'They shall separate themselves from wine and strong drink; they shall drink no wine vinegar or other vinegar, and shall not drink any grape juice or eat grapes, fresh or dried. All their days as nazirites they shall eat nothing that is produced by the grapevine, not even the seeds or the skins' (Numbers 6:3–4). The Rechabites were also pledged to abstain from wine. The Book of Jeremiah tells how Jeremiah went and set before the Rechabites wine and cups: 'But they answered, "We will drink no wine; for our ancestor Jonadab son of Rechab commanded us, 'You shall never drink wine, neither you nor your children; nor shall you ever build a house, or sow seed; nor shall you plant a vine-yard'"' (Jeremiah 35:6–7). Now, Timothy was on one side a Jew – his mother was Jewish (Acts 16:1) – and it may well be that from his mother he had inherited this abstemious way of living. On his father's side, he was a Greek. We have already seen that behind the Pastorals there is the heresy of Gnosticism, which saw all matter as evil and often resulted in self-denial; and it may well be that Timothy was unconsciously influenced by this Greek abstinence as well.

Here we have a great truth which Christians forget at their peril – that we dare not neglect the body, for often spiritual dullness and sterility come from the simple fact that the body is tired and neglected. No machine will run well unless it is cared for, and neither will the body. We cannot do Christ's work well unless we are physically fit to do it. There is no virtue – rather the reverse – in neglect of or contempt for the body. *Mens sana in corpore sano*, a healthy mind in a healthy body, was the old Roman ideal – and it is the Christian ideal too.

This is a text which has much troubled those who are advocates of total abstinence. It must be remembered that it does not give anyone a licence to indulge in drink to excess; it simply approves the use of wine where it may be medicinally helpful. If it does lay down any principle at all, E. F. Brown has well stated it: 'It shows that while total abstinence may be recommended as a wise counsel, it is never to be enforced as a religious obligation.' Paul is simply saying that there is no virtue in the self-denial which does the body more harm than good.

THE IMPOSSIBILITY OF
ULTIMATE CONCEALMENT

I Timothy 5:24-5

> Some men's sins are plain for all to see, and lead the way to judgment; the sins of others will duly catch up on them. Even so, there are good deeds which are plain for all to see, and there are things of a very different quality which cannot be hidden.

THIS saying tells us to leave things to God and be content. There are obvious sinners, whose sins are clearly leading to their disaster and their punishment; and there are secret sinners who, behind a façade of blameless virtue, live a life that is in essence evil and ugly. What other people cannot see, God does. As the thirteenth-century theologian Thomas Aquinas said, 'Man sees the deed, but God sees the intention.' There is no escape from the ultimate confrontation with the God who sees and knows everything.

There are some whose good deeds are plain for all to see, and who have already won the praise and thanks and congratulations of others. There are some whose good deeds have never been noticed, never appreciated, never thanked, never praised, never valued as they ought to have been. They need not feel either disappointed or embittered. God knows the good deed also, and he will repay, for he is never in anyone's debt.

Here, we are told that we must neither grow angry at the apparent escape of some people nor grow embittered at the apparent thanklessness of others, but that we must be content to leave all things to the ultimate judgment of God.

HOW TO BE A SLAVE AND A CHRISTIAN

I Timothy 6:1–2

> Let all those who are slaves under the yoke hold their own masters to be worthy of all respect, in order that no one may have an opportunity to speak evil of the name of God and the Christian teaching. If they have masters who are believers, let them not try to take advantage of them because they are brothers, but rather let them render even better service, because those who lay claim to that service are believers and beloved.

BENEATH the surface of this passage, there are certain supremely important Christian principles for everyday life and work.

Christian slaves were in a peculiarly difficult position. If they were the slaves of a non-Christian master, they might very easily make it clear that they regarded their master as bound for damnation and themselves as the heirs of salvation. Their Christianity might well give them a feeling of intolerant superiority, which would create an impossible situation. On the other hand, if their master was a Christian, the slaves might be tempted to take advantage of the relationship and to trade upon it, using it as an excuse for producing inefficient work in the expectation of escaping all punishment. They might think that the fact that they and their master were Christians entitled them to all kinds of special consideration. There was an obvious problem here. We must note two general things.

(1) In those early days, the Church did not emerge as the would-be destroyer of slavery by violent and sudden means. And it was wise. There were something like 60,000,000 slaves in the Roman Empire. Simply because of their numbers, they were always regarded as potential enemies. If ever there was a slave revolt, it was put down with merciless force, because the Roman Empire could not afford to allow the slaves to rebel. If slaves ran away and were caught, they were either executed or branded on their foreheads with the letter F, standing for *fugitivus*, which means *runaway*. There was indeed a Roman law which stated that, if a master was murdered, all his slaves could be questioned under torture and could indeed be put to death in a body. E. K. Simpson wisely writes: 'Christianity's spiritual campaign would have been fatally compromised by stirring the smouldering embers of class-hatred into a devouring flame, or opening an asylum for runaway slaves in its bosom.'

For the Church to have encouraged slaves to revolt against their masters would have been fatal. It would simply have caused civil war, mass murder and the complete discredit of the Church. What happened was that, as the centuries went on, Christianity so permeated civilization that in the end the slaves were freed voluntarily and not by force. Here is a tremendous lesson. It is the proof that neither individuals nor the world nor society can be reformed by force and by legislation. The reform must come through the slow penetration of the Spirit of Christ into the human situation. Things have to happen in God's time, not in ours. In the end, the slow way is the sure way, and the way of violence always defeats itself.

(2) There is here the further truth, that 'spiritual equality does not efface civil distinctions'. It is a continual danger that people may unconsciously regard their Christianity as an excuse for slackness and inefficiency. Because they and their employer are both Christians, they may expect to be treated with special consideration. But the fact that employer and employees are Christian does not release the employees from doing a good day's work and earning wages. Christians are under the same obligation to submit to discipline and to earn their pay as everyone else.

(3) What then is the duty of Christian slaves as the Pastorals see it? It is to be good slaves. If they are not, if they are slack and careless, if they are disobedient and insolent, they merely supply the world with ammunition to criticize the Church. Christian workers must commend their Christianity by being better at their work than other people. In particular, their work will be done in a new spirit. They will not now think of themselves as being unwillingly compelled to work; they will think of themselves as rendering service to their master, to God and to other people. Their aim will be not to see how little can be forced out of them, but how much they can willingly do. As George Herbert had it in that fine hymn 'Teach Me My God and King':

> A servant with this clause
>   Makes drudgery divine:
> Who sweeps a room, as for thy laws,
>   Makes that and the action fine.

FALSE TEACHERS AND FALSE TEACHING

I Timothy 6:3–5

> If any man offers a different kind of teaching, and does not apply himself to sound words (it is the words of our Lord Jesus Christ I mean) and to godly teaching, he has become inflated with pride. He is a man of no understanding; rather he has a diseased addiction to subtle speculations and battles of words, which can be only a source of envy, strife, the exchange of insults, evil suspicions, continual altercations of men whose minds are corrupt and who are destitute of the truth, men whose belief is that religion is a means of making gain.

THE circumstances of life in the ancient world presented the false teachers with an opportunity which they were not slow to take. On the Christian side, the Church was full of wandering prophets whose very way of life gave them a certain prestige. The Christian service was much more informal than it is now. Anyone who felt called to deliver a message was free to give it, and the door was wide open to those who were out to propagate a false and misleading message. On the non-Christian side, there were men called *sophists, wise men*, who made it their business to sell philosophy. They had two lines. They claimed – for a fee – to be able to teach people to argue cleverly; they were the men who with their smooth tongues and their adroit minds were skilled in what John Milton refers to in *Paradise Lost* as 'making the worse appear the better reason'. They had turned philosophy into a way of becoming rich. Their other line was to give demonstrations of public speaking. The Greeks had always been fascinated by the spoken word; they loved an orator; and these wandering sophists went from town to town, giving their demonstrations in the art of oratory. They went in for advertising on an intensive scale and even went as far as delivering by hand personal invitations to their displays. The most famous of them drew people literally by the thousand to their lectures; they were in their day the equivalent of the modern pop star. Philostratus, the Greek philosopher and teacher, tells us that Adrian, one of the most famous of them, had such a popular power that, when his messenger appeared with the news that he was to speak, even the senate and the circus emptied, and the whole population flocked to the Athenaeum to hear him. These sophists had three great faults.

Their speeches were quite unreal. They would offer to speak on any subject, however remote and obscure and un-likely, that any member of the audience might propose. This is the kind of question they would argue; it is an actual example. A man goes into the citadel of a town to kill a tyrant who has been grinding down the people; not finding the tyrant, he kills the tyrant's son; the tyrant comes in and sees his dead son with the sword in his body, and in his grief kills himself; the man then claims the reward for killing the tyrant and liberating the people; should he receive it?

Their thirst was for applause. Competition between them was a bitter and cut-throat affair. Plutarch tells of a travelling sophist called Niger, who came to a town in Galatia where a prominent orator lived. A competition was immediately arranged. Niger had to compete or lose his reputation. He was suffering from a fishbone in his throat and had difficulty in speaking, but for the sake of his reputation he had to go on. Inflammation set in soon after, and in the end he died. Dio Chrysostom paints a picture of a public place in Corinth with all the different kinds of competitors in full blast: 'You might hear many poor wretches of sophists shouting and abusing each other, and their disciples, as they call them, squabbling, and many writers of books reading their stupid compositions, and many poets singing their poems, and many jugglers exhibiting their marvels, and many soothsayers giving the meaning of prodigies, and 1,000 rhetoricians twisting lawsuits, and no small number of traders driving their several trades.' There you have just that interchange of insults, that envy and strife, that constant wordy quarrelling of people with decadent minds that the writer of the Pastorals deplores. 'A sophist', wrote Philostratus, 'is put out in an extempore speech by a serious-looking audience and tardy praise and no clapping.' 'They are all agape', said Dio Chrysostom, 'for the murmur of the crowd . . . Like men walking in the dark they move always in the direction of the clapping and the shouting.' Lucian writes: 'If your friends see you breaking down, let them pay the price of the suppers you give them by stretching out their arms and giving you a chance of thinking of something to say in the intervals between the rounds of applause.' The ancient world was only too familiar with just the kind of false teacher who was invading the Church.

Their thirst was for praise, and their success was measured by numbers. The Greek Stoic philosopher Epictetus has some vivid pictures of the sophist talking to his disciples after his performance. '"Well, what did you think of me today?" "Upon my life, sir, I thought you were admirable." "What did you think of my best passage?" "Which was that?" "Where I described Pan and the Nymphs." "Oh, it was excessively well done." "A much larger audience today, I think", says the sophist. "Yes, much larger", responds the disciple. "Five hundred, I should guess." "O, nonsense! It could not have been less than 1,000." "Why, that is more than Dio ever had. I wonder why it was? They appreciated what I said, too." "Beauty, sir, can move a stone."' These performing sophists were 'the pets of society'. They became senators, governors and ambassadors. When they died, monuments were erected to them, with inscriptions such as 'The Queen of Cities to the King of Eloquence'.

The Greeks were intoxicated with the spoken word. Among them, if a man could speak, his fortune was made. It was against a background like that that the Church was growing up, and it is little wonder that this type of teacher invaded it. The Church gave such people a new area in which to show off their superficial gifts and to gain a cheap and showy fame and a not unprofitable following.

THE CHARACTERISTICS OF THE FALSE TEACHERS

I Timothy 6:3–5 (contd)

HERE in this passage are set out the characteristics of the false teachers.

(1) Their first characteristic is conceit. Their desire is not to display Christ but to display themselves. There are still preachers and teachers who are more concerned to gain a following for themselves than for Jesus Christ, more concerned to press their own views than to bring to men and women the word of God. In a lecture on his old teacher A. B. Bruce, W. M. Macgregor, who became Principal of Trinity College, Glasgow, said: 'One of our own Highland ministers tells how he had been puzzled by seeing Bruce again and again during lectures take up a scrap of paper, look at it and then proceed. One day he caught at the chance of seeing what this paper contained, and discovered on it an indication of the words: "O, send out thy light and thy truth", and thus he realized with awe that into his classroom the professor brought the majesty and the hopefulness of worship.' Great

teachers do not offer people their own small spark of illumination; they offer them the light and the truth of God.

(2) Their concern is with remote and obscure speculations. There is a kind of Christianity which is more concerned with argument than with life. To be a member of a discussion circle or a Bible study group and to spend enjoyable hours in talk about doctrines does not necessarily make a Christian. J. S. Whale in his book *Christian Doctrine* has certain scathing things to say about this pleasant intellectualism: 'We have, as Valentine said of Thurio, "an exchequer of words, but no other treasure". Instead of putting off our shoes from our feet because the place whereon we stand is holy ground, we are taking nice photographs of the Burning Bush from suitable angles: we are chatting about theories of the Atonement with our feet on the mantelpiece, instead of kneeling down before the wounds of Christ.' As Martin Luther, the founder of the Reformation, had it: 'He who merely studies the commandments of God (*mandata Dei*) is not greatly moved. But he who listens to God commanding (*Deum mandantem*), how can he fail to be terrified by majesty so great?' As Luther's fellow reformer Melanchthon had it: 'To know Christ is not to speculate about the mode of his Incarnation, but to know his saving benefits.' Writing in the fourth century, the Church father Gregory of Nyssa drew a revealing picture of Constantinople in his day: 'Constantinople is full of mechanics and slaves, who are all of them profound theologians, preaching in the shops and the streets. If you want a man to change a piece of silver, he informs you wherein the Son differs from the Father; if you ask the price of a loaf, you are told by way of reply that the Son is inferior to the Father; and if you inquire whether the bath is ready, the answer is that the Son is made out of nothing.' Subtle argumentation and glib theological statements do not

make a Christian. That kind of thing may well be nothing other than a mode of escape from the challenge of Christian living.

(3) The false teachers disturb the peace. They are instinctively competitive; they are suspicious of all who disagree with them; when they cannot win in an argument, they hurl insults at their opponents' theological positions, and even at their character; in any argument, the tone of their voices is bitterness and not love. They have never learned to speak the truth in love. The source of their bitterness is the exaltation of self, for their tendency is to regard any difference from or any criticism of their views as a personal insult.

(4) The false teachers commercialize religion. They are out for profit. They look on their teaching and preaching not as a vocation but as a career. One thing is certain – there is no place for those who seek advancement in the ministry of any church. The Pastorals are quite clear that the labourer deserves to be paid; but the motive for work must be public service and not private gain. The passion of the one who labours for Christ is not to get, but to spend and be spent in the service of Christ and of others.

THE CROWN OF CONTENTMENT

I Timothy 6:6–8

> And in truth godliness with contentment is great gain. We brought nothing into the world, and it is quite clear that we cannot take anything out of it either; but if we have food and shelter, we shall be content with them.

THE word here used for *contentment* is *autarkeia*. This was one of the great slogans of the Stoic philosophers. By it, they meant a complete *self-sufficiency*. They meant a frame of mind which was completely independent of all outward things, and which carried the secret of happiness within itself.

Contentment never comes from the possession of external things. As the poet George Herbert wrote:

> For he that needs five thousand pounds to live
> Is full as poor as he that needs but five.

Contentment comes from an inward attitude to life. In the third part of *Henry VI*, Shakespeare draws a picture of the king wandering in the country places unrecognized. He meets two gamekeepers and tells them that he is a king. One of them asks him: 'But, if thou be a king, where is thy crown?' And the king gives a magnificent answer:

> My crown is in my heart, not on my head;
> Not deck'd with diamonds and Indian stones,
> Nor to be seen; my crown is call'd content –
> A crown it is that seldom kings enjoy.

Long ago, the Greek philosophers had grasped the right meaning of contentment. Epicurus said of himself: 'To whom little is not enough nothing is enough. Give me a barley cake and a glass of water and I am ready to rival Zeus for happiness.' And when someone asked him for the secret of happiness, his answer was: 'Add not to a man's possessions but take away from his desires.'

The great men and women have always been content with little. One of the sayings of the Jewish Rabbis was: 'Who is rich? He that is contented with his lot.' In his commentary, Walter Lock quotes the kind of training on which a Jewish Rabbi engaged and the kind of life he lived: 'This is the path of the law. A morsel with salt shalt thou eat, thou shalt drink also water by measure, and shalt sleep upon the ground and live a life of trouble while thou toilest in the law. If thou doest this, happy shalt thou be, and it shall be well with thee; happy shalt thou be in this world and it shall be well with thee in the world to come.' The Rabbi had to learn to be content with enough. E. F. Brown quotes a passage from the great French Dominican preacher Henri Lacordaire: 'The rock of our present day is that no one knows how to live upon little. The great men of antiquity were generally poor . . . It always seems to me that the retrenchment of useless expenditure, the laying aside of what one may call the relatively necessary, is the high road to Christian disentanglement of heart, just as it was to that of ancient vigour. The mind that has learned to appreciate the moral beauty of life, both as regards God and men, can scarcely be greatly moved by any outward reverse of fortune; and what our age wants most is the sight of a man, who might possess everything, being yet willingly contented with little. For my own part, humanly speaking, I wish for nothing. A great soul in a small house is the idea which has touched me more than any other.'

It is not that Christianity pleads for poverty. There is no special virtue in being poor, or in having a constant struggle to make ends meet. But it does plead for two things.

It pleads for the realization that it is never in the power of things to bring happiness. E. K. Simpson says: 'Many a millionaire, after choking his soul with gold-dust, has died from melancholia.' Happiness always comes from personal relationships. All the things in the world will not make people happy if they know neither friendship nor love. Christians know that the secret of happiness lies not in things but in people.

It pleads for concentration upon the things which are permanent. We brought nothing into the world, and we cannot take anything out of it. The wise of every age and faith have known this. 'You cannot', said Seneca, 'take anything more out of the world than you brought into it.' The poet of the Greek anthology had it: 'Naked I set foot on the earth; naked I shall go below the earth.' The Spanish proverb grimly puts it: 'There are no pockets in a shroud.' Simpson comments: 'Whatever a man amasses by the way is in the nature of luggage, no part of his truest personality, but something he leaves behind at the toll-bar of death.'

We can take only two things to God. We can, and must, take ourselves, and therefore our great task is to build up a self that we can take without shame to God. We can, and must, take that relationship with God into which we have entered in the days of our life. We have already seen that the secret of happiness lies in personal relationships, and the greatest of all personal relationships is the relationship to God. And the supreme thing that we can take with us is the utter conviction that we go to one who is the friend and lover of our souls.

Contentment comes when we escape the slavery to things, when we find our wealth in the love and the fellowship of others, and when we realize that our most precious possession is our friendship with God, made possible through Jesus Christ.

THE PERIL OF THE LOVE OF MONEY

I Timothy 6:9–10

> Those who wish to be rich fall into temptation and a snare, and into many senseless and harmful desires for the forbidden things, desires which swamp men in a sea of ruin and total loss in time and in eternity. For the love of money is a root from which all evils spring; and some, in their reaching out after it, have been sadly led astray, and have transfixed themselves with many pains.

HERE is one of the most misquoted sayings in the Bible. Scripture does not say that *money* is the root of all evil; it says that *the love of money* is the root of all evil. This is a truth of which the great classical thinkers were as conscious as the Christian teachers. 'Love of money', said the Greek philosopher Democritus, 'is the metropolis of all evils.' Seneca speaks of 'the desire for that which does not belong to us, from which every evil of the mind springs'. 'The love of money', said the Cynic teacher Diogenes of Sinope, 'is the mother of all evils.' Philo, the Jewish writer, spoke of 'love of money which is the starting-place of the greatest transgressions of the law'. The Greek writer Athenaeus, who lived in the second century, quotes a saying: 'The belly's pleasure is the beginning and root of all evil.'

Money in itself is neither good nor bad, but the love of it may lead to evil. With it, people may selfishly serve their own desires; with it, they may answer the cry of their neighbour's need. With it, they may advance the path of wrongdoing; with it, they may make it easier for other people to live as God meant them to do. Money is not itself an evil, but it is a great responsibility. It has power for good and power for evil. What then are the special dangers involved in the love of money?

(1) The desire for money tends to be a thirst which cannot be satisfied. There was a Roman proverbial saying that wealth is like sea water; far from quenching thirst, it intensifies it. The more we get, the more we want.

(2) The desire for wealth is founded on an illusion. It is founded on the desire for security; but wealth cannot buy security. It cannot buy health, nor real love, and it cannot preserve from sorrow and from death. The security which is founded on material things is doomed to failure.

(3) The desire for money tends to make people selfish. If they are driven by the desire for wealth, it is nothing to them

that someone has to lose in order that they may gain. The desire for wealth fixes people's thoughts upon self, and others become merely means or obstacles in the path to their own enrichment. True, that *need* not happen; but in fact it often *does*.

(4) Although the desire for wealth is based on the desire for security, it ends in nothing but anxiety. The more people have to keep, the more they have to lose, and the tendency is for them to be obsessed by the risk of loss. There is an old story about a peasant who performed a great service to a king, who rewarded him with a gift of much money. For a time, the man was thrilled; but the day came when he begged the king to take back his gift, for into his life had entered the hitherto unknown worry that he might lose what he had. John Bunyan was right:

> He that is down needs fear no fall.
>   He that is low, no pride;
> He that is humble ever shall
>   Have God to be his guide.
>
> I am content with what I have,
>   Little be it or much;
> And, Lord, contentment still I crave,
>   Because Thou savest such.
>
> Fullness to such a burden is
>   That go on pilgrimage;
> Here little, and hereafter bliss,
>   Is best from age to age.

(5) The love of money may easily lead people into wrong ways of getting it, and therefore, in the end, into pain and remorse. That is true even physically. They may so drive their bodies in their passion to get that they ruin their health. They may discover too late what damage their desire has done to others and be saddled with remorse.

To seek to be independent and prudently to provide for the future is a Christian duty, but to make the love of money the driving force of life cannot ever be anything other than the most perilous of sins.

CHALLENGE TO TIMOTHY

I Timothy 6:11–16

> But you, O man of God, flee from these things. Pursue righteousness, godliness, faith, love, endurance, gentleness. Fight the good fight of faith; lay hold on eternal life, to which you are called, now that you have witnessed a noble profession of your faith in the presence of many witnesses. I charge you in the sight of God, who makes all things alive, and in the sight of Christ Jesus, who, in the days of Pontius Pilate, witnessed his noble confession, that you keep the commandment, that you should be without spot and without blame, until the day when our Lord Jesus Christ appears, that appearance which in his own good times the blessed and only Potentate, the King of kings and the Lord of lords, will show, he who alone possesses immortality, he who dwells in the light that no man can approach, he whom no man has seen or ever can see, to whom be honour and everlasting power. Amen.

THE letter comes to an end with a tremendous challenge to Timothy, a challenge all the greater because of the deliberate sonorous nobility of the words in which it is clothed.

Right at the outset, Timothy is challenged to excel. He is addressed as *man of God*. That is one of the great Old Testament titles. It is a title given to Moses. Deuteronomy 33:1 speaks of 'Moses, the man of God.' The title of Psalm 90 is 'A Prayer of Moses, the man of God.' It is a title of the prophets and the messengers of God. God's messenger to Eli is a man of God (1 Samuel 2:27). Samuel is described as a man of God (1 Samuel 9:6). Shemaiah, God's messenger to Rehoboam, is a man of God (1 Kings 12:22). John Bunyan in *The Pilgrim's Progress* calls Great-Grace 'God's Champion'.

Here is a tide of honour. When the challenge is presented to Timothy, he is not reminded of his own weakness and sin, which might well have reduced him to pessimistic despair; rather, he is challenged by the honour given to him, of being God's man. It is the Christian way, not to depress people by branding them as lost and helpless sinners, but rather to uplift them by summoning them to be what they have it in them to be. The Christian way is not to fling a humiliating past in someone's face, but to set before that person the splendour of the potential future. The very fact that Timothy was addressed as 'man of God' would make him stand up straight and throw his head back as one who has received his commission from the King.

The virtues and noble qualities set before Timothy are not just heaped haphazardly together. There is an order in them. First, there comes *righteousness*, *dikaiosunē*. This is defined as 'giving both to other people and to God their due'. It is the most comprehensive of the virtues; the righteous are those who do their duty to God and to their neighbours.

Second, there comes a group of three virtues which look towards God. *Godliness*, *eusebeia*, is the reverence of the person who never ceases to be aware that all life is lived in the presence of God. *Faith*, *pistis*, here means *fidelity*, and is the virtue of the person who, through all the chances and the changes of life, down even to the gates of death, is loyal to God. *Love*, *agape*, is the virtue possessed by those who, even if they tried, could not forget what God has done for them nor the love of God to all people.

Third, there comes the virtue which looks to the conduct of life. It is *hupomonē*. The Authorized Version translates this as *patience*; but *hupomonē* never means the spirit which sits quietly and simply puts up with things, letting the experiences of life flow like a tide over it. It is victorious endurance. 'It is unswerving constancy to faith and piety in spite of adversity and suffering.' It is the virtue which does not so much accept the experiences of life as conquer them.

Fourth, there comes the virtue which considers others. The Greek word is *paupatheia*. It is translated as *gentleness*, but is really untranslatable. It describes the spirit which never blazes into anger for its own wrongs but can be devastatingly angry about wrongs done to other people. It describes the spirit which knows how to forgive and yet knows how to wage the battle of righteousness. It describes the spirit which walks in humility and yet also in pride of its high calling from God. It describes the virtue which enables people to keep a true balance between concern and respect for others and self-esteem.

MEMORIES WHICH INSPIRE

1 Timothy 6:11–16 (*contd*)

As Timothy is challenged to the task of the future, he is inspired with the memories of the past.

(1) He is to remember his baptism and the vows he took there. In the circumstances of the early Church, baptism was inevitably adult baptism, for men and women were coming straight from the old religions to Christ. It was confession of faith and witness to all that the baptized person had taken Jesus Christ as Saviour, Master and Lord. The earliest of all Christian confessions was the simple creed: 'Jesus Christ

is Lord' (Romans 10:9; Philippians 2:11). But it has been suggested that behind these words to Timothy lies a confession of faith which said: 'I believe in God the Almighty, Creator of heaven and earth, and in Christ Jesus who suffered under Pontius Pilate and will return to judge; I believe in the resurrection from the dead and in the life immortal.' It may well have been a creed like that to which Timothy gave his allegiance. So, first of all, he is reminded that he is a man who has given his promise. Christians are first and foremost men and women who have pledged themselves to Jesus Christ.

(2) He is to remember that he has made the same confession of his faith as Jesus did. When Jesus stood before Pilate, Pilate said: 'Are you the king of the Jews?' and Jesus answered: 'You say so' (Luke 23:3). Jesus had witnessed that he was a king, and Timothy had always witnessed to the lordship of Christ. When Christians confess their faith, they do what their Master has already done; when they suffer for their faith, they undergo what their Master has already undergone. When we are engaged on some great enterprise, we can say: 'We are treading where the saints have trod', but when we confess our faith before others, we are able to say even more; we can say: 'I stand with Christ'; and surely this must lift up our hearts and inspire our lives.

(3) He is to remember that Christ comes again. He is to remember that his life and work must be made fit for him to see. Christians are not working to satisfy other people; they are working to satisfy Christ. The question a Christian must always ask is not: 'Is this good enough to pass the judgment of others?' but: 'Is it good enough to win the approval of Christ?'

(4) Above all, he is to remember God. And what a memory that is! He is to remember the one who is King of every king

and Lord of every lord; the one who possesses the gift of life eternal to give to men and women; the one whose holiness and majesty are such that no one can ever dare to look upon them. Christians must always remember God and say: 'If God is for us, who is against us?' (Romans 8:31).

ADVICE TO THE RICH

I Timothy 6:17–19

> Charge those who are rich in this world's goods not to be proud, and not to set their hopes on the uncertainty of riches, but on God who gives them all things richly to enjoy. Charge them to do good; to find their wealth in noble deeds; to be ready to share all that they have; to be men who never forget that they are members of a fellowship; to lay up for themselves the treasure of a fine foundation for the world to come, that they may lay hold on real life.

SOMETIMES we think of the early Church as composed entirely of poor people and slaves. Here we see that, even as early as this, it had its wealthy members. They are not condemned for being wealthy, nor told to give all their wealth away; but they are told what not to do and what to do with it.

Their riches must not make them proud. They must not think themselves better than other people because they have more money. Nothing in this world gives anyone the right to look down on another person, least of all the possession of wealth. They must not set their hopes on wealth. In the chances and the changes of life, we may be wealthy today and find ourselves in poverty tomorrow; and it is folly to set one's hopes on what can so easily be lost.

They are told that they must use their wealth to do good, that they must always be ready to share, and that they must remember that every Christian is a member of a fellowship. And they are told that such wise use of wealth will build for them a good foundation in the world to come. As it has been put, 'What I kept, I lost; what I gave, I have.'

There is a famous Jewish Rabbinic story. A man called Monobaz had inherited great wealth, but he was a good, a kindly and a generous man. In time of famine, he gave away all his wealth to help the poor. His brothers came to him and said: 'Your fathers laid up treasure, and added to the treasure that they had inherited from their fathers, and are you going to waste it all?' He answered: 'My fathers laid up treasure below: I have laid it up above. My fathers laid up treasure of Mammon: I have laid up treasure of souls. My fathers laid up treasure for this world: I have laid up treasure for the world to come.'

Every time we could give and do not give lessens the wealth laid up for us in the world to come; every time we give increases the riches laid up for us when this life comes to an end.

The teaching of the Christian ethic is not that wealth is a sin but that it is a very great responsibility. If wealth ministers to nothing but personal pride and enriches no one but the wealthy individual, it becomes that person's ruination, because it impoverishes the soul. But if wealth is used to bring help and comfort to others, in becoming poorer, the wealthy person really becomes richer. In time and in eternity, 'it is more blessed to give than to receive' (Acts 20:35).

A FAITH TO HAND ON

I Timothy 6:20–1

> O Timothy, guard the trust that has been entrusted to you. Avoid irreligious empty talking; and the paradoxes

of that knowledge which has no right to be called knowledge, which some have professed, and by so doing have missed the target of the faith.

Grace be with you.

It may well be that the name *Timothy* is here used in the fullness of its meaning. It comes from two words, *timan*, *to honour*, and *theos*, *God*, and literally means *the one who honours God*. It may well be that this concluding passage begins by reminding Timothy of his name and urging him to be true to it.

The passage talks of the *trust* that has been entrusted to him. The Greek word for *trust* is *parathēkē*, which literally means a *deposit*. It is the word for money deposited with a banker or with a friend. When such money was in time demanded back, it was a sacred duty to hand it back in its entirety. Sometimes children were called a *parathēkē*, a sacred trust. If the gods gave a man a child, it was his duty to present that child trained and equipped to the gods.

The Christian faith is like that, something which we received from our ancestors, and which we must pass on to our children. E. F. Brown quotes a famous passage from the fifth-century saint Vincent of Lérins: 'What is meant by the *deposit* (*parathēkē*)? That which is committed to thee, not that which is invented by thee; that which thou hast received, not that which thou hast devised; a thing not of wit, but of learning; not of private assumption, but of public tradition; a thing brought to thee, not brought forth of thee; wherein thou must not be an author, but a keeper; not a leader, but a follower. Keep the deposit. Preserve the talent of the Catholic faith safe and undiminished; let that which is committed to thee remain with thee, and that deliver. Thou hast received gold, render gold.'

We do well to remember that our duty is not only to ourselves but also to our children and our children's children. If in our time the Church were to become weak; if the Christian ethic were to be more and more submerged in the world; if the Christian faith were to be twisted and distorted, we would not be the only losers. Those of generations still to come would be robbed of something infinitely precious. We are not only the possessors but also the trustees of the faith. That which we have received, we must also hand on.

Finally, the Pastorals condemn those who, as the Authorized Version has it, have given themselves to 'the oppositions of science falsely so-called'. First, we must note that here the word *science* is used in its original sense; it simply means *knowledge (gnōsis)*. What is being condemned is a false intellectualism and a false emphasis on human knowledge.

But what is meant by *oppositions*? The Greek word is *antitheseis*. Very much later than Timothy, there was a heretic called Marcion who produced a book called *The Antitheses*, in which he quoted Old Testament texts and set beside them New Testament texts which contradicted them. This might very well mean: 'Don't waste your time seeking out contradictions in Scripture. Use the Scriptures to live by and not to argue about.' But there are two meanings which are more probable than that.

(1) The word *antithesis* could mean a *controversy*, and this might mean: 'Avoid controversies; don't get yourself mixed up in useless and bitter arguments.' This would be a very relevant bit of advice to a Greek congregation in Ephesus. The Greeks had a passion for going to law. They would even go to law with their own brothers, just for the pleasure of it. This may well mean: 'Don't make the Church a battle ground

of theological arguments and debates. Christianity is not something to argue about, but something to live by.'

(2) The word *antithesis* can mean a *rival thesis*. This is the most likely meaning, because it suits Jews and Gentiles alike. The Christian scholars in later times used to argue about questions like: 'How many angels can stand on the point of a needle?' The Jewish Rabbis would argue about hair-splitting points of the law for hours and days and even years. The Greeks were the same, only in a still more serious way. There was a school of Greek philosophers – and a very influential school it was – called the Academics. The Academics held that, in the case of everything in the realm of human thought, you could by logical argument arrive at precisely opposite conclusions. They therefore concluded that there is no such thing as absolute truth, that there were always two hypotheses of equal weight. They went on to argue that, this being so, the wise will never make up their minds about anything but will hold themselves forever in a state of suspended judgment. The effect was of course to paralyse all action and to reduce people to a state of complete uncertainty. So, Timothy is told: 'Don't waste your time in subtle arguments; don't waste your time in trying to score points. Don't be too clever to be wise. Listen rather to the clear and unquestionable voice of God than to the subtle disputations of over-clever minds.'

So, the letter draws to a close with a warning which our own generation needs. Clever argument can never be a substitute for Christian action. The duty of the Christian is not to sit in a study and weigh arguments but to live the Christian life in the dust and heat of the world. In the end, it is not intellectual cleverness but conduct and character which count.

Then comes the closing blessing – 'Grace be with you.' The letter ends with the beauty of the grace of God.

2 TIMOTHY

AN APOSTLE'S GLORY AND
AN APOSTLE'S PRIVILEGE

2 Timothy 1:1–7

This is a letter from Paul, who was made an apostle of
Christ Jesus by the will of God, and whose apostleship
was designed to make known to all men God's promise
of real life in Christ Jesus, to Timothy his own beloved
child. Grace, mercy and peace be to you from God, the
Father, and from Christ Jesus, our Lord.

I thank God, whom I serve with a clear conscience,
as my forefathers did before me, for all that you are to
me, just as in my prayers I never cease to remember
you, for, remembering your tears when we parted, I
never cease to yearn to see you, that I may be filled
with joy. And I thank God that I have received a fresh
reminder of that sincere faith which is in you, a faith of
the same kind as first dwelt in your grandmother Lois
and in your mother Eunice, and which, I am convinced,
dwells in you too. That is why I send you this reminder
to keep at white heat the gift that is in you and which
came to you through the laying of my hands upon you;
for God did not give us the spirit of craven fear, but of
power and love and self-discipline.

When Paul speaks of his own apostleship, there are always certain unmistakable notes in his voice. To Paul, his apostleship always meant certain things.

(1) His apostleship was an *honour*. He was chosen for it by the will of God. All Christians must regard themselves as God-chosen men and women.

(2) His apostleship was a *responsibility*. God chose him because he wanted to do something with him. He wanted to make him the instrument by which the tidings of new life went out to all people. Christians are never chosen entirely for their own sake, but for what they can do for others. Christians are people who are lost in wonder, love and praise at what God has done for them and aflame with eagerness to tell others what God can do for them too.

(3) His apostleship was a *privilege*. It is most significant to see what Paul believed it his duty to bring to others – God's *promise*, not his *threat*. To Paul, Christianity was not the threat of damnation; it was the good news of salvation. It is worth remembering that the greatest evangelist and missionary the world has ever seen was out not to terrify people by shaking them over the flames of hell but to move them to astonished submission at the sight of the love of God. The driving force of his gospel was love, not fear.

As always when he speaks to Timothy, there is a warmth of loving affection in Paul's voice. 'My beloved child', he calls him. Timothy was his child in the faith. Timothy's parents had given him physical life, but it was Paul who gave him eternal life. Many people who never knew physical parenthood have had the joy and privilege of being a father or a mother in the faith – and there is no joy in all the world like that of bringing one soul to Christ.

THE INSPIRING OF TIMOTHY

2 Timothy 1:1–7 (*contd*)

PAUL'S object in writing is to inspire and strengthen Timothy for his task in Ephesus. Timothy was young, and he had a hard task in battling against the heresies and the infections that were bound to threaten the Church. So, in order to keep his courage high and his effort strenuous, Paul reminds Timothy of certain things.

(1) He reminds him of his own confidence in him. There is no greater inspiration than to feel that someone believes in us. An appeal to the best in someone is always more effective than a threat of punishment. The fear of letting down those who love us is a sobering thing.

(2) He reminds him of his family tradition. Timothy was walking in a fine heritage; and, if he failed, not only would he damage his own reputation but he would lessen the honour of his family name as well. A fine parentage is one of the greatest gifts anyone can have. It is something to thank God for and should never be dishonoured.

(3) He reminds him of his setting apart for office and of the gift which was conferred upon him. Once we enter upon the service of any association with a tradition, anything that we do affects not only us. We do not do it in our own strength. There is the strength of a tradition to draw upon and the honour of a tradition to preserve. That is especially true of the Church. Those who serve it have its honour in their hands; those who serve it are strengthened by the consciousness of the communion of all the saints.

(4) He reminds him of the qualities which should characterize the Christian teacher. These, as Paul at that moment saw them, were four.

(a) There was *courage*. It was not cowardly fear but courage that Christian service should bring. It always takes courage to be a Christian, and that courage comes from the continual consciousness of the presence of Christ.

(b) There was *power*. In true Christians, there is the power to cope, the power to shoulder the backbreaking task, the power to stand firm when faced with the shattering situation, the power to retain faith when confronted by the soul-destroying sorrow and the wounding disappointment. Christians are characteristically people who could pass the breaking point and not break.

(c) There was *love*. In Timothy's case, this was love for the brothers and sisters, for the congregation of the people of Christ over whom he was set. It is precisely that love which gives Christian pastors other qualities. They must love their people so much that they will never find any toil too great to undertake for them or any situation threatening enough to daunt them. No one should ever enter the ministry of the Church without a deep love for Christ's people.

(d) There was *self-discipline*. The word is *sōphronismos*, one of these great untranslatable Greek words. It has been defined as 'the sanity of saintliness'. In his book on *The Pastorals*, Sir Robert Falconer defines it as 'control of oneself in face of panic or of passion'. It is Christ alone who can give us that command of self which will keep us both from being swept away and from running away.

No one can ever rule others without having complete self-control. *Sōphronismos* is that divinely given control of self which makes people great rulers of others because they are first of all the servants of Christ and in complete control of themselves.

A GOSPEL WORTH SUFFERING FOR

Timothy 1:8–11

> So, then, do not be ashamed to bear your witness to our
> Lord; and do not be ashamed of me his prisoner; but
> accept with me the suffering which the gospel brings,
> and do so in the power of God, who saved us, and who
> called us with a call to consecration, a call which had
> nothing to do with our own achievements, but which
> was dependent solely on his purpose, and on the grace
> which was given to us in Christ Jesus: and all this was
> planned before the world began, but now it stands
> full-displayed through the appearance of our Saviour
> Christ Jesus, who abolished death and brought life and
> incorruption to light by means of the good news which
> he brought, good news in the service of which I have
> been appointed a herald, and an apostle and a teacher.

It is inevitable that loyalty to the gospel will bring trouble.
For Timothy, it meant loyalty to a man who was regarded as
a criminal, because as Paul was writing he was in prison in
Rome. But here Paul sets out the gospel in all its glory,
something worth suffering for. Sometimes by implication and
sometimes by direct statement, he brings out element after
element in that glory. Few passages in the New Testament
have in them and behind them such a sense of the sheer
grandeur of the gospel.

(1) It is the gospel of *power*. Any suffering which it in-
volves is to be borne in the power of God. To the ancient
world, the gospel was the power to live. That very age in
which Paul was writing was the great age of suicide. The
highest-principled of the ancient thinkers were the Stoics;
but they had their own way out when life became intolerable.
They had a saying: 'God gave men life, but God gave men

the still greater gift of being able to take their own lives away.'
The gospel was, and is, power – power to conquer self, power
to take control of circumstances, power to go on living when
life is unlivable, power to be a Christian when being a
Christian looks impossible.

(2) It is the gospel of *salvation*. God is the God who saves
us. The gospel is rescue. It is rescue from sin; it liberates
people from the things which have them in their grip; it
enables them to break with the habits which are unbreakable.
The gospel is a rescuing force which can make bad people
good.

(3) It is the gospel of *consecration*. It is not simply rescue
from the consequences of past sin; it is a summons to walk
the way of holiness. In *The Bible in World Evangelism*,
A. M. Chirgwin quotes two amazing instances of the miraculous changing power of Christ.

There was a New York gangster who had recently been in
prison for robbery with violence. He was on his way to join
his old gang with a view to taking part in another robbery
when he picked a man's pocket in Fifth Avenue. He went
into Central Park to see what he had succeeded in stealing,
and discovered to his disgust that it was a New Testament.
Since he had time to spare, he began idly to turn over the
pages and to read. Soon he was deep in the book, and he read
to such effect that a few hours later he went to his old
comrades and broke with them forever. For that ex-convict,
the gospel was the call to holiness.

There was a young Arab in Aleppo who had a bitter quarrel
with a former friend. He told a Christian evangelist: 'I hated
him so much that I plotted revenge, even to the point of
murder. Then, one day I ran into you and you induced me to
buy a copy of St Matthew. I only bought it to please you. I
never intended to read it. But, as I was going to bed that

night, the book fell out of my pocket, and I picked it up and started to read. When I reached the place where it says: 'You have heard that it was said to those of ancient times, "You shall not murder . . . But I say to you that if you are angry with a brother or sister, you will be liable to judgment", I remembered the hatred I was nourishing against my enemy. As I read on, my uneasiness grew until I reached the words: "Come to me, all you that are weary and carry heavy burdens, and I will give you rest. Take my yoke upon you, and learn of me; for I am gentle and humble in heart, and you will find rest for your souls." Then I was compelled to cry: "God be merciful to me a sinner." Joy and peace filled my heart, and my hatred disappeared. Since then I have been a new man, and my chief delight is to read God's word.'

It was the gospel which set the ex-convict in New York and the would-be murderer in Aleppo on the road to holiness. It is here that so much of our church Christianity falls down. It does not change people, and therefore it is not real. Those who have known the saving power of the gospel are changed men and women, in their work, their leisure, their home life, and in their character. There should be an essential difference between Christians and non-Christians, because Christians have obeyed the summons to walk the road to holiness.

A GOSPEL WORTH SUFFERING FOR

2 Timothy 1:8–11 (*contd*)

(4) It is the gospel of *grace*. It is not something which we achieve, but something which we accept. God did not call us because we are holy; he called us to make us holy. If we had to deserve the love of God, our situation would be helpless

and hopeless. The gospel is the free gift of God. He does not love us because we deserve his love; he loves us out of the sheer generosity of his heart.

(5) It is the gospel of *God's eternal purpose*. It was planned before time began. We must never think that God was once stern law and that only since the life and death of Jesus has he been forgiving love. From the beginning of time, God's love has been searching for us, and his grace and forgiveness have been offered to us. Love is the essence of the eternal nature of God.

(6) It is the gospel of *life and immortality*. It is Paul's conviction that Christ Jesus brought life and immortality to light. The ancient world feared death; or, if it did not fear it, regarded it as extinction. It was the message of Jesus that death was the way to life, and that far from separating us from God it brought us into his nearer presence.

(7) It is the gospel of *service*. It was this gospel which made Paul a herald, an apostle and a teacher of the faith. It did not leave him with the comfortable feeling that now his own soul was saved and he did not need to worry any more. It laid on him the inescapable task of wearing himself out in the service of God and of other people. This gospel laid three obligations on Paul.

(a) It made him a herald. The word is *kērux*, which has three main lines of meaning, each with something to suggest about our Christian duty. The *kērux* was the herald who brought the announcement from the king. The *kērux* was the one who was sent when two armies were opposed to each other, who brought the terms of or the request for truce and peace. The *kērux* was the person whom an auctioneer or a merchant employed to advertise the wares and invite people to come and buy. So, the Christian is to be the one who brings the message to others; the one who brings men and women into peace with God; the one who calls on others to accept the rich offer which God is making to them.

(b) It made him an *apostle*, *apostolos*, literally *one who is sent out*. The word can mean an *envoy* or an *ambassador*. The *apostolos* did not speak for himself, but for the one who sent him. He did not come in his own authority, but in the authority of the one who sent him. Christians are the ambassadors of Christ, whose task is to speak for him and to represent him to the world.

(c) It made him a *teacher*. There is a very real sense in which the teaching task of Christians and of the Church is the most important of all. Certainly, the task of the teacher is very much harder than the task of the evangelist. The evangelist's task is to appeal to people and confront them with the love of God. In a vivid moment of emotion, someone may respond to that summons. But a long road remains. That person must learn the meaning and discipline of the Christian life. The foundations have been laid, but the main structure still has to be built. The flame of evangelism has to be followed by the steady glow of Christian teaching. It may well be that people drift away from the Church after their first decision, for the simple yet fundamental reason that they have not been taught about the full meaning of the Christian faith.

Herald, ambassador, teacher – here is the threefold function of all Christians who would serve their Lord and their Church.

(8) It is the gospel of *Christ Jesus*. It was fully displayed through his *appearance*. The word Paul uses for *appearance* is one with a great history. It is *epiphaneia*, a word which the Jews repeatedly used of the great saving manifestations of God in the terrible days of the Maccabaean struggles, when the enemies of Israel were deliberately seeking to obliterate God.

In the days of the high priest Onias, a certain Heliodorus came to plunder the Temple treasury at Jerusalem. Neither prayers nor pleading would stop him carrying out this sacrilege. And, so the story runs, as Heliodorus was about to set hands on the treasury, 'the Sovereign of spirits and of all authority caused so great a manifestation [*epiphaneia*] . . . For there appeared to them a magnificently caparisoned [harnessed] horse with a rider of fighting mien . . . it rushed furiously at Heliodorus and struck at him with its front hooves . . . When he suddenly fell to the ground and deep darkness came over him' (2 Maccabees 3:24–7). What exactly happened, we may never know; but in Israel's hour of need there came this tremendous *epiphaneia* of God. When Judas Maccabaeus and his little army were confronted with the might of Nicanor, they prayed: 'O Lord, you sent your angel in the time of King Hezekiah of Judah, and he killed fully 185,000 in the camp of Senacharib [cf. 2 Kings 19:35–6]. So now, O Sovereign of the heavens, send a good angel to spread terror and trembling before us. By the might of your arm may these blasphemers who come against your holy people be struck down.' And then the story goes on: 'Nicanor and his troops advanced with trumpets and battle songs, but Judas and his troops met the enemy in battle with invocations to God and prayers. So, fighting with their hands and praying to God in their hearts, they laid low at least 35,000, and were greatly gladdened by God's manifestation [*epiphaneia*]' (2 Maccabees 15:22–7). Once again, we do not know exactly what happened; but God made a great and saving appearance for his people. To the Jews, *epiphaneia* denoted a rescuing intervention of God.

To the Greeks, this was an equally great word. The accession of the emperor to his throne was called his *epiphaneia*. It was his manifestation. Every emperor came to the throne with high hopes; his coming was hailed as the dawn of a new and precious day, and of great blessings to come.

The gospel was fully displayed with the *epiphaneia* of Jesus; the very word shows that he was God's great, rescuing intervention and manifestation into the world.

TRUST HUMAN AND DIVINE

2 Timothy 1:12–14

> And that is the reason why I am going through these things I am going through. But I am not ashamed, for I know him in whom my belief is fixed, and I am quite certain that he is able to keep safe what I have entrusted to him until the last day comes. Hold fast the pattern of health-giving words you have received from me, never slackening in that faith and love which are in Christ Jesus. Guard the fine trust that has been given to you through the Holy Spirit who dwells in you.

THIS passage uses a very vivid Greek word in a significant double way which is full of meaning. Paul talks of that which he has entrusted to God, and he urges Timothy to safeguard the trust God has placed in him. In both cases, the word is *parathēkē*, which means *a deposit committed to someone's trust*. A man might deposit something with a friend to be kept for his children or his loved ones; or he might deposit his valuables in a temple for safe-keeping, for the temples were the banks of the ancient world. In each case, the thing deposited was a *parathēkē*. In the ancient world, there was no more sacred duty than the safe-guarding of such a deposit and the returning of it when in due time it was claimed.

There was a famous Greek story which told just how sacred such a trust was (*Herodotus*, 6:89; Juvenal, *Satires*, 13:199–208). The Spartans were famous for their strict honour and honesty. A certain man of Miletus came to a certain Glaucus of Sparta. He said that he had heard such great reports of the honesty of the Spartans that he had turned half his possessions into money and wished to deposit that money with Glaucus until he or his heirs should claim it again. Certain symbols were given and received which would identify the rightful claimant when he should make his claim. The years passed on; the man of Miletus died; his sons came to Sparta to see Glaucus, produced the identifying tallies and asked for the return of the deposited money. But Glaucus claimed that he had no memory of ever receiving it. The sons from Miletus went sorrowfully away, but Glaucus went to the famous oracle at Delphi to see whether he should admit the trust or, as Greek law entitled him to do, should swear that he knew nothing about it. The oracle answered:

> Best for the present it were, O Glaucus, to do as thou
>   wishest,
> Swearing an oath to prevail, and so to make prize of
>   the money.
> Swear then – death is the lot even of those who never
>   swear falsely.
> Yet hath the Oath-god a son who is nameless, footless
>   and handless;
> Mighty in strength he approaches to vengeance, and
>   whelms in destruction
> All who belong to the race, or the house of the man
>   who is perjured.
> But oath-keeping men leave behind them a flourishing
>   offspring.

Glaucus understood; the oracle was telling him that if he wanted instant gain, he should deny the trust, but such a denial would inevitably bring eternal loss. He begged the oracle to pardon his question, but the answer was that to have tempted the god was as bad as to have done the deed. He sent for the sons of the man of Miletus and restored the money. Herodotus goes on: 'Glaucus at this present time has not a single descendant; nor is there any family known as his; root and branch has he been removed from Sparta. It is a good thing therefore, when a pledge has been left with one, not even in thought to doubt about restoring it.' To the Greeks, a *parathēkē* was completely sacred.

Paul says that he has made his deposit with God. He means that he has entrusted both his work and his life to him. It might seem that he had been cut off in mid-career; that he should end as a criminal in a Roman prison might seem the undoing of all his work. But he had sowed his seed and preached his gospel, and he left the result in the hands of God. Paul had entrusted his life to God; and he was sure that in life and in death he was safe. Why was he so sure? Because he knew in *whom* he had believed. We must always remember that Paul does not say that he knew *what* he had believed. His certainty did not come from the intellectual knowledge of a creed or a theology; it came from a personal knowledge of God. He knew God personally and intimately; he knew what he was like in love and in power; and to Paul it was inconceivable that he should fail him. If we have worked honestly and done the best that we can, we can leave the result to God, however meagre that work may seem to us. With him in this or any other world, life is safe, for nothing can separate us from his love in Christ Jesus our Lord.

TRUST HUMAN AND DIVINE

2 Timothy 1:12–14 (*contd*)

BUT there is another side to this matter of trust; there is another *parathēkē*. Paul urges Timothy to safeguard and keep unbroken the trust God has placed in him. Not only do we put our trust in God; he also puts his trust in us. The idea of God's dependence on men and women is never far from New Testament thought. When God wants something done, he has to find someone to do it. If he wants a child taught, a message brought, a sermon preached, a wanderer found, a sorrowing one comforted, a sick one healed, he has to find some instrument to do his work.

The trust that God had particularly placed in Timothy was the oversight and the strengthening of the Church. If Timothy was truly to discharge that trust, he had to do certain things.

(1) He had to hold fast to *the pattern of health-giving words*. That is to say, he had to see to it that Christian belief was maintained in all its purity and that false and misleading ideas were not allowed to enter in. That is not to say that in the Christian Church there must be no new thinking and no development in doctrine and belief; but it does mean that there are certain great Christian truths which must always be preserved intact. And it may well be that the one Christian truth which must stand forever is summed up in the creed of the early Church: 'Jesus Christ is Lord' (Philippians 2:11). Any theology which seeks to remove Christ from the highest place or take from him his unique position in the scheme of revelation and salvation has to be wrong. The Christian Church must always be restating its faith – but the faith restated must be faith in Christ.

(2) He must never slacken in *faith*. Faith here has two ideas at its heart. (a) It has the idea of *fidelity*. Christian leaders

must always be true and loyal to Jesus Christ. They must never be ashamed to show whose they are and whom they serve. Fidelity is the oldest and the most essential virtue in the world. (b) But faith also contains the idea of *hope*. Christians must never lose their confidence in God; they must never despair. As the nineteenth-century poet A. H. Clough wrote:

> Say not, 'The struggle naught availeth;
>   The labour and the wounds are vain;
> The enemy faints not, nor faileth,
>   And as things have been they remain.'
>
> For while the tired waves, vainly breaking,
>   Seem here no painful inch to gain,
> Far back, through creeks and inlets making,
>   Comes silent, flooding in, the main.

In the hearts of Christians, there must be no pessimism, either for themselves or for the world.

(3) He must never slacken in *love*. To love other people is to see them as God sees them. It is to refuse ever to do anything but seek their highest good. It is to meet bitterness with forgiveness; it is to meet hatred with love; it is to meet indifference with a burning passion which cannot be extinguished. Christian love insistently seeks to love all people as God loves them and as he has first loved us.

THE FAITHLESS MANY AND THE FAITHFUL ONE

2 Timothy 1:15–18

> You know this, that as a whole the people who live in Asia deserted me, and among the deserters are Phygelus and Hermogenes. May the Lord give mercy to the family of Onesiphorus, because he often refreshed me, and was

not ashamed of my chain. So far from that, when he
arrived in Rome he eagerly sought me out and found
me – may the Lord grant to him mercy from the Lord
on that day – and you know better than I do the many
services he rendered in Ephesus.

HERE is a passage in which pathos and joy are combined. In
the end, the same thing happened to Paul as happened to
Jesus, his Master. His friends forsook him and fled. In the
New Testament, *Asia* is not the continent of Asia, but the
Roman province which consisted of the western part of Asia
Minor. Its capital was the city of Ephesus. When Paul was
imprisoned, his friends abandoned him – most probably out
of fear. The Romans would never have proceeded against
him on a purely religious charge; the Jews must have persuaded them that he was a dangerous troublemaker and
disturber of the public peace. There can be no doubt that in
the end Paul would be held on a political charge. To be a
friend of a man like that was dangerous, and in his hour of
need his friends from Asia abandoned him because they were
afraid for their own safety.

But, although others deserted Paul, one man was loyal to
the end. His name was Onesiphorus, which means *profitable*.
In his book, *The Problem of the Pastoral Epistles*, P. N.
Harrison draws a vivid picture of Onesiphorus' search for
Paul in Rome: 'We seem to catch glimpses of one purpose-
ful face in a drifting crowd, and follow with quickening
interest this stranger from the far coasts of the Aegean, as he
threads the maze of unfamiliar streets, knocking at many
doors, following up every clue, warned of the risks he is taking
but not to be turned from his quest; till in some obscure
prison-house a known voice greets him, and he discovers Paul
chained to a Roman soldier. Having once found his way
Onesiphorus is not content with a single visit, but, true to his

name, proves unwearied in his ministrations. Others have
flinched from the menace and ignominy of that chain; but
this visitor counts it the supreme privilege of his life to
share with such a criminal the reproach of the Cross. One
series of turnings in the vast labyrinth (of the streets of
Rome) he comes to know as if it were his own Ephesus.'
There is no doubt that, when Onesiphorus sought out Paul
and came to see him again and again, he took his life in his
hands. It was dangerous to keep asking where a certain
criminal could be found; it was dangerous to visit him; it was
still more dangerous to keep on visiting him; but that is what
Onesiphorus did.

Again and again, the Bible brings us face to face with a
question which is real for every one of us. Again and again,
it introduces and dismisses a man from the stage of history
with a single sentence. Hermogenes and Phygelus – we know
nothing whatever of them beyond their names and the fact
that they were traitors to Paul. Onesiphorus – we know nothing
of him except that in his loyalty to Paul he risked – and perhaps
lost – his life. Hermogenes and Phygelus go down in history
branded as deserters; Onesiphorus goes down in history as
the friend who stuck closer than a brother. If we were to be
described in one sentence, what would it be? Would it be
the verdict on a traitor, or the verdict on a disciple who was
true?

Before we leave this passage, we must note that in one
particular connection it is a source of controversy. We have
to make our own judgment on this, but there are many
who feel that the implication is that Onesiphorus is dead.
It is for his family that Paul first prays. Now, if he was dead,
this passage shows us Paul praying for the dead, for it shows
him praying that Onesiphorus may find mercy on the last
day.

Prayers for the dead are a much-disputed problem which we do not intend to discuss here. But one thing we can say – to the Jews, prayers for the dead were by no means unknown. In the days of the Maccabaean wars, there was a battle between the troops of Judas Maccabaeus and the army of Gorgias, the governor of Idumaea, which ended in a victory for Judas Maccabaeus. After the battle, the Jews were gathering the bodies of those who had fallen in battle. On each one of them they found 'sacred tokens of the idols of Jamnia, which is forbidden the Jews by the law'. What is meant is that the dead Jewish soldiers were wearing Gentile charms in a superstitious attempt to protect their lives. The story goes on to say that every man who had been slain was wearing such a charm, and it was because of this that he was in fact killed. Seeing this, Judas and all the people prayed that the sin of these men 'might be wholly blotted out'. Judas then collected money and made a sin offering for those who had fallen, because they believed that, since there was a resurrection, it was not superfluous 'to pray for the dead'. The story ends with the saying of Judas Maccabaeus that it was a holy and good thing to pray for the dead. 'Therefore he made atonement for the dead, so that they might be delivered from their sin' (2 Maccabees 12:39–45).

It is clear that Paul was brought up in a way of belief which saw in prayers for the dead not a hateful but a lovely thing. This is a subject on which there has been long and bitter dispute; but this one thing we can and must say – if we love a person with all our hearts, and if the remembrance of that person is never absent from our minds and memories, then, whatever the intellect of the theologian may say about it, the instinct of the heart is to remember such a loved one in prayer, whether he or she is in this or in any other world.

THE CHAIN OF TEACHING

2 Timothy 2:1–2

> As for you, my child, find your strength in the grace
> which is in Christ Jesus; and entrust the things which
> you have heard from me, and which are confirmed by
> many witnesses, to faithful men who will be competent
> to teach others too.

HERE we have in outline two things – the reception and the
transmission of the Christian faith.

(1) The reception of the faith is founded on two things. It
is founded on hearing. It was from Paul that Timothy heard
the truth of the Christian faith. But the words he heard were
confirmed by the witness of many who were prepared to say:
'These words are true – and I know it, because I have found
it so in my own life.' It may be that there are many of us who
do not have the gift of expression, and who can neither teach
nor expound the Christian faith. But even those among us
who do not have the gift of teaching are able to witness to the
living power of the gospel.

(2) It is not only a privilege to receive the Christian faith;
it is a duty to transmit it. All Christians must look on themselves as the link between two generations. In his commentary,
E. K. Simpson writes on this passage: 'The torch of heavenly
light must be transmitted unquenched from one generation to
another, and Timothy must count himself an intermediary
between apostolic and later ages.'

(3) The faith is to be transmitted to faithful men and women
who in their turn will teach it to others. The Christian Church
is dependent on an unbroken chain of teachers. When the
letter known as 1 Clement was sent to the church at Corinth,
the author sketched that chain. 'Our apostles appointed the

aforesaid persons (that is, the elders) and afterwards they provided a continuance, that, if these should fall asleep, other approved men should succeed to their ministry.' The teacher is a link in the living chain which stretches unbroken from this present moment back to Jesus Christ.

These teachers are to be *faithful*. The Greek for *faithful*, *pistos*, is a word with a rich variety of closely connected meanings. A person who is *pistos* is someone who is *believing*, *loyal* and *reliable*. All these meanings are there. Falconer said that these believing people are such 'that they will yield neither to persecution nor to error'. The teachers' hearts must be so set on Christ that no threat of danger will lure them from the path of loyalty and no seduction of false teaching cause them to stray from the straight path of the truth. They must be steadfast both in life and in thought.

THE SOLDIER OF CHRIST

2 Timothy 2:3–4

> Accept your share in suffering like a fine soldier of Christ Jesus. No soldier who is on active service entangles himself in ordinary civilian business; he lays aside such things, so that by good service he may please the commander who has enrolled him in his army.

THE picture of every individual as a soldier and of life as a campaign is one which the Romans and the Greeks knew well. 'To live', said Seneca, 'is to be a soldier' (*Epistles*, 96:5). 'The life of every man', said Epictetus, 'is a kind of campaign, and a campaign which is long and varied' (*Discourses*, 3:24:34). Paul took this picture and applied it to all Christians, but especially to the leaders and outstanding servants of the Church. He urges Timothy to fight a fine campaign (1 Timothy

1:18). He calls Archippus, in whose house a church met, 'our fellow soldier' (Philemon 2). He calls Epaphroditus, the messenger of the Philippian church, 'my fellow-soldier' (Philippians 2:25). Clearly, in the life of the soldier Paul saw a picture of the life of the Christian. What then were the qualities of the soldier which Paul wanted to see repeated in the Christian life?

(1) The soldiers' service must be a *concentrated service*. Once soldiers have enlisted on a campaign, they can no longer involve themselves in the ordinary daily business of life and living; they must concentrate on their service as soldiers. The Roman code of Theodosius said: 'We forbid men engaged on military service to engage in civilian occupations.' A soldier is a soldier and nothing else; Christians must concentrate on their Christianity. That does not mean that they must not engage on any worldly tasks or business. They must still live in this world, and they must still make a living; but it does mean that they must use whatever task they are engaged upon to demonstrate their Christianity.

(2) Soldiers are conditioned to *obedience*. The early training of soldiers is designed to make them obey unquestioningly the word of command. There may come a time when such instinctive obedience will save their lives and the lives of others. There is a sense in which it is no part of a soldier's duty 'to know the reason why'. Involved as they are in the midst of the battle, they cannot see the overall picture. They must leave the decisions to the commander who sees the whole field. The first Christian duty is obedience to the voice of God, and acceptance even of what is not fully understood.

(3) Soldiers are conditioned to *sacrifice*. Professor A. J. Gossip of Trinity College, Glasgow, tells how, as a chaplain in the First World War, he was going up the line for the first time. War and blood, and wounds and death were new to

him. On his way, he saw by the roadside, left behind after the battle, the body of a young kilted Highlander. Oddly, perhaps, there flashed into his mind the words of Christ: 'This is my body broken for you.' Christians must always be ready to sacrifice themselves, their wishes and their fortunes for God and for other people.

(4) Soldiers are conditioned to *loyalty*. When a Roman soldier joined the army, he took the *sacramentum*, the oath of loyalty to his emperor. A conversation was reported between the French commander Marshal Foch and an officer in the First World War. 'You must not retire,' said Foch, 'you must hold on at all costs.' 'Then,' said the officer aghast, 'that means we must all die.' And Foch answered: 'Precisely!' The supreme virtue of all soldiers is that they are faithful even to death. Christians too must be loyal to Jesus Christ, through all the chances and the changes of life, even down to the gates of death.

THE ATHLETE OF CHRIST

2 Timothy 2:5

> And if anyone engages in an athletic contest, he does not win the crown unless he observes the rules of the game.

PAUL has just used the picture of the soldier to represent the Christian, and now he uses two other pictures – those of the athlete and of the toiling farmer. He uses the same three pictures close together in 1 Corinthians 9:6, 9:7, 9:24–7.

Paul says that no athlete can win the crown of victory without observing the rules of the contest. There is a very interesting point in the Greek here which is difficult to bring out in translation. The Authorized Version speaks of *striving lawfully*. The Greek is *athlein nomimōs*. In fact, that is the Greek phrase which was used by the later writers to describe a *professional* as opposed to an *amateur* athlete. The person who strove *nomimōs* was the one who concentrated completely on the struggle. That struggle was not just a spare-time concern, as it might be for an amateur; it was a full-time dedication of that individual's life to excellence in the chosen contest. Here, then, we have the same idea as in Paul's picture of the Christian as a soldier. Christians must concentrate their lives upon their Christianity just as professional athletes concentrate upon their chosen contest. The spare-time Christian is a contradiction in terms; the whole of life should be an endeavour to live out our Christianity. What then are the characteristics of an athlete which are in Paul's mind?

(1) Athletes are under *discipline* and *self-denial*. They must keep to their schedule of training and let nothing interfere with it. There will be days when they would like to drop their training and relax the discipline; but they must not do so. There will be pleasures and indulgences they would like to allow themselves; but they must refuse them. Athletes who want to excel know that they must let nothing interfere with that standard of physical fitness which they have set themselves. There must be discipline in the Christian life. There are times when the easy way is very attractive; there are times when the right thing is the hard thing; there are times when we are tempted to relax our standards. Christians must train themselves never to relax in the life-long attempt to make their souls pure and strong.

(2) Athletes are people who *observe the rules*. After the discipline and the rules of the training, there come the contest and the rules of the contest. It is not possible to win without playing the game. Christians, too, are often brought into contest with others. They must defend their faith; they must

seek to convince and to persuade; they will have to argue and to debate. They must do so by the Christian rules. No matter how heated the argument, they must never resort to rudeness. They must never be anything but honest about their own position and fair to that of their opponents. The *odium theologicum*, the hatred of theologians, has become notorious. There is often no bitterness like religious bitterness. But true Christians know that the supreme rule of the Christian life is love, and they will carry that love into every debate in which they are engaged.

THE WORKER FOR CHRIST

2 Timothy 2:6–7

> It is the toiling husbandman who must be first to receive
> his share of the fruits. Think of what I am saying, for
> the Lord will give you understanding in all things.

To represent the Christian life, Paul has used the picture of the soldier and of the athlete, and now he uses the picture of the farmer. It is not the lazy farmer, but the farmer who works hard, who must be the first to receive the share of the fruits of the harvest. What then are the characteristics of the farmer which Paul would wish to see in the life of the Christian?

(1) Often, farmers must be content, first to work and then to wait. More than any other worker, farmers have to learn that there is no such thing as quick results. Christians too must learn to work and to wait. Often, they must sow the good seed of the word into the hearts and minds of their hearers and see no immediate result. Teachers often have to teach and see no difference in those they teach. Parents often have to seek to train and guide, and see no difference in the children. It is only when the years go by that the result is

seen; for it often happens that, when those young people have grown to adulthood, they are faced with some irresistible temptation, some terrible decision or some intolerable effort, and back into their minds comes some word of God or some flash of remembered teaching; and the teaching, the guidance and the discipline bear fruit and bring honour where without it there would have been dishonour, salvation where without it there would have been ruin. The farmer has learned to wait with patience, and so must the Christian teacher and the Christian parent.

(2) One special thing characterizes the farmer – and that is a readiness to work at any hour. At harvest time, we can see farmers at work in their fields as long as the last streak of light is left; they know no hours. Neither must the Christian. The trouble with so much Christianity is that it is spasmodic. But, from dawn to sunset, Christians must always be working at their challenge of being Christians.

One thing remains in all three pictures. The soldier is upheld by the thought of final victory. The athlete is upheld by the vision of the crown. The farmer is upheld by the hope of the harvest. Each submits to the discipline and the toil for the sake of the glory which will come in the end. It is the same with the Christian. The Christian struggle is not without a goal; it is always going somewhere. Christians can be certain that after the effort of the Christian life there comes the joy of heaven; and the greater the struggle, the greater the joy.

REMEMBER JESUS CHRIST

2 Timothy 2:8–10

Remember Jesus Christ, risen from the dead, born of the seed of David, as I preached the gospel to you, that

gospel for which I suffer, even to the length of fetters,
on the charge of being a criminal. But though I am
fettered, the word of God is not bound. Therefore I
endure everything for the sake of God's chosen ones,
that they too may obtain the salvation which is in Christ
Jesus, with eternal glory.

RIGHT from the beginning of this letter, Paul has been trying
to inspire Timothy to his task. He has reminded him of his
own belief in him and of the godly parentage from which he
has come; he has shown him the picture of the Christian
soldier, the Christian athlete and the Christian worker. And
now he comes to the greatest appeal of all – *Remember Jesus
Christ*. Sir Robert Falconer calls these words 'The heart of
the Pauline gospel'. Even if every other appeal to Timothy's
strength of character should fail, surely the memory of Jesus
Christ cannot. In the words which follow, Paul is really urging
Timothy to remember three things.

(1) Remember Jesus Christ *risen from the dead*. The tense
of the Greek does not imply one definite act in time, but a
continued state which lasts forever. Paul is not so much saying to Timothy: 'Remember the actual resurrection of Jesus',
but rather: 'Remember your risen and ever-present Lord.'
Here is the great Christian inspiration. We do not depend on
a memory, however great. We enjoy the power of a presence.
When Christians are summoned to some great task that they
feel is beyond them, they must go about it in the certainty
that they do not go alone, but that the presence and the power
of their risen Lord is always with them. When fears threaten,
when doubts invade the mind, when inadequacy depresses,
remember the presence of the risen Lord.

(2) Remember Jesus Christ *born of the seed of David*. This
is the other side of the question. 'Remember', says Paul to
Timothy, 'that the Master shared our humanity.' We do not

remember one who is only a spiritual presence; we remember one who trod this road, and lived this life, and faced this struggle, and who therefore knows what we are going through. We have with us the presence not only of the glorified Christ, but also of the Christ who knew the desperate struggle of being human and followed the will of God to the bitter end.

(3) Remember the *gospel*, the good news. Even when the gospel demands much, even when it leads to an effort which seems to be beyond human ability and to a future which seems dark with every kind of threat, remember that it is good news, and remember that the world is waiting for it. However hard the task the gospel offers, that same gospel is the message of liberation from sin and victory over circumstances for us and for all people.

So, Paul fires up Timothy to courageous action by calling on him to remember Jesus Christ, to remember the continual presence of the risen Lord, to remember the sympathy which comes from the humanity of the Master, to remember the glory of the gospel for himself and for the world which has never heard it and is waiting for it.

THE CRIMINAL OF CHRIST

2 Timothy 2:8–10 (*contd*)

WHEN Paul wrote these words, he was in a Roman prison, bound by a chain. This was literally true, for all the time he was in prison night and day he would be chained to the arm of a Roman soldier. Rome took no risks that its prisoners might escape.

Paul was in prison on the charge of being a criminal. It seems strange that even a hostile government should be able to regard a Christian, and especially Paul, as a criminal. There were two possible ways in which Paul might seem to the Roman government to be a criminal.

First, Rome had an empire which extended almost as far as the known world of that time. It was obvious that such an empire was subject to stresses and to strains. The peace had to be kept, and every possible centre of discontent had to be eliminated. One of the things about which Rome was very particular was the formation of associations. In the ancient world, there were many associations. There were, for instance, dinner clubs whose members met at regular intervals. There were what are known as friendly societies designed for charity for the dependants of members who had died. There were burial societies to see that their deceased members were decently buried. But so particular were the Roman authorities about associations that even these humble and harmless societies had to receive special permission from the emperor before they were allowed to meet. Now, the Christians were in effect an illegal association; and that is one reason why Paul, as a leader of such an association, might well be in the very serious position of being a political criminal.

Second, the first persecution of the Christians was intimately connected with one of the greatest disasters which ever hit the city of Rome. On 19th July AD 64, the great fire broke out. It burned for six days and seven nights and devastated the city. The most sacred shrines and the most famous buildings perished in the flames. But worse – the homes of the ordinary people were destroyed. By far the greater part of the population lived in great tenements built largely of wood, and these went up in flames like tinder. People were killed and injured; they lost their nearest and dearest; they were left homeless and destitute. The population of Rome was reduced to what has been called 'a vast brotherhood of hopeless wretchedness'.

It was believed that Nero, the emperor, himself was responsible for the fire. It was said that he had watched the fire from the Tower of Maecenas and declared himself charmed with 'the flower and loveliness of the flames'. It was said that, when the fire showed signs of dying down, men were seen rekindling it with burning torches, and that these men were the servants of Nero. Nero had a passion for building, and it was said that he had deliberately set fire to the city so that from the ruins he might build a new and nobler Rome. Whether the story was true or not – the chances are that it was – one thing was certain. Nothing would kill the rumour. The destitute citizens of Rome were sure that Nero had been responsible.

There was only one thing for the Roman government to do; they must find a scapegoat. And a scapegoat was found. Let Tacitus, the Roman historian, tell how it was done: 'But all human efforts, all the lavish gifts of the emperor, and the propitiations of the gods did not banish the sinister belief that the conflagration was the result of an order. Consequently, to get rid of the report, Nero fastened the guilt and inflicted the most exquisite tortures on a class hated for their abominations, called Christians by the populace' (*Annals*, 15:44). Obviously, slanders were already circulating regarding the Christians. It has been suggested that the influential Jews were responsible. And the hated Christians were saddled with the blame for the disastrous fire of Rome. It was from that event that the first great persecution sprang. Paul was a Christian. More importantly, he was recognized as the leader of the Christians. And it may well be that part of the charge against Paul was that he was one of those responsible for the fire of Rome and the resulting misery of the people.

So, Paul was in prison as a criminal, a political prisoner, member of an illegal association and leader of that hated sect of fire-raisers, on whom Nero had pinned the blame for the destruction of Rome. It can easily be seen how helpless Paul was in the face of charges like that.

IN CHAINS YET FREE

2 Timothy 2:8–10 (*contd*)

EVEN though he was in prison on charges which made release impossible, Paul was not dismayed and was very far from despair. He had two great uplifting thoughts.

(1) He was certain that, though he might be bound, nothing could bind the word of God. Andrew Melville was one of the earliest heralds of the Scottish Reformation in the sixteenth century. One day, the Regent Morton sent for him and denounced his writings. 'There will never be quietness in this country', he said, 'till half a dozen of you be hanged or banished the country.' 'Tush! sir,' answered Melville, 'threaten your courtiers in that fashion. It is the same to me whether I rot in the air or in the ground. The earth is the Lord's; my fatherland is wherever well-doing is. I have been ready to give my life when it was not half as well worn, at the pleasure of my God. I lived out of your country ten years as well as in it. Yet God be glorified, it will not lie in your power to hang nor exile his truth!'

You can exile an individual, but you cannot exile the truth. You can imprison a preacher, but you cannot imprison the word that is preached. The message is always greater than the individual; the truth is always mightier than the bearer. Paul was quite certain that the Roman government could never find a prison which could contain the word of God. And it is one of the facts of history that if human effort could have obliterated Christianity, it would have perished long ago; but you cannot kill that which is immortal.

(2) Paul was certain that what he was going through would in the end be a help to other people. His suffering was not pointless and profitless. The blood of the martyrs has always been the seed of the Church, and the lighting of the pyre where Christians were burned has always been the lighting of a fire which could never be put out. When people have to suffer for their Christianity, let them remember that their suffering makes the road easier for someone else who is still to come. In suffering, we bear our own small portion of the weight of the cross of Christ and do our own small part in the bringing of God's salvation to the world.

THE SONG OF THE MARTYR

2 Timothy 2:11–13

This is a saying which can be relied upon:

> If we die with him,
>> we shall also live with him.
> If we endure,
>> we shall also reign with him.
> If we deny him,
>> he too will deny us.
> If we are faithless,
>> he remains faithful
> For he cannot deny himself.

THIS is a particularly precious passage because in it is enshrined one of the first hymns of the Christian Church. In the days of persecution, the Christian Church put its faith into song. It may be that this is only a fragment of a longer hymn. Polycarp (*To the Philippians*, 5:2) seems to give us a little more of it when he writes: 'If we please Christ in the present world, we shall inherit the world to come; as he has promised to raise us from the dead, and has said:

> "If we walk worthily of him,
>   So shall we reign with him."'

There are two possible interpretations of the first two lines – 'If we die with him, we shall also live with him.' There are those who want to take these lines as a reference to baptism. In Romans 6, baptism is likened to dying and rising with Christ. 'Therefore we have been buried with him by baptism into death, so that, as Christ was raised from the dead by the glory of the Father, we too might walk in newness of life.' 'But if we have died with Christ, we believe that we will also live with him' (Romans 6:4, 6:8). No doubt the language is the same; but the thought of baptism is quite irrelevant here; it is the thought of martyrdom that is in Paul's mind. Martin Luther, in a great phrase, said: '*Ecclesia haeres crucis est*', 'The Church is the heir of the cross.' Christians inherit Christ's cross, but they also inherit Christ's resurrection. They are partners both in the shame and in the glory of their Lord.

The hymn goes on: 'If we endure, we shall also reign with him.' It is the one who endures to the end who will be saved. Without the cross, there cannot be the crown.

Then comes the other side of the matter: 'If we deny him, he too will deny us.' That is what Jesus himself said: 'Everyone therefore who acknowledges me before others, I also will acknowledge before my Father in heaven; but whoever denies me before others, I also will deny before my Father in heaven' (Matthew 10:32–3). Jesus Christ cannot vouch in eternity for someone who has refused to have anything to do with him in

time; but he is always true to those who, however much they
have failed, have tried to be true to him.

These things are so because they are part of the very nature
of God. We may deny ourselves, but God cannot. 'God is
not a human being that he should lie, or a mortal, that he
should change his mind' (Numbers 23:19). God will never
fail those who have tried to be true to him; but not even he
can help someone who has refused to have anything to do
with him.

Long ago in the third century, the Church father Tertullian
said: 'The man who is afraid to suffer cannot belong to him
who suffered' (*De Fuga*, 14). Jesus died to be true to the will
of God; and Christians must follow that same will, whatever
light may shine or shadow fall.

THE DANGER OF WORDS

2 Timothy 2:14

> Remind your people of these things; and charge them
> before the Lord not to engage in battles of words – a
> thing of no use at all, and a thing which can only result
> in the undoing of those who listen to it.

ONCE again, Paul returns to the inadequacy of words. We must
remember that the Pastoral Epistles were written against a
background of those Gnostics who produced their long
words and their fantastic theories, and who tried to make
Christianity into an obscure philosophy instead of an adventure
of faith.

There is both fascination and danger in words. They can
become a substitute for actions. There are people who are
more concerned to talk than to act. If the world's problems
could have been solved by discussion, they would have been

solved long ago. But words cannot replace deeds. As Charles
Kingsley wrote in 'A Farewell':

> Be good, sweet maid, and let who will be clever;
> Do noble things, not dream them, all day long.

As Philip James Bailey wrote in *Festus*:

> We live in deeds, not years; in thoughts, not breaths;
> In feelings, not in figures on a dial.
> We should count time by heart-throbs. He most lives
> Who thinks most – feels the noblest – acts the best.

The eighteenth-century man of letters Dr Johnson was one
of the great talkers of all time; the founder of Methodism,
John Wesley, was one of the great men of action of all time.
They knew each other, and Johnson had only one complaint
about Wesley: 'John Wesley's conversation is good, but he
is never at leisure. He is always obliged to go at a certain
hour. This is very disagreeable to a man who loves to fold
his legs and have his talk out, as I do.' But the fact remains
that Wesley, the man of action, wrote his name across England
in a way in which Johnson, the man of talk, never did.

It is not even true that talk and discussion fully solve
intellectual problems. One of the most significant things
Jesus ever said was: 'Anyone who resolves to do the will of
God will know whether the teaching is from God' (John 7:17).
Often, understanding comes not by talking but by doing. In
the old Latin phrase, *solvitur ambulando*, the thing will solve
itself as you go on. It often happens that the best way to
understand the deep things of Christianity is to embark on
the unmistakable duties of the Christian life.

There remains one further thing to be said. Too much
talk and too much discussion can have two dangerous
effects.

First, they may give the impression that Christianity is nothing but a collection of questions for discussion and problems for solution. The discussion group is a characteristic phenomenon of our age. As the writer G. K. Chesterton once said: 'We have asked all the questions which can be asked. It is time we stopped looking for questions, and started looking for answers.' In any society, the discussion group must be balanced by the action group.

Second, discussion can be invigorating for those whose approach to the Christian faith is intellectual, for those who have a background of knowledge and of culture, for those who have a real knowledge of, or interest in, theology. But it sometimes happens that people with uncomplicated views find themselves in a group which is tossing heresies about and putting forward unanswerable questions; and their faith, far from being helped, is disturbed. It may well be that that is what Paul means when he says that wordy battles can undo those who listen to them. The normal word used for building a person up in the Christian faith, for *edification*, is the same as is used for literally *building a house*; the word which Paul uses here for ruin (*katastrophē*) is what might well be used for the *demolition* of a house. And it may well happen that clever, subtle, speculative, intellectually reckless discussion may have the effect of demolishing, and not building up, the faith of some of those who happen to become involved in it. As in all things, there is a time to discuss and a time to be silent.

THE WAY OF TRUTH AND THE WAY OF ERROR

2 Timothy 2:15–18

> Put out every effort to present yourself to God as one
> who has stood the test, as a workman who has no need

> to be ashamed, as one who rightly handles the word of truth.
>
> Avoid these godless chatterings, for the people who engage in them only progress further and further into ungodliness, and their talk eats its way into the Church like an ulcerous gangrene.
>
> Among such people are Hymenaeus and Philetus, who, as far as the truth is concerned, have lost the way, when they say that the resurrection has already happened, and who by such statements are upsetting the faith of some.

PAUL urges Timothy to present himself, amid the false teachers, as a real teacher of the truth. The word he uses for *to present* is *parastēsai*, which characteristically means *to present oneself for service*. The following words and phrases all develop this idea of usefulness for service.

The Greek for *one who has stood the test* is *dokimos*, which describes anything which has been tested and is fit for service. For instance, it describes gold or silver which has been purified of all alloy in the fire. It is therefore the word for money which is genuine, or, as we would say, *sterling*. It is the word used for a stone which is fit to be slotted into its place in a building. A stone with a flaw in it was marked with a capital A, standing for *adokimastos*, which means *tested and found wanting*. Timothy was to be tested to be sure that he was suitable for the work of Christ and was therefore a worker who had no need to be ashamed.

Further, Timothy is urged in a famous phrase *rightly to divide* the word of truth. The Greek word translated as *to divide rightly* is interesting. It is *orthotomein*, which literally means *to cut rightly*. It is a word containing many pictures. The reformer John Calvin connected it with a father dividing out the food at a meal and cutting it up so that each member of the family received the right portion. The sixteenth-century Calvinist theologian Theodore Beza connected it with the cutting up of sacrificial victims so that each part was correctly apportioned to the altar or to the priest. The Greeks themselves used the word in three different contexts. They used it for driving a straight road across country, for ploughing a straight furrow across a field, and for the work of a mason in cutting and squaring a stone so that it fitted into its correct place in the structure of the building. So, the person who rightly divides the word of truth drives a straight road through the truth and refuses to be lured down pleasant but irrelevant byways; such a person ploughs a straight furrow across the field of truth or takes each section of the truth and fits it into its correct position, as a mason does a stone, allowing no part to take an inappropriate place and so knock the whole structure out of balance.

On the other hand, the false teacher engages in what Paul would call 'godless chatterings'. Then Paul uses a vivid phrase. The Greeks had a favourite word for making progress (*prokoptein*). It literally means *to cut down in front*; to remove the obstacles from a road so that straight and uninterrupted progress is possible. Paul says of these senseless talkers that they progress further and further into ungodliness. They progress in reverse. The more they talk, the further they get from God. Here then is the test. If at the end of our talk we are closer to one another and to God, then all is well; but if we have put up barriers between one another and have left God more distant, then all is not well. The aim of all Christian discussion and of all Christian action is to bring people nearer to one another and to God.

THE LOST RESURRECTION

2 Timothy 2:15–18 (*contd*)

AMONG the false teachers, Paul numbers especially Hymenaeus and Philetus. Who these men were, we do not know.
But we get a brief glimpse of their teaching in at least one of
its aspects. They said that the resurrection had already
happened. This of course does not refer to the resurrection
of Jesus; it refers to the resurrection of Christians after death.
We do know of two false views of the resurrection of
Christians which had some influence in the early Church.

(1) It was claimed that the real resurrection of Christians
took place at baptism. It is true that, in Romans 6, Paul had
written vividly about how the Christian dies in the moment
of baptism and rises to new life. There were those who taught
that the resurrection happened in that moment of baptism
and that it was resurrection to new life in Christ here and
now, not after death.

(2) There were those who taught that the meaning of
individual resurrection was nothing more than that people
lived on in their children.

The trouble was that this kind of teaching found an echo
in both the Jewish and the Greek side of the Church. On the
Jewish side, the Pharisees believed in the resurrection of the
body but the Sadducees did not. Any teaching which did away
with the concept of life after death would appeal to the
Sadducees; the trouble with the Pharisees was that they were
wealthy materialists who had so big a stake in this world that
they were not interested in any world to come.

On the Greek side, the trouble was much greater. In the
early days of Christianity, the Greeks, generally speaking,
believed in immortality but not in the resurrection of the body.
The highest belief was that of the Stoics. They believed that

God was what might be called fiery spirit. The life in human beings was a spark of that spirit, a spark of God himself, a *scintilla* – a hint – of deity. But they believed that, when someone died, that spark went back to God and was re-absorbed in him. That is a noble belief, but it clearly does away with *personal* survival after death. Further, the Greeks believed that the body was entirely evil. They had their play on words as a slogan: '*Sōma Sēma*', 'The body is a tomb.' The last thing they wanted or believed in was the resurrection of the body, and therefore they, too, were open to receive any teaching about the resurrection which fitted their beliefs.

It is obvious that Christians do not believe in the resurrection of *this* body. No one could conceive of someone smashed in an accident or dying of cancer reawakening in heaven with the same body. But Christians do believe in the survival of personal identity; they believe most strenuously that after death you will still be you and I will still be I. Any teaching which removes that certainty of the personal survival of each individual person strikes at the very root of Christian belief.

When Hymenaeus and Philetus and others like them taught that the resurrection had already happened, either at the moment of baptism or in a person's children, they were teaching something which Sadducean Jews and philosophic Greeks would be by no means averse to accepting, but they were also teaching something which undermined one of the central beliefs of the Christian faith.

THE FIRM FOUNDATION

2 Timothy 2:19

> But the firm foundation of God stands fast with this inscription: 'The Lord knows those who are his', and

'Let everyone who names the name of the Lord depart from unrighteousness.'

In English, we use *foundation* in a double sense. We use it to mean the basis on which a building is erected, and also in the sense of an association, a college, a city which has been *founded* by someone. For instance, we talk about the *foundation* of a house; and we also say that King's College, Cambridge, is a *foundation* of Henry VI. Greek used the word *themelios* in the same two ways, and the *foundation* of God here means the *Church*, the association which he has founded.

Paul goes on to say that the Church has a certain *inscription* on it. The word he uses is *sphragis*, whose usual meaning is *seal*. The *sphragis* is the seal which proves genuineness or ownership. The seal on a sack of goods proved that the contents were genuine and had not been interfered with, and it also indicated the ownership and the source of the goods. But *sphragis* had other uses. It was used to denote the *brandmark*, what we would call the *trademark*. Galen, the Greek doctor, speaks of the *sphragis* on a certain phial of eye ointment, meaning the mark which showed what brand of eye ointment the phial contained. Still further, the *sphragis* was the *architect's mark*. Architects always put their mark on a monument, or a statue, or a building, to show that they were responsible for its design. The *sphragis* can also be the inscription which indicates the purpose for which a building has been built.

The Church has a *sphragis* which shows at once what it is designed to be. Paul gives the sign on the Church in two quotations. But the way in which these two quotations are made is very illuminating in regard to the manner in which Paul and the early Church used Scripture. The two quotations are: 'The Lord knows those who are his' and 'Let everyone

who names the name of the Lord depart from unrighteousness.' The interesting thing is that neither is a literal
quotation from any part of Scripture.

The first is a reminiscence of a saying of Moses to the
rebellious friends and associates of Korah in the wilderness
days. When they gathered themselves together against him,
Moses said: 'The Lord will make known who is his' (Numbers
16:5). But that Old Testament text was read in the light of the
saying of Jesus in Matthew 7:22: 'On that day many will say
to me, "Lord, Lord, did we not prophesy in your name, and
cast out demons in your name, and do many deeds of power
in your name?" Then I will declare to them, "I never knew
you; go away from me, you evildoers."' The Old Testament
text is, as it were, retranslated into the words of Jesus.

The second is another reminiscence of the Korah story. It
was Moses' command to the people: 'Turn away from the
tents of these wicked men, and touch nothing of theirs'
(Numbers 16:26). But that, too, is read in the light of the
words of Jesus in Luke 13:27, where he says to those who
falsely claim to be his followers: 'Go away from me, all you
evildoers.'

Two things emerge. The early Christians always read the
Old Testament in the light of the words of Jesus, and they
were not interested in verbal niceties; but to any problem
they brought the general sense of the whole range of Scripture.
These are still excellent principles by which to read and use
Scripture.

The two texts give us two broad principles about the
Church.

The first tells us that the Church consists of those who
belong to God, who have given themselves to him in such a
way that they no longer possess themselves and the world no
longer possesses them, but God possesses them.

The second tells us that the Church consists of those who have turned away from wickedness. That is not to say that it consists of perfect people. If that were so, there would be no Church. It has been said that the great interest of God is not so much in where someone has reached as in the direction in which that person is facing. And the Church consists of those whose faces are turned away from wickedness and towards righteousness. They may often fall, and the goal may sometimes seem distressingly far away, but their faces are always set in the right direction.

The Church consists of those who belong to God and have dedicated themselves to the struggle for righteousness.

VESSELS OF HONOUR AND OF DISHONOUR

2 Timothy 2:20–1

> In any great house, there are not only gold and silver vessels; there are also vessels of wood and earthenware. And some are put to a noble use and some to an ignoble use. If anyone purifies himself from these things, he will be a vessel fit to be put to a noble use, ready for any good work.

THE connection between this passage and the one which immediately precedes it is very practical. Paul had just given a great and high definition of the Church as consisting of those who belong to God and are on the way to righteousness. The obvious response is: how do you explain the existence of the chattering heretics in the Church? How do you explain the existence of Hymenaeus and Philetus? Paul's reply is that in any great house there are all kinds of utensils; there are things of precious metal and things of base metal; there are things which have a dishonourable use and things which have an honourable use. It must be so in the Church. As long as it is an earthly institution, it must be a mixture. As long as it consists of men and women, it must remain a cross-section of humanity. Just as it takes all kinds of people to make a world, so it takes all kinds of people to make the Church.

That is a practical truth which Jesus had stated long before, in the parable of the wheat and the tares (Matthew 13:24–30, 13:36–43). The point of that parable is that the wheat and the tares grow together, and, in the early stages, are so like each other that it is impossible to separate them. He stated it again in the parable of the dragnet (Matthew 13:47–8). The dragnet gathered *of every kind*. In both parables, Jesus teaches that the Church is necessarily a mixture and that human judgment must be suspended, but that God's judgment will in the end make the necessary separations.

Those who criticize the Church because there are imperfect people in it are criticizing it because it is composed of men and women. It is not given to us to judge; judgment belongs to God.

But it is the duty of Christians to keep themselves free from polluting influences. And if they do that, their reward is not special honour and special privilege but special service.

Here is the very essence of the Christian faith. A really good person does not regard goodness as offering an entitlement to special honour; that person's one desire will be to have more and more work to do, for that work will be the greatest privilege. The last thing a good person will do will be to seek to stand aloof from others. On the contrary, that person will seek to be among them, at their worst, serving God by serving them. The good person's glory will not be in exemption from service; it will be in still more demanding service. No Christian should ever think of being fit for honour but always as becoming fit for service.

ADVICE TO A CHRISTIAN LEADER

2 Timothy 2:22–6

> Flee from youthful passions; run in pursuit of righteousness in the company of those who call on the Lord from a clean conscience. Have nothing to do with foolish and stupid arguments, for you know that they only breed quarrels. The servant of the Lord must not fight, rather he must be kindly to all, apt to teach, forbearing, disciplining his opponents by gentleness. It may be that God will enable them to repent, so that they will come to know the truth, and so that they will escape from the snare of the devil, when they are captured alive by God's servant that they may do God's will.

Here is a passage of most practical advice for Christian leaders and teachers.

Timothy is told to flee from youthful lusts. Many commentators have made suggestions as to what these youthful lusts are. They are far more than the passions of the flesh. They include that *impatience*, which has never learned to make haste slowly and has still to discover that too much haste can do far more harm than good; that *self-assertion*, which is intolerant in its opinions and arrogant in its expression of them, and which has not yet learned to see the good in points of view other than its own; that *love of debate*, which tends to argue long and act little, and which will talk the night away and be left with nothing but a litter of unsolved problems; and that *love of novelty*, which tends to condemn a thing simply because it is old and to desire a thing simply because it is new, underrating the value of experience. One thing is to be noted – the faults of youth are the faults of idealism. It is simply the freshness and intensity of the vision which makes youth run into these mistakes. Such faults are matters not for austere condemnation but for sympathetic correction, for every one has a virtue hidden beneath it.

Christian teachers and leaders are to aim at *righteousness*, which means giving both to other people and to God their due; at *faith*, which means loyalty and reliability which both come from trust in God; at *love*, which is the utter determination never to seek anything but the highest good of our neighbours, no matter what they do to us, and which has put away forever all bitterness and all desire for vengeance; and at *peace*, which is the right relationship of loving fellowship with God and with one another. And all these things are to be sought *in the company of those who call upon the Lord*. Christians must never seek to live apart and aloof from others. They must find their strength and their joy in the Christian fellowship. As John Wesley said: 'A man must have friends or make friends; for no one ever went to heaven alone.'

Christian leaders must not get involved in senseless controversies which are the curse of the Church. In the modern Church, Christian arguments are usually particularly senseless, for they are seldom about great matters of life and doctrine and faith, but almost always about unimportant and trivial things. Once leaders become involved in senseless and un-Christian controversy, they have forfeited all right to lead.

Christian leaders must be *kindly* to all; even when they have to criticize and point out a fault, it must be done with the gentleness which never seeks to hurt. They must be *apt teachers*; they must not only know the truth but also be able to communicate it, and they will do that not so much by talking about it as by living in such a way that they show Christ to others. They must be *forbearing*; like their Master, if they are criticized they must not respond with similar criticism; they must be able to accept insult and injury, slights and

humiliations, as Jesus accepted them. There may be greater
sins than touchiness, but there is none which does greater
damage in the Christian Church. They must discipline their
opponents in *gentleness*; their hands must be like the hands
of a surgeon, unerring to find the diseased spot, yet never for
a moment causing unnecessary pain. They must love people,
not browbeat them into submission to the truth.

The last sentence of this passage is in very complex Greek,
but it seems to be a hope that God will awaken repentance
and the desire for the truth in people's hearts, so that those
who are trapped by the devil may be rescued while their souls
are still alive and brought into obedience to the will of God
by the work of his servants. It is God who awakes the
repentance; it is the Christian leaders who open the door of
the Church to all who have penitent hearts.

TIMES OF TERROR

2 Timothy 3:1

> You must realize this – that in the last days difficult
> times will set in.

THE early Church lived in an age when the time was growing
late; they expected the second coming at any moment.
Christianity developed within Judaism, and it very naturally
thought largely in Jewish terms and pictures. Jewish thought
had one basic idea. The Jews divided all time into *this present
age* and *the age to come*. This present age was altogether
evil; and the age to come would be the golden age of God. In
between, there was *the day of the Lord*, a day when God
would personally intervene and shatter the world in order to
remake it. That day of the Lord was to be preceded by a time
of terror, when evil would gather itself for its final assault,

and the world would be shaken to its moral and physical foundations. It is in terms of these last days that Paul is thinking in this passage.

He says that, in them, *difficult* times would set in. *Difficult* is the Greek word *chalepos*. It is the normal Greek word for *difficult*, but it has certain usages which explain its meaning here. It is used in Matthew 8:28 to describe the two demoniacs who met Jesus among the tombs. They were violent and dangerous. It is used in Plutarch to describe what we would call an *ugly* wound. It is used by ancient writers on astrology to describe what we would call a *threatening* conjunction of the heavenly bodies. There is the idea of menace and of danger in this word. In the last days, there would come times which would menace the very existence of the Christian Church and of goodness itself, a final tremendous assault of evil before its ultimate defeat.

In the Jewish pictures of these last terrible times, we get exactly the same kind of picture as we get here. There would come a kind of terrible flowering of evil, when the moral foundations seemed to be shaken. In the Testament of Issachar, one of the books written between the Old and the New Testaments, we get a picture like this:

Know you, therefore, my children, that in the last times
Your sons will forsake singleness
And will cleave unto insatiable desire;
And leaving guilelessness, will draw near to malice;
And forsaking the commandments of the Lord,
They will cleave unto Beliar.
And leaving husbandry,
They will follow after their own wicked devices,
And they shall be dispersed among the Gentiles,
And shall serve their enemies.

(Testament of Issachar 6:1–2)

In 2 Baruch, we get an even more vivid picture of the moral chaos of these last times:

> And honour shall be turned into shame,
> And strength humiliated into contempt,
> And probity destroyed,
> And beauty shall become ugliness . . .
> And envy shall rise in those who had not thought aught of
>   themselves,
> And passion shall seize him that is peaceful,
> And many shall be stirred up in anger to injure many;
> And they shall rouse up armies in order to shed blood,
> And in the end they shall perish together with them.
>
>   (2 Baruch 27)

In this picture which Paul draws, he is thinking in terms familiar to the Jews. There was to be a final showdown with the forces of evil.

Nowadays, we have to restate these old pictures in modern terms. They were never meant to be anything other than visions; we do violence to Jewish and to early Christian thought if we take them with a crude literalness. But they do enshrine the permanent truth that some time there must come the consummation when evil meets God in head-on collision, and the final triumph of God comes.

THE QUALITIES OF GODLESSNESS

2 Timothy 3:2–5

> For men will live a life that is centred in self; they will
> be lovers of money, braggarts, arrogant, lovers of insult,
> disobedient to their parents, thankless, regardless
> even of the ultimate decencies of life, without human
> affection, implacable in hatred, revelling in slander,

ungovernable in their passions, savage, not knowing
what the love of good is, treacherous, headlong in word
and action, inflated with pride, lovers of pleasure rather
than lovers of God. They will maintain the outward form
of religion, but they will deny its power. Avoid such
people.

HERE is one of the most terrible pictures in the New Testament
of what a godless world would be like, with the terrible
qualities of godlessness set out in a ghastly list. Let us look
at them one by one.

It is no accident that the first of these qualities will be *a
life that is centred in self*. The adjective used is *philautos*,
which means *self-loving*. Love of self is the basic sin, from
which all others flow. The moment anyone makes self-will
the centre of life, divine and human relationships are destroyed, and obedience to God and charity to other people
both become impossible. The essence of Christianity is not
the enthronement but the obliteration of self.

People would become *lovers of money* (*philarguros*). We
must remember that Timothy's work lay in Ephesus, perhaps
the greatest market in the ancient world. In those days, trade
tended to flow down river valleys; Ephesus was at the
mouth of the River Cayster, and commanded the trade of one
of the richest hinterlands in all Asia Minor. At Ephesus,
some of the greatest roads in the world met. There was the
great trade route from the Euphrates valley which came by
way of Colosse and Laodicaea and poured the wealth of
the middle east into the lap of Ephesus. There was the road
from north Asia Minor and from Galatia which came in via
Sardis. There was the road from the south which centred the
trade of the Maeander valley in Ephesus. Ephesus was
called 'the treasure-house of the ancient world', 'the Vanity
Fair of Asia Minor'. It has been pointed out that the writer

of the Book of Revelation may well have been thinking of Ephesus when he wrote that haunting passage which describes the cargo of the merchants: 'Cargo of gold, silver, jewels and pearls, fine linen, purple, silk and scarlet, all kinds of scented wood, all articles of ivory, all articles of costly wood, bronze, iron and marble, cinnamon, spice, incense, myrrh, frankincense, wine, olive oil, choice flour and wheat, cattle and sheep, horses and chariots, slaves – and human lives' (Revelation 18:12–13). Ephesus was the town of a prosperous, materialistic civilization; it was the kind of town where men and women could so easily lose their souls.

There is peril when people assess prosperity by material things. It is to be remembered that we may lose our souls far more easily in prosperity than in adversity; and we are on the way to losing our souls when we assess the value of life by the number of things which we possess.

THE QUALITIES OF GODLESSNESS

2 Timothy 3:2–5 (*contd*)

In these terrible days, people would be *braggarts* and *arrogant*. In Greek writings, these two words often went together – and they are both picturesque.

Braggart has an interesting derivation. It is the word *alazōn* and was derived from the *alē*, which means *a wandering about*. Originally, the *alazōn* was a wandering quack. Plutarch uses the word to describe a quack doctor. The *alazōn* was someone with no qualification at all who travelled round the country with medicines and spells and methods of exorcism which, he claimed, were remedies for all diseases. He boasted of the virtues of these medicines wherever he went. In time, the word went on to widen its meaning until it meant any boastful person.

The Greek moralists wrote much about this word. The *Platonic Definitions* defined the corresponding noun (*alazoneia*) as 'The claim to good things which a man does not really possess'. Aristotle (*Nicomachean Ethics*, 7:2) defined the *alazōn* as 'the man who pretends to creditable qualities that he does not possess, or possesses in a lesser degree than he makes out'. The Greek historian Xenophon tells us how Cyrus, the Persian king, defined the *alazōn*: 'The name *alazōn* seems to apply to those who pretend that they are richer than they are or braver than they are, and to those who promise to do what they cannot do, and that, too, when it is evident that they do this only for the sake of getting something or making some gain' (*Cyropoedia*, 2:2:12). Xenophon in the *Memorabilia* tells how Socrates utterly condemned such impostors. Socrates said that they were to be found in every walk of life but were worst of all in politics. 'Much the greatest rogue of all is the man who has gulled his city into the belief that he is fit to direct it.'

The world is full of these braggarts to this day – the clever know-alls who deceive people into thinking that they are wise, the politicians who claim that their parties have a programme which will bring in the Utopia and that they alone are born to lead, the people who crowd the pages of advertisements with claims to give beauty, knowledge or health, the people in the Church who have a kind of ostentatious goodness.

Closely allied with the *braggarts*, but – as we shall see – even worse, are people who are arrogant. The word is *huperēphanos*. It is derived from two Greek words that mean *to show oneself above*. The man who is *huperēphanos*, said Theophrastus, the master of the character sketch, has a kind of contempt for everyone except himself. He is the man who is guilty of the 'sin of the high heart'. He is the man whom God resists, for it is repeatedly said in Scripture that God receives the humble but resists those who are proud, *huperēphanos* (James 4:6; 1 Peter 5:5; Proverbs 3:34). The eleventh-century theologian Theophylact called this kind of pride *akropolis kakōn*, the stronghold of evils.

The difference between the braggart and the person who is arrogant is this. The braggart is a swaggering individual, who tries to bluster a way into power and importance. No one can possibly mistake someone like that. But the sin of the person who is *arrogant* is in the heart. The arrogant person might even seem to be humble; but deep down there is contempt for everyone else. People like that nourish an all-consuming, all-pervading pride; and in their hearts there is a little altar where they bow down before their own images of self.

THE QUALITIES OF GODLESSNESS

2 Timothy 3:2–5 (*contd*)

THESE twin qualities of the braggart and the arrogant person inevitably result in *love of insult* (*blasphēmia*). *Blasphēmia* is the word which is translated directly into English as *blasphemy*. In English, we usually associate it with insult against God, but in Greek it means insult both against individuals and against God. Pride always gives rise to insult. It encourages disregard of God, thinking that it does not need him and that it knows better than he. It breeds a contempt for others which can result in hurtful actions and in wounding words. The Jewish Rabbis placed what they called *the sin of insult* high in the list of sins. The insult which comes from anger is bad but is forgivable, for it is delivered in the heat of the moment; but the cold insult which comes from arrogant pride is an ugly and an unforgivable thing.

People will be *disobedient to their parents*. The ancient world considered duty to parents very important. The oldest Greek laws took away all rights from the man who struck his parents; to strike a father was in Roman law as bad as murder; in the Jewish law, honour for father and mother comes high in the list of the Ten Commandments. It is the sign of a supremely decadent civilization when youth loses all respect for age and fails to recognize the unpayable debt and the basic duty it owes to those who gave it life.

People will be *thankless* (*acharistos*). They will refuse to recognize the debt they owe both to God and to others. The strange characteristic of ingratitude is that it is the most hurtful of all sins because it is completely blind. The words of Shakespeare's King Lear remain true:

> How sharper than a serpent's tooth it is
> To have a thankless child!

It is the sign of honour to pay one's debts; and for everyone there is a debt to God and there are debts to others which must be remembered and repaid.

People will *refuse to recognize even the ultimate decencies of life*. The Greek word is that people will become *anosios*. *Anosios* does not so much mean that they will break the written laws; it means that they will offend against the unwritten laws which are part and parcel of the essence of life. To the Greeks, it was *anosios* to refuse burial to the dead; it was *anosios* for a brother to marry a sister, or a son a mother. The person who is *anosios* offends against the fundamental decencies of life. Such offence can and does still happen. People who are ruled by their passions will gratify them in the most shameless ways. Those who have exhausted the normal pleasures of life and are still unsatisfied will seek their thrills in any new pleasures which are on offer.

People will be *without human affection* (*astorgos*). *Storgē* is the word used especially of *family love*, the love of child for parent and parent for child. If there is no human affection, the family cannot exist. In the terrible times, men and women will be so centred on self that even the closest ties will be nothing to them.

People will be *implacable in their hatreds* (*aspondos*). *Spondē* is the word for a truce or an agreement. *Aspondos* can mean two things. It can mean that someone is so bitter as to be completely unable to come to terms with the person with whom he or she has quarrelled. Or it can mean being so dishonourable as to break the terms of an agreement. In either case, the word describes a certain harshness of mind which separates people from their neighbours in unrelenting bitterness. It may be that, since we are only human, we cannot live entirely without differences with one another; but to perpetuate these differences is one of the worst – and also one of the most common – of all sins. When we are tempted to do so, we should hear again the voice of our blessed Lord saying on the cross: 'Father, forgive them.'

THE QUALITIES OF GODLESSNESS

2 Timothy 3:2–5 (*contd*)

In these terrible days, people will be *slanderers*. The Greek for *slanderer* is *diabolos*, which is precisely the English word *devil*. The devil is the patron saint of all slanderers, and of all slanderers he is chief. There is a sense in which slander is the most cruel of all sins. If our possessions are stolen, we can set to and build up our fortunes again; but, if our good name is taken away, irreparable damage has been done. It is one thing to start an evil and untrue report on its malicious way; it is entirely another thing to stop it. As Shakespeare had it in Iago's words to Othello:

> Good name in man and woman, dear my lord,
> Is the immediate jewel of their souls:
> Who steals my purse steals trash; 'tis something,
>   nothing;
> 'Twas mine, 'tis his, and has been slave to thousands:
> But he that filches from me my good name
> Robs me of that which not enriches him
> And makes me poor indeed.

Many men and women, who would never dream of stealing, think nothing of – even find pleasure in – passing on a story which ruins someone else's good name, without even trying to find out whether or not it is true. There is slander enough in many churches to make the recording angel weep as he records it.

People will be *ungovernable in their desires* (*akratēs*). The Greek verb *kratein* means *to control*. It is possible to reach a stage when, far from controlling a habit or desire, a person becomes a slave to it. That is the inevitable way to ruin, for no one can take control of anything without first taking control of self.

People will be *savage*. The word is *anēmeros* and would be more fittingly applied to a wild animal than to a human being. It denotes a savagery which has neither sensitivity nor sympathy. People can be savage in rebuke and savage in pitiless action. Even a dog may show signs of being sorry when it has hurt its owner; but there are people who, in their treatment of others, can be lost to human sympathy and feeling.

THE QUALITIES OF GODLESSNESS

2 Timothy 3:2–5 (*contd*)

In these last terrible days, people will come *to have no love for good things or good persons* (*aphilagathos*). There can come a time in life when the company of good people and the presence of good things is simply an embarrassment. Those who feed their minds on cheap literature can in the end find nothing in the great classics. Their mental palate loses its taste. Finding even the presence of good people something which is best avoided is a true sign of having reached the very depths.

People will be *treacherous*. The Greek word (*prodotēs*) means nothing less than a *traitor*. We must remember that this was written just at the beginning of the years of persecution, when it was becoming a crime to be a Christian. At this particular time in the ordinary matters of politics, one of the curses of Rome was the existence of *informers* (*delatores*). Things were so bad that the Roman historian Tacitus could say: 'He who had no foe was betrayed by his friend.' There were those who would revenge themselves on an enemy by informing against him. What Paul is thinking of here is more than faithlessness in friendship – although that in all truth is wounding enough – he is thinking of those who, to pay back an old score, would inform against the Christians to the Roman government.

People would be *headlong* in words and action. The word is *propetēs*, precipitate or reckless. It describes the person who is swept on by passion and impulse to such an extent that he or she is totally unable to think sensibly. Far more harm is done from lack of thought than by almost anything else. Time after time, we would be saved from hurting ourselves and from wounding other people if we would only stop to think.

People will be *inflated with conceit* (*tetuphōmenos*). The word is almost exactly the English *swollen-headed*. They will be inflated with a sense of their own importance. There are still church officials whose main thought is their own dignity; but Christians are the followers of the one who was meek and lowly in heart.

They will be *lovers of pleasure rather than lovers of God*. Here, we come back to where we started: such people place their own wishes in the centre of life. They worship self instead of God.

The final condemnation of these people is that they retain the outward form of religion but deny its power. That is to say, they go through all the correct movements and maintain all the external forms of religion, but they know nothing of Christianity as a dynamic power which changes the lives of men and women. It is said that, after hearing an evangelical sermon, the nineteenth-century statesman Lord Melbourne once remarked: 'Things have come to a pretty pass when religion is allowed to invade the sphere of private life.' It may well be that the greatest handicap to Christianity is not the most notorious sinner but the sleek devotee of a faultless orthodoxy and a dignified convention, who is horrified when it is suggested that real religion is a dynamic power which changes an individual's personal life.

SEDUCTION IN THE NAME OF RELIGION

2 Timothy 3:6–7

> For from among these there come those who enter into houses, and take captive foolish women, laden with sins and driven by varied desires, ready to listen to any teacher but never able to come to a knowledge of the truth.

THE Christian emancipation of women inevitably brought its problems. We have already seen how secluded the life of the respectable Greek woman was, how she was brought up under the strictest supervision, how she was not allowed 'to see anything, to hear anything, or to ask any questions', how she never appeared alone on the streets, even on a shopping expedition, and how she was never allowed even to appear at a public meeting. Christianity changed all that, and a new set of problems arose. It was only to be expected that certain women would not know how to use their new liberty. There were false teachers who were quick to take advantage of that.

Irenaeus, who was the Bishop of Lyons at the end of the second century, draws a vivid picture of the methods of just such a teacher in his day. True, he is telling of something which happened later than this; but the wretched story would be the same (*Against Heresies*, 1:13:3). There was a certain heretic called Marcus, who dealt in magic. 'He devotes himself specially to women, and those such as are well-bred, and elegantly attired, and of great wealth.' He tells such women that by his spells and incantations he can enable them to prophesy. One woman protests that she has never done so and cannot do so. He says: 'Open your mouth, speak whatsoever occurs to you, and you shall prophesy.' The woman, thrilled to the heart, does so and is deluded into thinking that she can prophesy. 'She then makes the effort to reward Marcus, not only by the gift of her possessions (in which way he has collected a very large fortune), but also by yielding up to him her person, desiring in every way to be united to him, that she may become altogether one with him.' The technique would be the same in the days of Timothy as it was in the later days of Irenaeus.

There would be two ways in which these heretics in the time of Timothy could exert an evil influence. We must remember that they were Gnostics and that the basic principle of Gnosticism was that spirit was altogether good and matter altogether evil. We have already seen that that teaching resulted in one of two things. The Gnostic heretics taught either that, since matter is altogether evil, a rigid self-denial must be practised and all the things of the body as far as possible eliminated, or that it does not matter what we do with the body, and its desires can be indulged in to the limit because they do not matter. The Gnostics who were infiltrating the churches would teach these doctrines to impressionable women. The result would often be either that the woman broke off married relationships with her husband in order to live the life of self-denial, or that she gave her physical instincts full play and abandoned herself to promiscuous relationships. In either case, home and family life were destroyed.

It is still possible for some teachers to gain an undue and unhealthy influence over others, especially when those people are impressionable.

It is Paul's charge that such people are 'willing to learn from anyone, and yet never able to come to a knowledge of the truth'. E. F. Brown has pointed out the danger of what he calls 'intellectual curiosity without moral earnestness'. There is a type of person who is eager to discuss every new theory, who is always to be found deeply involved in the latest fashionable religious movement, but who is quite unwilling to accept the day-to-day discipline – even drudgery – of living the Christian life.

No amount of intellectual curiosity can ever take the place of serious moral resolve. We are not meant to titillate our minds with the latest intellectual crazes; we are meant to purify and strengthen ourselves in the moral battle to live the Christian life.

THE OPPONENTS OF GOD

2 Timothy 3:8–9

> In the same way as Jannes and Jambres opposed Moses,
> so these also oppose the truth, men whose minds are
> corrupt, and whose faith is counterfeit. But they will
> not get much further, for their folly will be as clear to
> all as that of those ancient impostors.

In the days between the Old and the New Testaments, many
Jewish books were written which expanded the Old Testament
stories. In certain of these books, Jannes and Jambres figured
largely. These were the names given to the court magicians
of Pharaoh who opposed Moses and Aaron, when Moses was
leading the children of Israel out of their slavery in Egypt. At
first, these magicians were able to match the wonders which
Moses and Aaron did, but in the end they were defeated and
discredited. In the Old Testament they are not named, but
they are referred to in Exodus 7:11, 8:7 and 9:11.

A whole collection of stories gathered round their names.
They were said to be the two servants who accompanied
Balaam when he was disobedient to God (Numbers 22:22);
they were said to have been part of the great mixed multitude
who accompanied the children of Israel out of Egypt (Exodus
12:38); some said that they perished at the crossing of the
Red Sea; other stories said that it was Jannes and Jambres
who were behind the making of the golden calf and that
they perished among those who were killed for that sin
(Exodus 32:28); still other stories said that in the end they
became converts to Judaism. Amid all the stories, one fact
stands out – Jannes and Jambres became legendary figures
typifying all those who opposed the purposes of God and the
work of his true leaders.

The Christian leader will never lack opponents. There will always be those who have their own twisted ideas of the Christian faith, and who wish to win others to their mistaken beliefs. But of one thing Paul was sure – the days of the deceivers were numbered. Their falsehood and deception would be demonstrated, and they would receive their appropriate reward.

The history of the Christian Church teaches us that false teaching cannot survive. It may flourish for a time, but when it is exposed to the light of truth it is bound to shrivel and die. There is only one test for such misrepresentation – 'You will know them by their fruits' (Matthew 7:16, 7:20). The best way to overcome and to banish the false is to live in such a way that the loveliness and the graciousness of the truth are plain for all to see. The defeat of error depends not on skill in controversy but in the demonstration in life of the more excellent way.

THE DUTIES AND THE QUALITIES
OF AN APOSTLE

2 Timothy 3:10–13

> But you have been my disciple in my teaching, my training, my aim in life, my faith, my patience, my love, my endurance, my persecutions, my sufferings, in what happened to me at Antioch, at Iconium, at Lystra, in the persecutions which I underwent; and the Lord rescued me from them all. And those who wish to live a godly life in Christ Jesus will be persecuted, while evil men and impostors will go from bad to worse, deceived themselves and deceiving others.

PAUL contrasts the conduct of Timothy, his loyal disciple, with the conduct of the heretics who were doing their utmost to wreck the Church. The word we have translated as *to be a disciple* includes so much that is beyond translation in any single English word. It is the Greek *parakolouthein* and literally means *to follow alongside*, but it is used with a magnificent breadth of meaning. It means to follow someone *physically*, to stick by that person through thick and thin. It means to follow someone *mentally*, to attend diligently to that person's teaching and fully to understand the meaning of what is being said. It means to follow someone *spiritually*, not only to understand what is being said, but also to carry out that person's ideas and become everything that that person would want us to be. *Parakolouthein* is indeed the word for the disciple, for it includes the unwavering loyalty of the true comrade, the full understanding of the true scholar and the complete obedience of the dedicated servant.

Paul goes on to list the things in which Timothy has been his disciple; and the interest of that list is that it consists of the strands out of which the life and work of an apostle are woven. In it, we find the *duties*, the *qualities* and the *experiences* of an apostle.

First, there are the *duties* of an apostle. There is *teaching*. We cannot teach what we do not know, and therefore before we can teach Christ to others we must know him for ourselves. When the father of the Scottish historian and essayist Thomas Carlyle was discussing the kind of minister his parish needed, he said: 'What this parish needs is a man who knows Christ other than at second hand.' Real teaching always comes out of real experience. There is *training*. The Christian life does not consist only in knowing something; it consists even more in being something. The task of the apostle is not only to tell men and women the truth; it is also to help them do it. The true leader gives training in living.

Second, there are the *qualities* of the apostle. First and foremost, he has an *aim in life*. Two men were talking about a great satirist who had been filled with serious moral resolve. 'He kicked the world about,' said one, 'as if it had been a football.' 'True,' said the other, 'but he kicked it to a goal.' As individuals, we should sometimes ask ourselves: what is our aim in life? As teachers, we should sometimes ask ourselves: what am I trying to do with these people whom I teach? Once Agesilaus, the king of Sparta, was asked: 'What shall we teach our boys?' His answer was: 'That which will be most useful to them when they are men.' Is it knowledge, or is it life, that we are trying to transmit?

As members of the Church, we should sometimes ask ourselves: what are we trying to do in it? It is not enough to be satisfied when a church is humming like a dynamo and every night in the week has its own crowded organization. We should be asking: what, if any, is the unifying purpose which binds all this activity together? In all life, there is nothing so creative of really productive effort as a clear sense of purpose.

Paul goes on to other qualities of an apostle. There is *faith*, complete belief that God's commands are binding and that his promises are true. There is *patience*. The word here is *makrothumia*; and *makrothumia*, as the Greeks used it, usually meant *patience with people*. It is the ability not to lose patience when people are foolish, not to grow irritable when they seem unteachable. It is the ability to accept the folly, the perversity, the blindness and the ingratitude of others and still to remain gracious, and still to labour on. There is *love*. This is God's attitude to us. It is the attitude which puts up with everything we can do and refuses to be either angry or embittered, and which will never seek anything but our highest good. To love others is to forgive them and care for them as God forgives and cares – and it is only God who can enable us to do that.

THE EXPERIENCES OF AN APOSTLE

2 Timothy 3:10–13 (*contd*)

PAUL completes the story of the things in which Timothy has shared and must share with him, by speaking of the *experiences* of an apostle; and he prefaces that list of experiences by setting down the quality of *endurance*. The Greek is *hupomonē*, which means not a passive sitting down and bearing things but a triumphant facing of them so that even out of evil there can come good. It describes not the spirit which *accepts* life but the spirit which *takes control of* it.

And that quality of conquering endurance is necessary, because persecution is an essential part of the experience of an apostle. Paul cites three instances when he had to suffer for Christ. He was driven from Antioch in Pisidia (Acts 13:50), he had to flee from Iconium to avoid lynching (Acts 14:5–6), and in Lystra he was stoned and left for dead (Acts 14:19). It is true that these things happened before the young Timothy had definitely entered on the Christian way; but they all happened in his home district, and he may well have been an eyewitness to them. It may well be a proof of Timothy's courage and consecration that he had seen very clearly what could happen to an apostle and still had not hesitated to throw in his lot with Paul.

It is Paul's conviction that the real follower of Christ cannot escape persecution. When trouble fell on the Thessalonians, Paul wrote to them: 'When we were with you, we told you beforehand that we were to suffer persecution; so it turned out, as you know' (1 Thessalonians 3:4). It is as if he said to them: 'You have been well warned.' He returned after the first missionary journey to visit the churches he had founded, where 'they strengthened the souls of the disciples, and encouraged them to continue in the faith, saying "It is through

many persecutions that we must enter the kingdom of God"'
(Acts 14:22). The kingdom had its price. And Jesus himself
had said: 'Blessed are those who are persecuted for righteousness' sake' (Matthew 5:10). Anyone who proposes to
accept a set of standards quite different from the world's is
bound to encounter trouble. For anyone who proposes to introduce into life a loyalty which surpasses all earthly loyalties,
there are bound to be clashes. And that is precisely what
Christianity demands that we should do.

Persecution and hardships will come; but of two things
Paul is sure.

He is sure that God will rescue those who put their faith in
him. He is sure that in the long run it is better to suffer with
God and the right than to prosper with the world and the
wrong. Certain of the temporary persecution, he is equally
certain of the ultimate glory.

He is sure that the ungodly will go from bad to worse and
that there is literally no future for those who refuse to accept
the way of God.

THE VALUE OF SCRIPTURE

2 Timothy 3:14–17

> But as for you, remain loyal to the things which you
> have learned, and in which your belief has been
> confirmed, for you know from whom you learned them,
> and you know that from childhood you have known the
> sacred writings which are able to give you the wisdom
> that will bring you salvation through the faith which is
> in Christ Jesus. All God-inspired Scripture is useful for
> teaching, for the conviction of error, for correction, and
> for training in righteousness, that the man of God may
> be complete, fully equipped for every good work.

PAUL concludes this section with an appeal to Timothy to remain loyal to all the teaching he had received. On his mother's side, Timothy was a Jew, although his father had been a Greek (Acts 16:1); and it is clear that it was his mother who had brought him up. It was the glory of the Jews that their children from their earliest days were trained in the law. They claimed that their children learned the law even from birth and drank it in with their mother's milk. They claimed that the law was so imprinted on the hearts and minds of Jewish children that they would sooner forget their own name than they would forget it. So, from his earliest childhood, Timothy had known the sacred writings. We must remember that the Scripture of which Paul is writing is the Old Testament; as yet, the New Testament had not come into being. If what he claims for Scripture is true of the Old Testament, how much truer it is of the even more precious words of the New.

We must note that Paul here makes a distinction. He speaks of 'all God-inspired Scripture'. The Gnostics had their own fanciful books; the heretics all produced their own literature to support their claims. Paul regarded these as manufactured things; but the great books for the human soul were the God-inspired ones which tradition and experience had sanctified.

Let us then see what Paul says of the usefulness of Scripture.

(1) He says that the Scriptures give *the wisdom which will bring salvation*. In *The Bible in World Evangelism*, A. M. Chirgwin tells the story of a ward sister in a children's hospital in England. She had been finding life, as she herself said, futile and meaningless. She had waded through book after book and laboured with philosophy after philosophy in an attempt to find satisfaction. She had never tried the Bible, for

a friend had convinced her by subtle arguments that it could not be true. One day, a visitor came to the ward and left a supply of gospels. The sister was persuaded to read a copy of St John's Gospel. 'It shone and glowed with truth,' she said, 'and my whole being responded to it. The words that finally convinced me were those in John 18:37: "For this I was born, and for this I came into the world, to testify to the truth. Everyone who belongs to the truth hears my voice." So I listened to that voice, and heard the truth, and found my Saviour.'

Again and again, Scripture has opened for men and women the way to God. In simple fairness, no one seeking for the truth has any right to neglect the reading of the Bible. A book with a record such as it has cannot be disregarded. Even unbelievers are acting unfairly unless they attempt to read it. The most amazing things may happen if they do, for there is a saving wisdom here that is in no other book.

(2) The Scriptures are of use in *teaching*. Only in the New Testament have we any picture of Jesus, any account of his life and any record of his teaching. For that very reason, it is undeniable that, whatever might be argued about the rest of the Bible, it is impossible for the Church ever to do without the gospels. It is perfectly true – as we have so often said – that Christianity is founded not on a printed book but on a living person. The fact remains that the only place in all the world where we get a first-hand account of that person and of his teaching is in the New Testament. That is why the church which has no Bible class is a church in whose work an essential element is missing.

(3) The Scriptures are valuable for *reproof*. It is not meant that the Scriptures are valuable for *finding fault*; what is meant is that they are valuable for convincing people of the error of their ways and for pointing them on the right path. A. M. Chirgwin has story after story of how the Scriptures

came by chance into the hands of people whose lives were changed by them.

In Brazil, Signor Antonio of Minas bought a New Testament, which he took home to burn. He went home and found that the fire was out. Deliberately, he lit it. He flung the New Testament on it. It would not burn. He opened out the pages to make it burn more easily. It opened at the Sermon on the Mount. He glanced at it as he consigned it to the flames. His attention was caught; he took it back. 'He read on, forgetful of time, through the hours of the night, and just as the dawn was breaking, he stood up and declared, "I believe."'

Vincente Quiroga of Chile found a few pages of a book washed up on the seashore by a tidal wave following an earthquake. He read them and never rested until he obtained the rest of the Bible. Not only did he become a Christian; he devoted the rest of his life to the distribution of the Scriptures in the forgotten villages of northern Chile.

One dark night in a forest in Sicily, a robber held up at gunpoint a man who distributed Bibles. He was ordered to light a bonfire and burn his books. He lit the fire, and then he asked if he might read a little from each book before he dropped it in the flames. He read the twenty-third psalm from one; the story of the good Samaritan from another; from another the Sermon on the Mount; from another 1 Corinthians 13. At the end of each reading, the robber said: 'That's a good book; we won't burn that one; give it to me.' In the end, not a book was burned; the robber left the bookseller and went off into the darkness with the books. Years later, that same robber turned up again. *This time, he was a Christian minister*, and it was to the reading of the books that he attributed his change.

It is beyond argument that the Scriptures can convict people of their error and convince them of the power of Christ.

(4) The Scriptures are of use for *correction*. The real meaning of this is that all theories, all theologies and all ethics are to be tested against the Bible. If they contradict the teaching of the Bible, they are to be refused. It is our duty to use and stimulate our minds; but the test must always be agreement with the teaching of Jesus Christ as the Scriptures present it to us.

(5) Paul makes a final point. The study of the Scriptures trains people in righteousness until they are equipped for every good work. Here is the essential conclusion. The study of the Scriptures must never be selfish, never simply for the good of an individual's own soul. Any conversion which makes someone think of nothing but the fact that *he or she* has been saved is no true conversion. We must study the Scriptures to make ourselves useful to God and to other people. No one is saved who does not have a burning desire to save others.

PAUL'S GROUNDS OF APPEAL

2 Timothy 4:1–5

> I charge you before God and Christ Jesus, who is going to judge the living and the dead – I charge you by his appearing and by his kingdom – herald forth the word; be urgent in season and out of season; convict, rebuke, exhort, and do it all with a patience and a teaching which never fail. For there will come a time when men will refuse to listen to sound teaching, but, because they have ears which have to be continually titillated with novelties, they will bury themselves under a mound of teachers, whose teaching suits their own lusts after forbidden things. They will avert their ears from the truth, and they will turn to extravagant tales. As for you, be steady in all things; accept the suffering which

> will come upon you; do the work of an evangelist; leave
> no act of your service unfulfilled.

As Paul comes to the end of his letter, he wants to encourage
and to challenge Timothy to his task. To do so, he reminds
him of three things concerning Jesus.

(1) Jesus is the judge of the living and the dead. Some
day, Timothy's work will be tested, and that by none other
than Jesus himself. Christians must do every task in such a
way that they can offer it to Christ. They are not concerned
with either the criticism or the verdict of others. The one
thing they long for is the 'Well done!' of Jesus Christ. If we
all did our work in that spirit, the difference would be
incalculable. It would save us from being so touchy that we
are offended by criticism; it would save us from the self-
importance which is concerned with personal rights and
personal prestige; it would save us from being self-centred
and demanding thanks and praise for everything we do; it
would even save us from being hurt by people's ingratitude.

(2) Jesus is the returning conqueror. 'I charge you', says
Paul, 'by his *appearing*.' The word is *epiphaneia*. *Epiphaneia*
was used in two special ways. It was used for the clear
intervention of some god, and it was especially used in connection with the Roman emperor. His accession to the throne
was his *epiphaneia*, and in particular – and this is the background of Paul's thought here – it was used of his visit to any
province or town. Obviously, when the emperor was due to
visit any place, everything was put in perfect order. The streets
were swept and decorated, and all work was brought up to
date so that the town might be fit for *epiphaneia*. So, Paul
says to Timothy: 'You know what happens when any town is
expecting the *epiphaneia* of the emperor; *you* are expecting
the *epiphaneia* of Jesus Christ. Do your work in such a way

that all things will be ready whenever he appears.' Christians should order their lives in such a way that at any moment they are ready for the coming of Christ.

(3) Jesus is king. Paul urges Timothy to action by the remembrance of the kingdom of Jesus Christ. The day comes when the kingdoms of the world will be the kingdom of the Lord; and so Paul says to Timothy: 'So live and work that you will have an honourable place on the roll of its citizens when the kingdom comes.'

Our work must be such that it will stand the scrutiny of Christ. Our lives must be such that they will welcome the appearance of the King. Our service must be such that it will demonstrate the reality of our citizenship of the kingdom of God.

CHRISTIAN DUTY

2 Timothy 4:1–5 (contd)

THERE can be few New Testament passages where the duties of Christian teachers are more clearly set out than here.

Christian teachers are to be urgent. The message they bring is literally a matter of life and death. The teachers who really get their message across are those who have the note of serious determination in their voice. The Baptist preacher Charles Spurgeon had a real admiration for James Martineau, who was a Unitarian and therefore denied the divinity of Jesus Christ, which Spurgeon believed in with passionate intensity. Someone once said to Spurgeon: 'How can you possibly admire Martineau? You don't believe what he preaches.' 'No,' said Spurgeon, '*but he does*.' Anyone whose voice has that note of urgency demands, and will receive, a hearing from others.

Christian teachers are to be *persistent*. They are to urge the claims of Christ 'in season and out of season'. As someone has put it: 'Take or make your opportunity.' As Theodore of Mospeuestia, the biblical scholar who lived in the late fourth and early fifth centuries, put it: 'The Christian must count every time an opportunity to speak for Christ.' It was said of George Morrison of Wellington Church in Glasgow that with him, wherever the conversation started, it went straight across country to Christ. This does not mean that we will not choose our time to speak, for there should be courtesy in evangelism as in every other human contact; but it does mean that perhaps we are far too shy in speaking to others about Jesus Christ.

Paul goes on to speak of the effect that those who witness to Christianity must produce.

They must *convict*. They must make sinners aware of their sin. The nineteenth-century economist and journalist Walter Bagehot once said: 'The road to perfection lies through a series of disgusts.' Somehow or other, sinners must be made to feel disgusted with their sin. Epictetus, the great Stoic philosopher, draws a contrast between the false philosopher, who is out for popularity, and the real philosopher, whose one aim is the good of his hearers. The false philosopher deals in flattery and panders to self-esteem. The real philosopher says: 'Come and be told that you are in a bad way.' 'The philosopher's lecture', he said, 'is a surgery; when you go away, you ought to have felt not pleasure but pain.' It was Alcibiades, the brilliant but spoiled darling of Athens, who used to say to Socrates: 'Socrates, I hate you, because every time I meet you, you make me see what I am.' The first essential is to compel people to see themselves as they really are.

They must *rebuke*. In the great days of the Church, there was an utter fearlessness in its voice, and because of that things happened. The missionary E. F. Brown tells of an incident from India. A certain young nobleman in the Viceroy's suite in Calcutta became notorious for his shameless behaviour. Bishop Wilson one day put on his robes, drove to Government House and said to the Viceroy: 'Your Excellency, if Lord —— does not leave Calcutta before next Sunday, I shall denounce him from the pulpit in the Cathedral.' Before Sunday came, that young man was gone.

Ambrose of Milan was one of the great figures of the early Church. He was a close friend of Theodosius, the emperor, who was a Christian but a man of violent temper. Ambrose never hesitated to tell the emperor the truth. 'Who', he demanded, 'will dare to tell you the truth if a priest does not dare?' Theodosius had appointed one of his friends, Botherich, as governor of Thessalonica. Botherich, a good governor, had occasion to imprison a famous charioteer for scandalous behaviour. The popularity of these charioteers was incredible, and the people rose in a riot and murdered Botherich. Theodosius was mad with anger. Ambrose pleaded with him for discrimination in punishment; but Rufinus, his minister of state, deliberately inflamed his anger, and Theodosius sent out orders for a massacre of vengeance. Later he countermanded the order, but too late for the new order to reach Thessalonica in time. The theatre was crammed to capacity with the doors shut, and the soldiers of Theodosius went to and fro slaughtering men, women and children for three hours. More than 7,000 people were killed. News of the massacre came back to Milan; and, when Theodosius presented himself at the church service the next Sunday, Ambrose refused him admission. The emperor pleaded for pardon. Eight months passed, and again he came to church. Again Ambrose refused him entry. In the end, the emperor of Rome had to lie prostrate on the ground with the penitents before he was allowed to worship with the church again. In its great days, the Church was fearless in rebuke.

In our personal relationships, a word of warning and rebuke would often save another person from sin and disaster. But that word must always be spoken with a consciousness of our common guilt. It is not our place to set ourselves up as moral judges; nonetheless, it is our duty to speak that warning word when it needs to be spoken.

They must *exhort*. Here is the other side of the matter. No rebuke should ever be such that it drives another person to despair and takes away all heart and hope. People should not only be rebuked, they should also be encouraged.

Further, the Christian duty of conviction, of rebuke and of encouragement must be carried out with tireless *patience*. The word is *makrothumia*, and it describes the spirit which never becomes irritated, never despairs and never regards anyone as beyond salvation. Christians patiently believe in others because they have a resolute belief in the changing power of Christ.

FOOLISH LISTENERS

2 Timothy 4:1–5 (*contd*)

PAUL goes on to describe the foolish listeners. He warns Timothy that the day is coming when people will refuse to listen to sound teaching and will surround themselves with teachers who will satisfy their desire with precisely the easy-going, comfortable things they want to hear.

In Timothy's day, it was tragically easy to find such teachers. They were called *sophists* and wandered from city to city, offering to teach anything in return for money. Isocrates, the Athenian orator, said of them: 'They try to attract pupils by low fees and big promises.' They were prepared to teach the whole of virtue for a modest fee. They would teach people to argue subtly and to use words cleverly until they could make 'the worse appear the better reason'. Plato described them savagely: 'Hunters after young men of wealth and position, with sham education as their bait, and a fee for their object, making money by a scientific use of quibbles in private conversation, while quite aware that what they are teaching is wrong.'

They competed for customers. Dio Chrysostom wrote of them: 'You might hear many poor wretches of sophists shouting and abusing each other, and their disciples, as they call them, squabbling, and many writers of books reading their stupid compositions, and many poets singing their poems, and many jugglers exhibiting their marvels, and many soothsayers giving the meaning of prodigies, and 10,000 rhetoricians twisting lawsuits, and no small number of traders driving their several trades.'

In the days of Timothy, people were surrounded by false teachers offering their sham knowledge. Their deliberate policy was to find arguments whereby people could justify anything they wanted to. Any teacher, even today, whose teaching tends to make people think less of sin is a menace to Christianity and to society as a whole.

In complete contrast to that, certain duties are to be laid on Timothy.

He is to be *steady in all things*. The word (*nēphein*) means that he is to be sober and self-disciplined, like an athlete who has all passions, appetites and nerves well under control. The biblical scholar F. J. A. Hort says that the word describes 'a mental state free from all perturbations or stupefactions . . . every faculty at full command, to look all facts and all considerations deliberately in the face'. Christians are not to be _ims of crazes; in an unbalanced and often insane world, they are to stand out for their stability.

He is to *accept whatever suffering comes upon him.* Christianity will cost something, and Christians are to pay the price of it without grumbling and without regret.

He is to do *the work of an evangelist.* In spite of the demand for conviction and rebuke, Christians are essentially *the bringers of good news.* If they insist on discipline and self-denial, it is because an even greater happiness may be attained than common and easily bought pleasures can bring.

He is to leave *no act of service unfulfilled.* Christians should have only one ambition – to be of use to the Church of which they are a part and the society in which they live. The opportunity not to be missed is not that of a cheap profit but that of being of service to God, to the Church and to other people.

PAUL COMES TO THE END

2 Timothy 4:6–8

> For my life has reached the point when it must be sacrificed, and the time of my departure has come. I have fought the good fight: I have completed the course: I have kept the faith. As for what remains, there is laid up for me the crown of righteousness which on that day the Lord, the righteous judge, will give to me – and not only to me, but also to all who have loved his appearing.

FOR Paul, the end is very near, and he knows it. When the Dutch reformer Erasmus was growing old, he said: 'I am a veteran, and have earned my discharge, and must leave the fighting to younger men.' Paul, the veteran warrior, is laying down his arms in order that Timothy may take them up.

No passage in the New Testament is more full of vivid pictures than this.

'My life', says Paul, 'has reached the point where it must be sacrificed.' The word he uses for *sacrifice* is the verb *spendesthai*, which literally means *to pour out as a libation, a drink offering, to the gods*. Every Roman meal ended with a kind of sacrifice. A cup of wine was taken and was poured out (*spendesthai*) to the gods. It is as if Paul were saying: 'The day is ended; it is time to rise and go; and my life must be poured out as a sacrifice to God.' He did not think of himself as going to be executed; he thought of himself as going to offer his life to God. Ever since his conversion, he had offered everything to God – his money, his scholarship, his time, his physical strength, the acuteness of his mind and the devotion of his heart. Only life itself was left to offer, and gladly he was going to lay it down.

He goes on to say: 'The time of my departure has come.' The word (*analusis*) he uses for *departure* is a vivid one. It contains many pictures, and each one tells us something about leaving this life. (1) It is the word for unyoking an animal from the shafts of the cart or the plough. Death to Paul was rest from labour. As Edmund Spenser had it in *The Faerie Queene*, sleep after toil, port after stormy seas, ease after war, death after life, are lovely things. (2) It is the word for loosening bonds or fetters. Death for Paul was a release. He was to exchange the confines of a Roman prison for the glorious liberty of the courts of heaven. (3) It is the word for loosening the ropes of a tent. For Paul, it was time to strike camp again. He had made many journeys across the roads of Asia Minor and of Europe. Now he was setting out on his last and greatest journey: he was taking the road that led to God. (4) It is the word for loosening the mooring ropes of a ship. On many occasions, Paul had felt his ship leave the harbour for the deep waters. Now he is to launch out into the greatest deep of all, setting sail to cross the waters of death to arrive in the haven of eternity.

So, for Christians, death is laying down the burden in order to rest; it is laying aside the shackles in order to be free; it is dismantling a temporary campsite in order to take up residence in the heavenly places; it is casting off the ropes which bind us to this world in order to set sail on the voyage which ends in the presence of God. Who then shall fear it?

THE JOY OF THE WELL-FOUGHT CONTEST

2 Timothy 4:6–8 (contd)

PAUL goes on, still speaking in the vivid pictures which he drew so skilfully: 'I have fought the good fight: I have completed the race: I have kept the faith.' It is likely that he is not using different pictures from three different spheres of life, but using one picture from the Greek and Roman games.

(1) 'I have fought the good fight.' The word he uses for *fight* is *agōn*, which is the word for a contest in the arena. When athletes can really say that they have done their best, then, win or lose, there remains a deep satisfaction. Paul has come to the end, and he knows that he has put up a good show. When his mother died, the writer J. M. Barrie made a great claim. 'I can look back,' he said, 'and I cannot see the smallest thing undone.' There is no satisfaction in all the world like knowing that we have done our best.

(2) 'I have finished the race.' It is easy to begin but hard to finish. The one thing necessary for life is staying power, and that is what so many people lack. It was suggested to a certain very famous man that his biography should be written while he was still alive. He absolutely refused to give permission, and his reason was: 'I have seen so many men fall out on the

last lap.' It is easy to wreck a noble life or a fine record by some foolishness at the end. But it was Paul's claim that he had finished the race. There is a deep satisfaction in reaching the goal.

Perhaps the world's most famous race is the marathon. The Battle of Marathon was one of the decisive battles of the world. In it, the Greeks met the Persians; and, if the Persians had conquered, the glory that was Greece would never have flowered upon the world. Against fearful odds, the Greeks won the victory; and, after the battle, a Greek soldier ran all the way, day and night, to Athens with the news. He ran straight to the magistrates. 'Rejoice,' he gasped, 'we have conquered' – and, even as he delivered his message, he fell down dead. He had completed his course and done his work, and there is no finer way for any individual to die.

(3) 'I have kept the faith.' This phrase can have more than one meaning. If we are to keep the background of the games, it is this. The great games in Greece were the Olympics, to which came all the finest athletes in the world. On the day before the games, all the competitors met and took a solemn oath before the gods that they had done not less than ten months' training and that they would not resort to any trickery to win. So, Paul may be saying: 'I have kept the rules: I have played the game.' It would be a great thing to die knowing that we had never transgressed the rules of honour in the race of life.

But this phrase may have other meanings. It is also a business phrase. It was the regular Greek for: 'I have kept the conditions of the contract; I have been true to my engagement.' If Paul used it in that way, he meant that he had engaged himself to serve Christ and had stood by that engagement and never let his Master down. Further, it could mean: 'I have kept my faith: I have never lost my confidence and my hope.' If Paul used it in that way, he meant that through thick and thin, in freedom and in imprisonment, in all his perils by land and sea, and now in the very face of death, he had never lost his trust in Jesus Christ.

Paul goes on to say that there is laid up for him the crown. In the games, the greatest prize was the laurel wreath. With it the victor was crowned, and to wear it was the greatest honour which could come to any athlete. But, in a few short days, this crown would wither. Paul knew that there awaited him a crown which would never fade.

In this moment, Paul is turning from the verdict of the world to the verdict of God. He knew that in a very short time he would stand before the Roman judgment seat and that his trial could have only one end. He knew what Nero's verdict would be, but he also knew what God's verdict would be. Those whose lives are dedicated to Christ are indifferent to the world's verdict. They do not care if the world condemns them as long as they hear their Master's 'Well done!'

Paul sounds yet one more note – this crown awaits not only him but all who wait with expectation for the coming of the King. It is as if he said to the young Timothy: 'Timothy, my end is near, and I know that I am going to my reward. If you follow in my steps, you will feel the same confidence and the same joy when the end comes to you.' The joy of Paul is open to everyone who also fights that fight and finishes the race and keeps the faith.

A ROLL OF HONOUR AND DISHONOUR

2 Timothy 4:9–15

> Do your best to come and see me soon. Demas has deserted me, because he loved this present world, and

has gone to Thessalonica. Crescens has gone to Galatia,
Titus to Dalmatia. Luke alone is with me. Take Mark
and bring him with you, for he is very useful in service.
I have sent Tychicus to Ephesus.

When you come, bring with you the cloak which I
left behind at Troas at Carpus' house, and bring the
books, especially the parchments.

Alexander, the coppersmith, did me a great deal of
harm. The Lord will reward him according to his deeds.
You yourself must be on your guard against him, for he
hotly opposed our words.

PAUL draws up a roll of honour and of dishonour of his friends.
Some are only names to us; of some, as we read the Acts of
the Apostles as well as the Epistles, we get the occasional
revealing glimpse. If we are allowed to use our imagination,
we can reconstruct some of the stories.

1. THE SPIRITUAL PILGRIMAGE OF DEMAS

First on the list comes Demas. There are three mentions of
him in Paul's letters, and it may well be that they have in
them the story of a tragedy. (1) In Philemon 24, he is listed
among a group of those whom Paul calls his *fellow workers*.
(2) In Colossians 4:14, he is mentioned without any comment
at all. (3) Here, he has forsaken Paul because he loved this
present world. First, Demas the fellow worker, then just
Demas, and finally Demas the deserter who loved the world.
Here is the history of a spiritual degeneration. Bit by bit, the
fellow worker has become the deserter; the title of honour
has become the name of shame.

What happened to Demas? We cannot tell for sure, but we
can guess.

(1) It may be that he had begun to follow Christ without
first counting the cost, and it may be that he was not altogether

̣e. There is a kind of evangelism which proclaims:
̣t Christ, and you will have rest and peace and joy.'
There is a sense, the deepest of all senses, in which that is
profoundly and blessedly true. But it is also true that when
we accept Christ our troubles begin. Up to this time, our lives
have conformed to the world and its standards. Because of
that, life has been easy, because we followed the line of least
resistance and went with the crowd. But once people accept
Christ, they accept an entirely new set of standards and are
committed to an entirely new kind of life at work, in personal
relationships and in pleasure, and there is bound to be conflict.
It may be that Demas was swept into the Church in a moment
of emotion without ever thinking things through – and then,
when unpopularity, persecution, the necessity of sacrifice,
loneliness and imprisonment came, he quit because he had
never bargained for anything like that. When we undertake
to follow Christ, the first essential is that we should know
what we are doing.

(2) It may be that there came to Demas the inevitable
weariness of the years. Time has a way of taking our ideals
away, of lowering our standards, of accustoming us to defeat.

The Roman Catholic doctor, Halliday Sutherland, tells how
he felt when he first qualified as a medical practitioner. If on
the street or in any company there came the call: 'Is there a
doctor here?', he was thrilled by it, proud and eager to step
forward and help. But, as the years went on, a request like
that became a nuisance. The thrill had gone.

W. H. Davies, the tramp who was also one of the greatest
poets, has a revealing passage about himself. He had walked
to see Tintern Abbey, which he had last seen twenty-seven
years before. He says: 'As I stood there now, twenty-seven
years after, and compared that young boy's enthusiasm with
my present lukewarm feelings, I was not very well pleased

with myself. For instance, at that time I would sacrifice both food and sleep to see anything wonderful; but now in my prime I did not go seeking things of beauty, and only sang of things that came my way by chance.'

William Inge, who was Dean of St Paul's Cathedral, had a sermon on Psalm 91:6 – 'the destruction that wastes at noonday', which he called 'The Peril of Middle Age'. There is no threat so dangerous as the threat of the passing years to our ideals; and it can be kept at bay only by living constantly in the presence of Jesus Christ.

(3) Paul said of Demas that 'he loved this present world'. His trouble may have been quite simple, and yet very terrible. It may simply be that he loved comfort more than he loved Christ, that he loved the easy way more than he loved the way which led first to a cross and then to the stars.

We think of Demas not to condemn but to sympathize, for so many of us are like him.

It is just possible that this is neither the beginning nor the end of the story of Demas. The name Demas is a shortened and familiar form of Demetrius, and twice we come upon a Demetrius in the New Testament story. There was a Demetrius who led the riot of the silversmiths at Ephesus and wanted to lynch Paul because he had taken their temple trade away (Acts 19:25). There was a Demetrius of whom John wrote that he had a good report of all and of the truth itself, a fact to which John bore willing and decisive witness (3 John 12). Might this be the beginning and the end of the story? Did Demetrius the silversmith find something about Paul and Christ which entwined itself round his heart? Did the hostile leader of the riot become the convert to Christ? Did he for a time fall away from the Christian path and become Demas, the deserter, who loved this present world? And did the grace of God lay hands on him again, and bring him back,

and make him the Demetrius of Ephesus of whom John wrote
that he was a servant of the truth of whom all spoke well?
That we will never know, but it is a lovely thought that the
charge of being a deserter may not have been the final verdict
on the life of Demas.

A ROLL OF HONOUR AND DISHONOUR

2. The Gentile of whom All Spoke Well

2 Timothy 4:9–15 (*contd*)

AFTER Paul has spoken of the man who was the deserter, he
goes on to speak of the man who was faithful to the death.
'Luke alone is with me', he says. We know very little about
Luke, and yet even from that little knowledge he emerges as
one of the loveliest characters in the New Testament.

(1) One thing we know by implication – Luke accompanied Paul on his last journey to Rome and to prison. He
was the writer of the Acts of the Apostles. Now, there are
certain passages of Acts which are written in the first-person
plural, and we can be quite sure that Luke is here describing
occasions on which he himself was actually present. Acts 27
describes Paul setting out under arrest for Rome, and the story
is told in the first person. Therefore we can be sure that Luke
was there. From that, we may deduce something else. It is
thought that, when an arrested prisoner was on his way to
trial at Rome, he was allowed to be accompanied by only
two slaves, and it is therefore probable that Luke signed up
as Paul's slave in order to be allowed to accompany him to
Rome and to prison. Little wonder that Paul speaks of him
with love in his voice. Surely devotion could go no further.

(2) There are only two other definite references to Luke
in the New Testament. In Colossians 4:14, he is described

as *the beloved physician*. Paul owed a great deal to Luke. All his life, he had the torturing thorn in his flesh (cf. 2 Corinthians 12:7), and Luke must have been the man who used his skill to ease his pain and enable him to go on. Luke was essentially a man who was kind. He does not seem to have been a great preacher of the gospel; he was the man who made his contribution in terms of personal service. God had given him healing skill in his hands, and Luke gave back that skill to God. Kindness is the quality which lifts men and women above the mass of ordinary people. Eloquence will be forgotten; mental cleverness may live on the printed page; but kindness lives on enthroned in people's hearts.

The man of letters Dr Johnson had certain contacts with a young man called Harry Hervey. Hervey was rich and rather a wild young man. But he had a London house where Johnson was always welcome. Years later, Harry Hervey was being unkindly discussed. Johnson said seriously: 'He was a vicious man, but very kind to me. If you call a dog Hervey, I shall love him.' Kindness covered a multitude of sins.

Luke was loyal and Luke was kind.

(3) The other definite reference to Luke is in Philemon 24, where Paul calls him his *fellow worker*. Luke was not content only to write, nor to confine himself to his job as a doctor; he got down to the work. The Church is full of talkers and of people who are there more for what they can get than for what they can give; Luke was one of these priceless people – the workers of the Church.

(4) There is one other possible reference to Luke in the New Testament, where 2 Corinthians 8:18 speaks of 'the brother who is famous among all the churches'. From the earliest times, that brother has been identified with Luke. He was the man of whom all spoke well. He was the man who

was loyal even though the consequence was death; he was the man who was essentially kind; he was the man who was dedicated to the work. Someone like that will always be a person of whom everyone speaks well.

A ROLL OF HONOUR AND DISHONOUR

3. The Man who Redeemed Himself

2 Timothy 4:9–15 (*contd*)

There is still another name with an untold, yet thrilling, story behind it in this list.

Paul urges Timothy to bring Mark with him, 'for he is profitable to me for the ministry'. The word *ministry* is not used in its narrower sense of the ministry of the Church but in its wider sense of *service*. 'Bring Mark,' says Paul, 'for he is very useful in service.' As E. F. Scott puts it in his commentary, 'Bring Mark, for he can turn his hand to anything.' Or, as we might put it, 'Bring Mark. He is a useful man to have about the place.'

Mark had a curiously chequered career. He was very young when the Church began, but he lived at the very centre of its life. It was to the house of Mary, Mark's mother, that Peter turned when he escaped from prison, and we may take it that this house was the central meeting place of the Jerusalem church (Acts 12:12).

When Paul and Barnabas set out on their first missionary journey, they took Mark with them – John Mark was his full name – to be their assistant (Acts 13:5). It looked as if he was earmarked for a great career in the company of Paul and in the service of the Church. Then something happened. When Paul and Barnabas left Pamphylia and set off inland on the hard and dangerous road that led to the central plateau of Asia Minor, Mark left them and went home (Acts 13:13). His nerve failed him, and he turned back.

Paul took that defection very hard. When he set out with Barnabas on their second missionary journey, Barnabas – who was related to Mark (Colossians 4:10) – planned to take Mark with them again. But, because he had quit, Paul absolutely refused to have Mark with them a second time, and so fierce was the argument and so acute the difference that Paul and Barnabas parted company and, as far as we know, never worked together again (Acts 15:36–40). So, there was a time when Paul had no use for Mark, when he looked on him as a spineless deserter and completely refused to have him on his staff.

What happened to Mark after that, we do not know. Tradition has it that he went to Egypt and that he was the founder of the Christian church in that country. But, whatever he did, he certainly redeemed himself. When Paul comes to write Colossians from his Roman prison, Mark is with him, and Paul commends him to the Colossian church and tells them to welcome him. And now, when the end is near, the one man Paul wants, besides his beloved Timothy, is Mark, for he is a useful man to have about. The quitter has become the man who can turn his hand to anything in the service of Paul and of the gospel.

The American Baptist Harry Emerson Fosdick had a sermon with the great and uplifting title: 'No man need stay the way he is.' Mark is proof of that. He is our encouragement and our inspiration, for he was the man who failed and yet made good. To this day, Jesus Christ can make cowards brave and give strength to those who are afraid. He can release the sleeping hero that lies in every soul. He can turn the shame of failure into the joy of triumphant service.

A ROLL OF HONOUR AND DISHONOUR

4. HELPERS AND A HINDERER AND A LAST REQUEST

2 Timothy 4:9–15 (*contd*)

So the list of names goes on. Of Crescens, we know nothing at all. Titus was another of Paul's most faithful companions. 'My loyal child', Paul calls him (Titus 1:4). When the trouble with the church at Corinth had been worrying him, Titus had been one of Paul's go-betweens in the struggle to put things right (2 Corinthians 2:13, 7:6, 7:13, 12:18). Tychicus had been entrusted with the delivery of the letter to the Colossians (Colossians 4:7) and of the letter to the Ephesians (Ephesians 6:21). The little group of helpers was being dispersed throughout the Church – for, even if Paul was in prison, the work still had to go on, and Paul's loneliness was the price of ensuring that his scattered people were strengthened and guided and comforted.

Then comes the mention of a man who had hindered instead of helping: 'Alexander, the coppersmith, did me a great deal of harm.' We do not know what Alexander had done, but perhaps we can work it out. The word that Paul uses for *did me a great deal of harm* is the Greek *endeiknumi*. That verb literally means *to display*, and was in fact often used for *giving information* against someone. Informers were one of the great curses of Rome at this time. And it may well be that Alexander had at one time been a Christian and had gone to the magistrates with false information against Paul, seeking to ruin him in the most dishonourable way.

Paul has certain personal requests to make. He wants the cloak he had left behind at the house of Carpus in Troas. The cloak (*phainolē*) was a great, circular, rug-like garment. It had a hole for the head in the middle and was rather like a tent, reaching right down to the ground. It was a garment for the wintertime, and no doubt Paul was feeling the cold of his Roman prison.

He wants the *books*. The word is *biblia*, which literally means papyrus rolls; and it may well be that these rolls contained the earliest forms of the gospels. He wanted the *parchments*. They could be one of two things. They might be Paul's necessary legal documents, especially his certificate of Roman citizenship; but more likely they were copies of the Hebrew Scriptures, for the Jews wrote their sacred books on parchment made from the skins of animals. It was the word of Jesus and the word of God that Paul wanted most of all, when he lay in prison awaiting death.

Sometimes history has a strange way of repeating itself: 1,500 years later, William Tyndale was lying in prison in Vilvorde, waiting for death because he had dared to give the people the Bible in their own language. It is a cold damp winter, and he writes to a friend: 'Send me, for Jesus' sake, a warmer cap, something to patch my leggings, a woollen shirt, and *above all my Hebrew Bible*.' When they were up against it and the chill breath of death was on them, these great Christians wanted more than anything else the word of God to put strength and courage into their souls.

LAST WORDS AND GREETINGS

2 Timothy 4:16–22

> At my first defence, no one was there to stand by me, but all forsook me. May it not be reckoned against them! But the Lord stood beside me, and he strengthened me, so that through me the proclamation of the gospel was fully made so that the Gentiles might hear it. So

I was rescued from the mouth of the lion. The Lord will rescue me from every evil, and will save me for his heavenly kingdom. Glory be to him for ever and ever. Amen.

Greet Prisca and Aquila, and the family of Onesiphorus. Erastus stayed in Corinth. I left Trophimus at Miletus. Exibulus sends greetings to you, as do Pudens, Linus and Claudia, and all the brothers.

The Lord be with your spirit.

Grace be with you.

A ROMAN trial began with a preliminary examination to formulate the precise charge against the prisoner. When Paul was brought to that preliminary examination, not one of his friends stood by him. It was too dangerous to proclaim oneself the friend of a man on trial for his life.

One of the curious things about this passage is the number of reminiscences of Psalm 22. 'Why have you forsaken me? – all forsook me.' 'There is no one to help – no one was there to stand by me.' 'Save me from the mouth of the lion! – I was rescued from the mouth of the lion.' 'All the ends of the earth shall remember and turn to the Lord – that the Gentiles might hear it.' 'Dominion belongs to the Lord – The Lord will save me for his heavenly kingdom.' It seems certain that the words of this psalm were running in Paul's mind. And the lovely thing is that this was the psalm which was in the mind of Jesus when he hung upon his cross. As Paul faced death, he took encouragement from the same psalm that his Lord used in the same circumstances.

Three things brought Paul courage in that lonely hour.

(1) Everyone had forsaken him; but the Lord was with him. Jesus had said that he would never leave his followers or forsake them, and that he would be with them to the end of the world. Paul is a witness that Jesus kept his promise. If to

do the right means to be alone, as Joan of Arc said, 'It is better to be alone with God.'

(2) Paul would use even a Roman court to proclaim the message of Christ. He obeyed his own commandment: in season and out of season, he pressed the claims of Christ on men and women. He was so busy thinking of the task of preaching that he forgot the danger. Those who are immersed in the task before them have conquered fear.

(3) He was quite certain of the ultimate rescue. He might seem to be the victim of circumstances and a criminal condemned by Roman justice, but Paul saw beyond the present time and knew that his eternal safety was assured. It is always better to be in danger for a moment and safe for eternity than to be safe for a moment and to jeopardize eternity.

A HIDDEN STORY?

2 Timothy 4:16–22 (*contd*)

FINALLY, there come greetings sent and given. There is a greeting to Priscilla and Aquila, that husband and wife whose home was a church, wherever it might be, and who had at some time risked their lives for Paul's sake (Acts 18:2; Romans 16:3; 1 Corinthians 16:19). There is a greeting to the gallant Onesiphorus, who had sought out Paul in prison in Rome (2 Timothy 1:16) and who had quite possibly paid for his loyalty with his life. There is a greeting to Erastus, whom Paul had once sent as his messenger to Macedonia (Acts 19:22) and who in all probability afterwards joined the church at Rome (Romans 16:23). There is a greeting to Trophimus, a Gentile whom Paul had been accused of bringing into the Temple precincts in Jerusalem, an incident which caused Paul's last imprisonment (Acts 20:4, 21:29).

Finally, there are greetings from Eubulus, Linus, Pudens and Claudia. In the later lists, Linus stands as the first Bishop of Rome.

A story has been woven around the names of Pudens and Claudia. The story may be impossible, or at least improbable, but it is too interesting not to quote. Martial was a famous Roman poet, a writer of epigrams, who flourished from AD 66–100. Two of his epigrams celebrate the marriage of Pudens, a distinguished Roman from an aristocratic family, to a lady called Claudia. In the second of them, Claudia is called a stranger in Rome, and it is said that she came from Britain. Now, Tacitus tells us that in AD 52, in the reign of the Emperor Claudius, certain territories in south-east Britain were given to a British king called Cogidubnus, for his loyalty to Rome; and in 1723 a marble tablet was dug up in Chichester which commemorates the building of a temple to the Roman gods by Cogidubnus, the king, and by Pudens, his son. In the inscription, the full name of the king is given; and, no doubt in honour of the Roman emperor, we find that the British king had taken the name of Tiberius Claudius Cogidubnus. If that king had a daughter, her name must have been Claudia, for that is the name that she would take from her father. We can take the story further. It may be that Cogidubnus sent his daughter Claudia to stay in Rome. That he should do so would be almost certain, for, when a foreign king entered into an alliance with Rome, as Cogidubnus had done, some members of his family were always sent to Rome as a guarantee of keeping the agreement. If Claudia went to Rome, she would certainly have stayed in the house of a Roman called Aulus Plautius, who had been the governor in Britain from AD 43–52, and to whom Cogidubnus had given his faithful service. The wife of Aulus Plautius was a lady called Pomponia, and we learn from Tacitus that she had been accused before the Roman courts in AD 57 because she was 'tainted with a foreign superstition'. That 'foreign superstition' may well have been Christianity. Pomponia may have been a Christian, and from her Claudia, the British princess, may have learned of Jesus also.

We cannot say whether that story is true. But it would be wonderful to think that this Claudia was actually a British princess who had come to stay in Rome and become a Christian, and that Pudens was her husband.

Paul comes to the end by commending his friends to the presence and the Spirit of his Lord and theirs; and, as always, his last word is grace.

The Letter to Titus

TITUS

THE TRUE NATURE OF APOSTLESHIP

Titus 1:1–4

> This is a letter from Paul, the slave of God and the
> envoy of Jesus Christ, whose task it is to awaken faith
> in God's chosen ones, and to equip them with a fuller
> knowledge of that truth, which enables a man to live a
> really religious life, and whose whole work is founded
> on the hope of eternal life, which God, who cannot lie,
> promised before time began. In his own good time, God
> set forth his message plain for all to see in the procla-
> mation with which I have been entrusted by the royal
> command of God our Saviour. This letter is to Titus,
> his true son in the faith they both share. Grace be to you
> and peace from God the Father and from Christ Jesus
> our Saviour.

WHEN Paul summoned one of his followers to a task, he always
began by setting out his own right to speak and, as it were,
laying again the foundations of the gospel. So, he begins here
by saying certain things about his apostleship.

(1) It set him in *a great succession*. Right at the beginning,
Paul calls himself 'the slave [*doulos*] of God'. That was a title
held with a mixture of humility and legitimate pride. It meant
that his life had been totally submitted to God; at the same
time – and this was where the pride came in – it was the title

that was given to the prophets and the great figures of the past. Moses was the slave of God (Joshua 1:2); and Joshua, his successor, would have claimed no higher title (Joshua 24:29). It was to the prophets, his slaves, that God revealed all his intentions (Amos 3:7); it was his slaves the prophets whom God had repeatedly sent to Israel throughout the history of the nation (Jeremiah 7:25). The title *slave of God* was one which gave Paul the right to take his place in a great succession.

When we join the Church, we do not join an institution which began yesterday. The Church has centuries of human history behind it and goes back into eternity in the mind and intention of God. When men and women take upon themselves any part of the preaching, or the teaching, or the serving work of the Church, they do not enter into a service which is without traditions; they follow in the footsteps of the saints who have gone before.

(2) It gave him *a great authority*. He was the messenger of Jesus Christ. Paul never thought of his authority as coming from his own mental excellence, still less from his own moral goodness. It was in the authority of Christ that he spoke. Those who preach the gospel of Christ or teach his truth, if they are truly dedicated, do not talk about their own opinions or offer their own conclusions; they come with Christ's message and with God's word. The true messenger of Christ has passed the stage of 'perhaps' and 'maybe' and 'possibly', and speaks with the certainty of one who knows.

AN APOSTLE'S GOSPEL

Titus 1:1–4 (*contd*)

FURTHER, in this passage we can see the essence of an apostle's gospel and the central things in an apostle's task.

(1) The whole message of the apostle is founded on *the hope of eternal life*. Again and again, the phrase *eternal life* recurs in the pages of the New Testament. The word for *eternal* is *aiōnios*; and properly the only person in the whole universe to whom that word may correctly be applied is God. The Christian offer is nothing less than the offer of a share in the life of God. It is the offer of God's power for our frustration, of God's serenity for our disquiet, of God's truth for our guessing, of God's goodness for our moral failure, of God's joy for our sorrow. The Christian gospel does not in the first place offer an intellectual creed or a moral code; it offers life, the very life of God.

(2) To enable people to enter into that life, two things are necessary. It is the apostle's duty to awaken *faith* in men and women. With Paul, faith always means one thing – absolute trust in God. The first step in the Christian life is to realize that all we have to do is receive. In every sphere of life, no matter how precious an offer may be, it remains ineffective until it is received. The first duty of Christians is to persuade others to accept the offer of God. In the last analysis, we can never argue anyone into Christianity. All we can say is: 'Try it, and see!'

(3) It is the apostle's duty also to equip others with *knowledge*. Christian evangelism and Christian education must go hand in hand. Faith may begin by being a response of the heart, but it must go on to be the possession of the mind. The Christian gospel must be thought out in order to be tried out. No one can live forever on the crest of a wave of emotion. The Christian life must be a process of loving Christ more and understanding him better each day.

(4) The result of faith and knowledge must be *a truly religious life*. Faith must always be evident in life; and Christian knowledge is not merely intellectual knowledge but

the knowledge of *how to live*. Many people have been great scholars and yet completely inefficient in the ordinary things of life and total failures in their personal relationships. A truly religious life is one in which we are on the right terms with God, with ourselves and with one another. It is a life in which we are able to cope both with the great moments and with the everyday duties. It is a life in which Jesus Christ lives again.

It is the duty of Christians to offer to everyone the very life of God, to awaken faith in people's hearts and to deepen knowledge in people's minds, to enable them to live in such a way that others will see the reflection of the Master in them.

GOD'S PURPOSE AND GOD'S GOOD TIME

Titus 1:1-4 (*contd*)

THIS passage tells us of God's purpose and of his way of working that purpose out.

(1) God's purpose for all humanity was always one of salvation. His promise of eternal life was there before the world began. It is important to note that here Paul applies the word *Saviour* both to God and to Jesus. We sometimes hear the gospel presented in a way that seems to draw a distinction between a gentle, loving and gracious Jesus and a hard, stern and severe God. Sometimes it sounds as if Jesus had done something to change God's attitude to men and women and had persuaded him to set aside his wrath and not to punish them. There is no justification for that in the New Testament. But behind the whole process of salvation is the eternal and unchanging love of God, and it was of that love that Jesus came to tell people. God is characteristically the Saviour God, whose last desire is to condemn and whose first desire is to

save. He is the Father who desires only that his children should come home so that he may gather them to himself.

(2) But this passage does more than speak of God's eternal purpose; it also speaks of his method. It tells us that he sent his message in *his own good time*. That means to say that all history was a preparation for the coming of Jesus. We cannot teach any kind of knowledge until those who are to be taught are fit to receive it. In all human knowledge, we have to start at the beginning; so people had to be prepared for the coming of Jesus. All the history of the Old Testament and all the searchings of the Greek philosophers were preparations for that event. The Spirit of God was moving both among the Jews and among all other peoples so that they should be ready to receive his Son when he came. We must look on all history as God's education.

(3) Further, Christianity came into this world at a time when it was uniquely possible for its message to spread. There were five elements in the world situation which made the spread of that message easy.

(a) Almost everyone spoke Greek. That is not to say that the nations had forgotten their own language, but that nearly everyone also spoke Greek. It was the language of trade, of commerce and of literature. Anyone who intended to take any part in public life and activity had to know Greek. People were bilingual, and the first age of Christianity was one of the very few when missionaries had no language problems to solve.

(b) To all intents and purposes, there were no frontiers. The Roman Empire extended throughout the known world. Wherever travellers might go, they were within that Empire. Nowadays, to cross Europe, we need passports and we may still be held up at frontiers. In the first age of Christianity, missionaries could move without hindrance from one end of the known world to the other.

(c) Travel was comparatively easy. True, it was slow, because there was no mechanized travel, and most journeys had to be done on foot, with the baggage carried by slow-moving animals. But the Romans had built their great roads from country to country and had, for the most part, cleared the land of robbers and the sea of pirates. Travel was easier than it had ever been before.

(d) The first age of Christianity was one of the few when the world was very largely at peace. If wars had been raging all over Europe, the progress of missionaries would have been impossible. But this was the time of the *pax Romana*, the Roman peace, and travellers could move within the Roman Empire in safety.

(e) It was a world which was conscious of its needs. The old faiths had broken down, and the new philosophies were beyond most people's understanding. People were looking, as Seneca, the Roman statesman and philosopher, said, *ad salutem*, towards salvation. They were increasingly conscious of 'their weakness in necessary things'. They were searching for 'a hand let down to lift them up'. They were looking for 'a peace, not of Caesar's proclamation, but of God's'. There was never a time when people were more receptive to the message of salvation which the Christian missionaries brought.

It was no accident that Christianity came when it did. It came in God's own time; all history had been a preparation for it; and the circumstances were such that the way was open for the good news to spread.

A FAITHFUL FOLLOWER

Titus 1:1–4 (*contd*)

WE do not know a great deal about Titus, to whom this letter was written; but, from the scattered references to him, a picture emerges of a man who was one of Paul's most trusted and most valuable helpers. Paul calls him his loyal child, so it is most likely that he himself converted Titus, perhaps at Iconium.

Titus was Paul's companion at an awkward and a difficult time. When Paul paid his visit to Jerusalem, to a church which viewed him with suspicion and was prepared to mistrust and dislike him, it was Titus whom he took with him along with Barnabas (Galatians 2:1). It was said of Henry Dundas, the famous Scottish politician, by one of his friends: 'Dundas is no orator; but he will go out with you in any kind of weather.' Titus was like that. When Paul was up against it, Titus was by his side.

Titus was the man for a tough assignment. When the trouble at Corinth was at its peak, it was he who was sent with one of the severest letters Paul ever wrote (2 Corinthians 8:16). Titus clearly had the strength of mind and character which enabled him to face and to handle a difficult situation. There are two kinds of people. There are the people who can make a bad situation worse, and there are the people who can bring order out of chaos and peace out of strife. Titus was the man to send to the place where there was trouble. He had a gift for practical administration. It was Titus whom Paul chose to organize the collection for the poor members of the church at Jerusalem (2 Corinthians 8:6, 8:10). It is clear that he had no great gifts of speech, but he was the man for practical administration. The Church ought to thank God for the people to whom we turn whenever we want a practical job done well.

Paul has certain titles for Titus.

He calls him his *loyal child*. That must mean that he was Paul's convert and child in the faith (Titus 1:4). Nothing in this world gives a preacher and teacher more joy than to see those whom they have taught rise to fulfil a useful position within the Church. Titus was the son who brought joy to the heart of Paul, his father in the faith.

He calls him his *brother* (2 Corinthians 2:13) and his *sharer in work and toil* (2 Corinthians 8:23). The great day for a preacher or a teacher is the day when children in the faith become brothers and sisters in the faith, when those who were once taught are able to take their place in the work of the Church, no longer as junior members but as equals with them.

He says that *Titus walked in the same spirit* (2 Corinthians 12:18). Paul knew that Titus would deal with things as he would have dealt with them himself. It is a great pleasure to have a deputy to whom we can commit our work, certain that it will be done in the way in which we ourselves would have wanted it done.

He gives to Titus a great task. He sends him to Crete to be a *model* to the Christians who are there (Titus 2:7). The greatest compliment Paul paid Titus was that he sent him to Crete, not to *talk* to them about what a Christian should be, but to *show* them what a Christian should be. There could be no greater responsibility and no higher compliment than that.

One very interesting suggestion has been made. Both 2 Corinthians 8:18 and 2 Corinthians 12:18 say that when Titus was sent to Corinth another brother was sent with him, described in the former passage as 'the brother who is famous among all the churches', and commonly identified with Luke. It has been suggested that Titus was Luke's brother. It is rather an odd fact that Titus is never mentioned in Acts; but we know that Luke wrote Acts and often tells the story in the first-person plural, saying: 'We did this' or 'We did that', and it has been suggested that in such passages he includes Titus with himself. Whether or not that suggestion is true we do not know, but certainly Titus and Luke have a family resemblance in that they were both men of practical service.

In the western Church, Titus is commemorated on 4th January, and in the eastern Church on 25th August.

THE ELDERS OF THE CHURCH

Titus 1:5–7a

> The reason why I left you in Crete was that any deficiencies in the organization of the Church should be rectified, and that you might appoint elders in each city as I instructed you. An elder is a man whose conduct must be beyond reproach, the husband of one wife, with children who are also believers, who cannot be accused of profligacy, and who are not undisciplined. For he who oversees the Church of God must be beyond reproach, as befits a steward of God.

WE have already studied in detail the qualifications of the elder as set out by Paul in 1 Timothy 3:1–7. It is therefore not necessary to examine them in detail again.

It was always Paul's custom to ordain elders as soon as a church had been founded (Acts 14:23). Crete was an island of many cities. Homer called it 'Crete of the hundred cities'. It was Paul's principle that his little churches should be encouraged to stand on their own feet as soon as possible.

In this repeated list of the qualifications of the elder, one thing is especially stressed. He must be someone who has taught his own family in the faith. The Council of Carthage later laid it down: 'Bishops, elders and deacons shall not be ordained to office before they have made all in their own households members of the Catholic Church.' Christianity begins at home. It is no virtue to be so engaged in public work that the result is neglect of those at home. All the church service in the world will not make amends for neglect of a church official's family.

Paul uses one very vivid word. The family of the elder must be such that they cannot be accused of *profligacy*. The Greek word is *asōtia*. It is the word used in Luke 15:13 for the *riotous* living of the prodigal son. The person who is *asōtos* is wasteful, extravagant and incapable of saving, and spends everything on personal pleasure. Such a person loses it all and in the end suffers personal ruin. One who is *asōtos* is the old English *scatterling*, the Scots *ne'er-do-well*, the modern *waster*. Aristotle, who always described a virtue as the mid-point between two extremes, declares that on the one hand there is stinginess, on the other there is *asōtia*, reckless and selfish extravagance, and the relevant virtue is generosity. The household of the elder must never be guilty of the bad example of reckless spending on personal pleasure.

Further, the family of the elder must not be *undisciplined*. Nothing can make up for the lack of parental control. In his book on the Pastorals, Sir Robert Falconer quotes a saying about the household of the English statesman and martyr Sir Thomas More: 'He controls his family with the same easy hand: no tragedies, no quarrels. If a dispute begins, it is promptly settled. His whole house breathes happiness, and no one enters it who is not the better for the visit.' The true training ground for the eldership is at least as much in the home as it is in the church.

WHAT THE ELDERS MUST NOT BE

Titus 1:7b

> He must not be obstinately self-willed; he must not be
> an angry man; he must not be given to drunken and

outrageous conduct; he must not be a man ready to come
to blows; he must not be a seeker of gain in disgraceful
ways.

HERE is a summary of the qualities from which the elders of
the church must be free – and every one is described by a
vivid word.

(1) Elders must not be *obstinately self-willed*. The Greek
is *authadēs*, which literally means *pleasing himself*. The
person who is *authadēs* has been described as someone 'who
is so pleased with himself that nothing else pleases him and
he is not interested in pleasing anybody'. R. C. Trench, the
Archbishop of Dublin, said of such a man that 'he obstinately
maintains his own opinion, or asserts his own rights, while
he is reckless of the rights, opinions and interests of others'.

The Greek ethical writers had much to say about this fault
of *authadeia*. Aristotle set on the one extreme the man who
pleases everybody (*areskos*), and on the other extreme the
man who pleases nobody (*authadēs*), and between them the
man who had in his life a proper dignity (*semnos*). He said of
the *authadēs* that he was the man who would not converse or
associate with anyone. Eudemus said that the *authadēs* was
the man who 'regulates his life with no respect to others, but
who is contemptuous'. Euripides said of him that he was 'harsh
to his fellow citizens through want of culture'. Philodemus
said that his character was made up in equal parts of conceit,
arrogance and contemptuousness. His conceit made him think
too highly of himself; his contemptuousness made him think
too meanly of others; and his arrogance made him act on his
estimate of himself and others.

Clearly, the person who is *authadēs* is an unpleasant character. People like that are intolerant, condemning everything
that they cannot understand and thinking that there is no way

of doing anything except their way. Such a quality, as W. Lock said in his commentary, 'is fatal to the rule of free men'. No one who shows contemptuous and arrogant intolerance is fit to be an office-bearer of the Church.

(2) Elders must not be quick-tempered. The Greek is *orgilos*. There are two Greek words for anger. There is *thumos*, which is the anger that quickly blazes up and just as quickly subsides, like a fire in straw. There is *orgē*, the noun connected with *orgilos*, and it means ingrained anger. It is not the anger of the sudden blaze, but the wrath which is continually fed to keep it alive. A blaze of anger is an unhappy thing, but this long-lived, purposely maintained anger is still worse. Those who nourish their anger against another person are not fit to be office-bearers of the Church.

(3) Elders must not be *given to drunken and outrageous conduct*. The word is *paroinos*, which literally means *given to overindulgence in wine*. But the word widened its meaning until it came to describe all conduct which is outrageous. The Jews, for instance, used it of the conduct of Jews who married Midianite women; the Christians used it of the conduct of those who crucified Christ. It describes the character of someone who, even in sober moments, acts with the outrageousness of a drunk.

(4) Elders must not be *ready to come to blows*. The word is *plēktēs*, which literally means *a striker*. It would seem that in the early Church there were overzealous bishops who disciplined erring members of their flock with physical violence, for the *Apostolic Canons* lay it down: 'We order that the bishop who strikes an erring believer should be deposed.' The fifth-century heretic Pelagius says: 'He cannot strike anyone who is the disciple of that Christ who, being struck, returned no answering blow.' The Greeks themselves widened the meaning of this word to include not only violence

in action but also violence in speech. The word came to mean one who *browbeats* others, and it may well be that it should be translated in this way here. Anyone who abandons love and resorts to violence of action or of speech is not fit to be an office-bearer of the Christian Church.

(5) Elders must not be *seekers of gain in disgraceful ways*. The word is *aischrokerdēs*, and it describes people who do not care how they make money as long as they make it. It so happens that this was a fault for which the Cretans were notorious. The Greek historian Polybius said: 'They are so given to making gain in disgraceful and acquisitive ways that among the Cretans alone of all men no gain is counted disgraceful.' Plutarch said that they stuck to money like bees to honey. The Cretans counted material gain far above honesty and honour. They did not care how much their money cost them; but every Christian knows that there are some things which cost too much. Anyone whose only aim in life is to amass material things, irrespective of how that is achieved, is not fit to be an office-bearer of the Christian Church.

WHAT THE ELDERS MUST BE

Titus 1:8–9

> Rather he must be hospitable, a lover of all good things and all good people, prudent, just, pious, self-controlled, with a strong grip on the truly reliable message which Christian teaching gave to him, that he may be well able to encourage the members of the Church with health-giving teaching, and to convict the opponents of the faith.

THE previous passage set out the things which the elders of the Church must not be; this one sets out what the elders must be. These necessary qualities group themselves into three sections.

(1) First, there are the qualities which elders of the Church must display *to other people*.

An elder must he *hospitable*. The Greek is *philoxenos*, which literally means *a lover of strangers*. In the ancient world, there were a great many who were constantly on the move. Inns were notoriously expensive, dirty and immoral; and it was essential that Christian travellers should find an open door within the Christian community. To this day, no one needs Christian fellowship more than the stranger in an unfamiliar place.

An elder must also be *philagathos*, a word which means either someone who loves good things or who loves good people, and which Aristotle uses in the sense of *unselfish*; that is, someone who loves good actions. We do not have to choose between these three meanings; they are all included. The Christian elder must be someone whose heart answers to the good in whatever person, wherever and in whatever circumstances it is found.

(2) Second, there comes a group of terms which tell us the *personal* qualities which Christian elders must possess.

They must be *prudent* (*sōphrōn*). Euripides called this prudence 'the fairest gift the gods have given to men'. Socrates called it 'the foundation stone of virtue'. Xenophon said that it was that spirit which shunned evil, not only when evil could be seen but even when no one would ever see it. R. C. Trench defined it as 'entire command over the passions and desires, so that they receive no further allowance than that which the law and right reason admit and approve'. *Sōphrōn* is the adjective to be applied to the person, as the Greeks said themselves, 'whose thoughts are saving thoughts'. The

Christian office-bearers must be people who wisely control every instinct.

They must be *just* (*dikaios*). The Greeks defined the just person as the one who gives both to other people and to the gods what is due to them. The Christian elders must be the kind of people who give to other people the respect, and to God the reverence, which are their due.

They must be *pious* (*hosios*). The Greek word is hard to translate, for it describes the person who reverences the fundamental decencies of life, the things which go back beyond any human law.

They must be *self-controlled* (*egkratēs*). The Greek word describes the person who has achieved complete self-control. Anyone who would serve others must first be in complete control of self.

(3) Finally, there comes a description of the qualities of the Christian elders *within the church*.

They must be able *to encourage* the members of the church. The navy has a rule which says that officers shall not speak discouragingly to other officers in the performance of their duties. There is always something wrong with preaching or teaching whose effect is to discourage others. The function of true Christian preachers and teachers is not to drive people to despair but to lift them up to hope.

They must be able *to convict* the opponents of the faith. The Greek is *elegchein* and is a most meaningful word. It means to rebuke people in such a way that they are compelled to admit the error of their ways. Trench says that it means 'to rebuke another, with such an effectual wielding of the victorious arms of the truth, as to bring him, if not always to a confession, yet at least to a conviction of his sin'. The Athenian orator Demosthenes said that it describes the situation in which a man unanswerably demonstrates the truth of the things that he has said. Aristotle said that it means to prove that things cannot be otherwise than as we have stated them. Christian rebuke means far more than flinging angry and condemning words at people. It means speaking in such a way that they see the error of their ways and accept the truth.

THE FALSE TEACHERS OF CRETE

Titus 1:10–11

> For there are many who are undisciplined, empty talkers, deceivers. Those of the circumcision are especially so. They must be muzzled. They are the kind of people who upset whole households, by teaching things which should not be taught in order to acquire a shameful gain.

HERE we have a picture of the false teachers who were troubling Crete. The worst offenders were apparently Jews. They tried to persuade the Cretan converts of two things. They tried to persuade them that the simple story of Jesus and the cross was not sufficient, but that, to be really wise, they needed all the subtle stories and the long genealogies and the elaborate allegories of the Rabbis. Further, they tried to teach them that grace was not enough, but that, to be really good, they needed to take upon themselves all the rules and regulations about foods and washings which were so characteristic of Judaism. The false teachers were seeking to persuade people that they needed more than Christ and more than grace in order to be saved. They were intellectuals for whom the truth of God was too simple and too good to be true.

One by one, the characteristics of these false teachers are described.

They were *undisciplined*; they were like disloyal soldiers who refused to obey the word of command. They refused to accept the creed or the control of the Church. It is perfectly true that the Church does not seek to impose a flat uniformity of belief on people; but there are certain things which everyone must believe in order to be Christians, the greatest of which is the all-sufficiency of Christ. Even in the Church today, discipline has its place.

They were *empty talkers*; the word is *mataiologoi*, and the adjective *mataios*, meaning *vain*, *empty*, *profitless*, was the adjective applied to the ancient worship of Greece and Rome. The main idea was of a worship which produced no goodness of life. These people in Crete could talk glibly, but all their talk was ineffective in bringing anyone a single step nearer to goodness. The Cynics used to say that all knowledge which is not profitable for virtue is pointless. The teacher who simply provides pupils with a forum for pleasant intellectual and speculative discussion teaches in vain.

They were *deceivers*. Instead of leading people to the truth, they led them away from it.

Their teaching *upset whole households*. There are two things to notice there. First, their teaching was fundamentally upsetting. It is true that truth must often make people rethink their ideas and that Christianity does not run away from doubts and questions but faces them fairly and squarely. But it is also true that teaching which ends in nothing but doubts and questionings is bad teaching. In true teaching, the challenging questioning that so often disturbs should in the end lead to a new and greater certainty. Second, they upset households. That is to say, they had a bad effect on family life. Any teaching which tends to disrupt the family is false, for the Christian Church is built on the basis of the Christian family.

Their teaching was designed for *gain*. They were more concerned with what they could get out of the people when they were teaching than with what they could put into them. In his commentary, R. St John Parry has said that this is indeed the greatest temptation for professional teachers. When they look on their teaching simply as a career designed for personal advancement and profit, they are in a perilous state.

These false teachers are to be *muzzled*. That does not imply that they are to be silenced by violence or by persecution. The Greek (*epistomizein*) does mean *to muzzle*, but it became the normal word for *to silence a person by reason*. The way to combat false teaching is to offer true teaching, and the only truly unanswerable teaching is the teaching of a Christian life.

A BAD REPUTATION

Titus 1:12

> One of themselves, a prophet of their own, has said:
>> 'The Cretans are always liars, wild and evil beasts,
>> lazy gluttons.'
> His testimony is true!

No nation ever had a worse reputation than the Cretans. The ancient world spoke of the three most evil C's – the Cretans, the Cilicians and the Cappadocians. The Cretans were famed as a drunken, insolent, untrustworthy, lying, gluttonous people.

Their greed was proverbial. 'The Cretans,' said the Greek historian Polybius, 'on account of their innate avarice, live in a perpetual state of private quarrel and public feud and civil strife . . . and you will hardly find anywhere characters more tricky and deceitful than those of Crete.' He writes of them: 'Money is so highly valued among them that its possession is not only thought to be necessary but highly creditable; and in fact greed and avarice are so native to the soil in Crete that they are the only people in the world among whom no stigma attaches to any sort of gain whatever.'

Polybius tells of a certain bargain that a traitor called Bolis made with a leader called Cambylus, also a Cretan. Bolis approached Cambylus 'with all the subtlety of a Cretan'. 'This was now made the subject of discussion between them in a truly Cretan spirit. They never took into consideration the saving of the person in danger, or their obligations of honour to those who had entrusted them with the undertaking, but confined the discussion entirely to questions of their own safety and their own advantage. As they were both Cretans, they were not long in coming to a unanimous agreement.'

So notorious were the Cretans that the Greeks actually formed a verb *krētizein*, *to cretize*, which meant *to lie and to cheat*; and they had a proverbial phrase, *krētizein pros Krēta*, to cretize against a Cretan, which meant *to match lies with lies*, as diamond cuts diamond.

The quotation which Paul cites is actually from a Greek poet called Epimenides. He lived about 600 BC and held the status of one of the seven wise men of Greece. The first phrase, 'The Cretans are chronic liars', had been made famous by a later and equally well-known poet called Callimachus. In Crete, there was a monument called the Tomb of Zeus. Obviously, the greatest of the gods cannot die and be buried in a tomb; and Callimachus quoted this as a perfect example of Cretan lying. In his *Hymn to Zeus*, he writes:

> Cretans are chronic liars,
> For they built a tomb, O King,
> And called it thine; but you die not;
> Your life is everlasting.

The Cretans were notorious liars and cheats and gluttons and traitors – but here is the wonderful thing. Knowing that, and actually experiencing it, Paul does not say to Timothy: 'Leave them alone. They are hopeless and everyone knows it.' He says: 'They are bad and we all know it. *Go and convert them.*' Few passages so demonstrate the divine optimism of the Christian evangelist who refuses to regard anyone as hopeless. The greater the evil, the greater the challenge. It is the Christian conviction that there is no sin too great for the grace of Jesus Christ to conquer.

THE PURE IN HEART

Titus 1:13–16

> For that very reason correct them with severity, that they may grow healthy in the faith and not pay attention to Jewish fables and to rules and regulations made by men who persist in turning their backs on the truth.
>
> 'To the pure, all things are pure.'
>
> But, to those who are defiled and who do not believe, nothing is pure, because their mind and conscience are defiled. They profess to know God, but they deny their profession by their deeds, because they are repulsive and disobedient and useless for any good work.

THE great characteristic of the Jewish faith was its thousands of rules and regulations. Many things were branded as unclean; many kinds of food were classified as forbidden. When Judaism and Gnosticism joined hands, even the body became unclean, and the natural instincts of the body were held to be evil. The inevitable result was that long lists of sins were constantly being created. It became a sin to touch certain things; it became a sin to eat certain foods; it even became a sin to marry and to have children. Things which were either good in themselves or quite natural were considered unclean.

So Paul declares the great principle – to the pure, all things are pure. He had already said that even more definitely in Romans 14:20 when, to those who were constantly involved in questions about clean and unclean foods, he said: 'Everything is indeed clean.' It may well be that this phrase is not only a proverb but an actual saying of Jesus. When Jesus was speaking about these numerous Jewish rules and regulations, he said: 'There is nothing outside a person that by going in can defile, but the things that come out are what defile' (Mark 7:15).

It is the heart which makes all the difference. If someone is pure in heart, all things are pure to that person. If someone is unclean in heart, then everything that person thinks about or speaks about or touches becomes unclean. This was a principle which the great classical writers had often stated. 'Unless the vessel is pure,' said Horace, 'everything you pour into it grows bitter.' Seneca said: 'Just as a diseased stomach alters the food which it receives, so the darkened mind turns everything you commit to it to its own burden and ruin. Nothing can come to evil men which is of any good to them, nay nothing can come to them which does not actually harm them. They change whatever touches them into their own nature. And even things which would be of profit to others become pernicious to them.' The person with a dirty mind makes everything dirty, taking even the loveliest things and covering them with smut. But the person whose mind is pure finds purity in everything.

It is said of these people that both their *minds* and their *consciences* are contaminated. We come to decisions and form conclusions by using two faculties. We use *intellect* to think things out; we use *conscience* to listen to the voice of God.

But if the intellect is warped in such a way that it sees the unclean everywhere and in all things, and if the conscience is darkened and numbed by continual consent to what is evil, it becomes impossible to take any good decision at all.

If we allow impurity to infect the mind, we will see all things through a mist of uncleanness. The infected mind soils every thought that enters into it; the imagination turns every picture which it forms into a source of lust. Every motive is misinterpreted. Every statement is given a double meaning. To escape that uncleanness, we must walk in the cleansing presence of Jesus Christ.

THE UGLY AND THE USELESS LIFE

Titus 1:13–16 (contd)

WHEN people get into this state of impurity, they may know God intellectually but their lives are a denial of that knowledge. Three things are singled out here about such people.

(1) They are repulsive. The word (bdeluktos) is the word particularly used of idols and images. It is the word from which the noun bdelugma, an abomination, comes. There is something repulsive about someone with an obscene mind, who makes sniggering jokes and whose comments are full of innuendo.

(2) They are disobedient. Such people cannot obey the will of God. Their consciences are darkened. They have made it almost impossible for themselves to hear the voice of God, let alone obey it. People like that cannot be anything but an evil influence and are therefore unfit to be instruments in the hand of God.

(3) That is just another way of saying that they have become useless to God and to others. The word used for useless

(*adokimos*) is interesting. It is used to describe a counterfeit coin which is below standard weight. It is used to describe a cowardly soldier who fails in the testing hour of battle. It is used of a candidate rejected for public office, someone whom the citizens regarded as useless. It is used of a stone which the builders rejected. (If a stone had a flaw in it, it was marked with a capital A, for *adokimos*, and left to one side, as being unfit to have any place in the building.) The ultimate test of life is usefulness, and those who are a bad influence and who have a contaminating effect are of no use to God or to other people. Instead of helping God's work in the world, they hinder it; and uselessness always invites disaster.

THE CHRISTIAN CHARACTER

1. THE SENIOR MEN

Titus 2:1–2

> You must speak what befits sound teaching. You must charge the senior men to be sober, serious, prudent, healthy in Christian faith and love and fortitude.

THIS whole chapter deals with what might be called *the Christian character in action*. It takes various groups of people by their age and status and lays down what they ought to be within the world. It begins with the *senior men*.

They must be *sober*. The word is *nēphalios*, and it literally means *sober* as opposed to *given to overindulgence in wine*. The point is that, when a man has reached years of seniority, he ought to have learned what are and what are not true pleasures. The senior men should have learned that the pleasures of self-indulgence cost far more than they are worth.

They must be *serious*. The word is *semnos*, and it describes the behaviour which is serious in the right way. It does not describe the appearance and manner of a person who is a gloomy killjoy, but the conduct of someone aware of living in the light of eternity, and expecting before very long to leave human fellowship for fellowship with God.

They must be *prudent*. The word is *sōphrōn*, and it describes someone with the mind which has everything under control. Over the years, the senior men must have acquired that cleansing, saving strength of mind which has learned to govern every instinct and passion until each has its proper place and no more.

The three words taken together mean that the senior man must have learned what can only be called *the gravity, the serious nature, of life*. A certain amount of recklessness and of thoughtlessness may be excusable in youth, but the years should bring their wisdom. One of the most tragic sights in life is the individual who has learned nothing through all the years.

Further, there are three great qualities in which the senior men must be healthy.

They must be healthy in *faith*. If we live really close to Christ, the passing of the years and the experiences of life – far from taking our faith away – will make our faith even stronger. The years must teach us not to trust God less but to trust him more.

They must be healthy in *love*. It may well be that the greatest danger of age is that it should drift into severe criticism and fault-finding. Sometimes the years take kindly sympathy away. It is fatally possible to become so settled in our ways that unconsciously we come to resent all new ideas and ways of doing things. But the years ought to bring not increasing intolerance but increasing sympathy with the views and mistakes of others.

They must be healthy in *fortitude*. The years should toughen us just as steel is strengthened in the fire, so that we

are able to bear more and more, and emerge more and more
as conquerors of life's troubles.

THE CHRISTIAN CHARACTER

2. The Older Women

Titus 2:3–5

> In the same way, you must charge the older women to
> be in demeanour such as befits those who are engaged
> in sacred things. You must charge them not to spread
> slanderous stories, not to be enslaved by overindulgence
> in wine. To be teachers of fine things, in order that they
> may train the young women to be devoted to their
> husbands and their children, to be prudent, to be chaste,
> to be home-keepers and home-minders, to be kindly, to
> be obedient to their own husbands, so that no one will
> have any opportunity to speak evil of the word of God.

IT is clear that, in the early Church, a most honoured and
responsible position was given to the older women. Kindly
grandmothers are the natural advisers of the young of both
sexes. The older women to whom the years have brought
serenity and sympathy and understanding have a part to play
in the life of the Church and of the community which is
peculiarly their own.

Here, the qualities which characterize them are laid down.
Their behaviour must be such as befits those *who are engaged
in sacred things*. As Clement of Alexandria had it: 'The
Christian must live as if all life was a sacred assembly.' It is
easy to see what a difference it would make to the peace and
fellowship of the Church if it was always remembered that
we are engaged in sacred things. Much of the embittered
argument and the touchiness and the intolerance which all

too frequently characterize church activities would vanish overnight.

They must not spread slanderous stories. It is a curious feature of human nature that most people would rather repeat and hear a malicious tale than one to someone's credit. It is no bad thing to resolve to make up our minds to say nothing at all about people if we cannot find anything good to say.

The older women must teach and train those who are younger. Sometimes it would seem that the only gift experience gives to some is that of pouring cold water on the plans and dreams of others. It is a Christian duty always to use experience to guide and encourage, and not to daunt and discourage.

THE CHRISTIAN CHARACTER

3. The Younger Women

Titus 2:3–5 (*contd*)

THE younger women are instructed to be devoted to their husbands and their children, to be prudent and chaste, to manage their households well, to be kindly to their servants and to be obedient to their husbands; and the object of such conduct is that no one will be able to speak evil of the word of God.

In this passage, there is both something that is of temporary value and something that is permanent.

In the ancient Greek world, the respectable woman lived a completely secluded life. In the house, she had her own quarters and seldom left them, not even to sit at meals with the male members of the family; and no man except her husband ever entered her rooms. She never attended any public assemblies or meetings; she seldom appeared on the streets, and, when she did, she never did so alone. In fact, it has been said that there was no honourable way in which a Greek woman could make a living. No trade or profession was open to her; and, if she tried to earn a living, she was driven to prostitution. If the women of the ancient Church had suddenly burst every limitation which the centuries had imposed upon them, the only result would have been to bring discredit on the Church and cause people to say that Christianity corrupted womanhood. The life laid down here seems narrow and restricted, but it is to be read against its background. In that sense, this passage is of its time and so is temporary.

But there is also a sense in which it is permanent. It is the simple fact that there is no greater task, responsibility and privilege in this world than to make a home. It may well be that, when women are involved in all the exhausting duties which children and a home bring with them, they may say: 'If only I could be done with all this, so that I could live a truly religious life.' There is in fact nowhere where a truly religious life can better be lived than within the home. As John Keble's hymn 'New Every Morning' has it:

> We need not bid, for cloistered cell,
> Our neighbour and our work farewell,
> Nor strive to wind ourselves too high
> For sinful man beneath the sky;
> The trivial round, the common task,
> Will furnish all we need to ask –
> Room to deny ourselves, a road
> To bring us daily nearer God.

In the last analysis, there can be no greater career than that of homemaking. Many who have made a mark in the world have been enabled to do so simply because someone at home loved them and looked after them. It is infinitely more important to be at home to put the children to bed and hear them say their prayers than to attend all the public and church meetings in the world.

THE CHRISTIAN CHARACTER

4. THE YOUNGER MEN

Titus 2:6

> In the same way, urge on the younger men the duty of prudence.

THE duty of the younger men is summed up in one sentence – but it is a loaded one. They are told to remember the duty of prudence. As we have already seen, the man who is *prudent*, *sōphrōn*, has that quality of mind which keeps life safe and the security which comes from having all things under control.

The time of youth is necessarily a time of danger.

(1) In youth, the blood runs hotter and the passions speak more commandingly. The tide of life runs strongest in youth, and it sometimes threatens to sweep a young person away.

(2) In youth, there are more opportunities for going wrong. Young people are thrown into company where temptation can speak with a most compelling voice. Often, they have to study or to work away from home and from the influences which would keep them on the right path. The young man has not yet taken upon himself the responsibility of a home and a family; he has not yet made the kind of attachments to people and things that cannot be easily given up; and he does not yet possess the anchors which hold an older person in the right way through a sheer sense of obligation. In youth, there are far more opportunities to encounter disaster and to wreck one's life.

(3) In youth, there is often that confidence which comes from lack of experience. In almost every sphere of life, a younger man will be more reckless than his elders, for the simple reason that he has not yet discovered all the things which can go wrong. To take a simple example, he will often drive a car much faster simply because he has not yet discovered how easily an accident can take place or on how slender a piece of metal the safety of a car depends. He will often shoulder a responsibility in a much more carefree spirit than an older person, because he has not known the difficulties and has not experienced how easily disaster may happen. No one can buy experience; that is something for which only the years can pay. There is a risk, as there is a glory, in being young.

For that very reason, the first thing at which any young person must aim is self-control. We can never serve others until we have full control of self. 'One who is slow to anger is better than the mighty, and one whose temper is controlled than one who captures a city' (Proverbs 16:32).

Self-discipline is not among the more glamorous of the virtues, but it is the very stuff of life. When the eagerness of youth is supported by the solidity of self-control, something really great comes into life.

THE CHRISTIAN CHARACTER

5. THE CHRISTIAN TEACHER

Titus 2:7–8

> And all the time you are doing this you must offer yourself as a pattern of fine conduct; and in your teaching you must display absolute purity of motive, dignity, a sound message which no one could condemn, so that

> your opponent may be turned to shame, because he can
> find nothing bad to say about us.

Iғ Titus' teaching is to be effective, it must be backed by the witness of his own life. He is himself to be the demonstration of all that he teaches.

(1) It must be clear that his motives are absolutely pure. The Christian teacher and preacher is always faced with certain temptations. There is always the danger of self-publicity, the temptation to demonstrate one's own cleverness and to seek to attract notice to oneself rather than to God's message. There is always the temptation to power. The teacher, the preacher, the pastor is always confronted with the temptation to be a dictator. Leader he must be, but dictator never. Titus will find that people can be led, but that they will never be driven. If there is one danger which confronts the Christian teacher and preacher more than another, it is to set store by the wrong standards of success. It can often happen that those who have never been heard of outside their own sphere of work are in God's eyes far more successful than those who have become household names.

(2) He must have dignity. Dignity is not aloofness, or arrogance, or pride; it is the consciousness of having the terrible responsibility of being the ambassador of Christ. Others may stoop to pettiness; Titus must be above it. Others may bear their grudges; he must have no bitterness. Others may be touchy about their status; he must have a humility which has forgotten that it has a place. Others may grow irritable or blaze into anger in an argument; he must have a serenity which cannot be provoked. Nothing so injures the cause of Christ as when leaders of the Church and pastors of the people descend to conduct and to words unworthy of Christ's servants.

(3) He must have a sound message. Christian teachers and preachers must be certain to pass on the truths of the gospel and not their own ideas. There is nothing easier than to spend time on side issues; but Titus might well have one prayer: 'God, give me a sense of proportion.' The central things of the faith will last him a lifetime. As soon as he becomes a propagandist either for his own ideas or for the interest of a particular group, he ceases to be an effective preacher or teacher of the word of God.

The duty laid on Titus is the tremendous task not of talking to people about Christ but of showing Christ to them. It must be true of him as it was of Chaucer's saintly parson in the *Canterbury Tales*:

> But Cristes love, and his apostles twelve
> He taught, but first he folwed it him-selve.

The greatest compliment that can be paid to a teacher is to say of him: 'First he wrought, and then he taught.'

THE CHRISTIAN CHARACTER

6. THE CHRISTIAN WORKER

Titus 2:9-10

> Impress upon slaves the duty of obeying their own masters. Urge them to seek to give satisfaction in every task, not to answer back, not to pilfer, but to display all fidelity with hearty goodwill, that they may in all things adorn the teaching which God our Saviour gave to them.

IN the early Church, the problem for Christian workers was acute. It was one which could operate in two directions.

If the master was not a Christian, the responsibility laid upon servants was heavy indeed, for it was perhaps only through their conduct that the master could ever come to see what Christianity was. It was the task of the workers to show the master what a Christian could be; and that responsibility still lies upon Christian employees. A large number of people never willingly darken a church door, a minister of the church seldom gets a chance to speak to them. How then is Christianity ever to make contact with them? The only possible way is for colleagues at work to *show* them what Christianity is. There is a famous story of St Francis. One day, he said to one of the young monks: 'Let us go down to the village and preach to the people.' So they went. Every so often, they stopped to talk to someone. They begged something to eat at one house. Francis stopped to play with the children, and exchanged a greeting with the passers-by. Then they turned to go home. 'But Father,' said the novice, 'when do we preach?' 'Preach?' smiled Francis. 'Every step we took, every word we spoke, every action we did, has been a sermon.'

There was another side to the problem. If the master was a Christian, a new temptation came into the lives of Christian workers. They might attempt to trade on the master's Christianity. They might think that, because they were Christians, special allowances would be made for them. They might expect to 'get away' with things because they and the master were members of the same church. It is perfectly possible for people to trade on their Christianity – and there is no worse advertisement for it than the person who does that.

Paul lists the qualities of Christian workers.

They are *obedient*. Christians are never above taking orders. Their Christianity teaches them how to serve. They are *efficient*. They are determined to give satisfaction. Christian workers can never put less than their best into any task that is given them to do. They are *respectful*. They do not think that their Christianity gives them a special right to be un-disciplined. Christianity does not obliterate the necessary lines of authority in the world of industry and of commerce. They are *honest*. Others may stoop to the petty dishonesties of which the world is full; but their hands are clean. They are *faithful*. The master can rely upon their loyalty.

It may well be that those who take their Christianity to work will run into trouble; but, if they stick to it, they will end by winning everyone's respect.

The missionary E. F. Brown tells of a thing which happened in India. 'A Christian servant in India was once sent by his master with a verbal message which he knew to be untrue. He refused to deliver it. Though his master was very angry at the time, he respected the servant all the more afterwards and knew that he could always trust him in his own matters.'

The truth is that in the end the world comes to see that the Christian worker is the one most worth having. In one sense, it is hard to be a Christian at our work; in another sense, it is easier than we think, for there is not an employer under the sun who is not desperately looking for employees whose loyalty and efficiency can be relied upon.

THE MORAL POWER OF THE INCARNATION

Titus 2:11–14

> For the grace of God, which brings salvation to all men, has appeared, schooling us to renounce godlessness and worldly desires for forbidden things, and to live in this world prudently, justly and reverently, because we expectantly await the realization of our blessed hope – I mean the glorious appearing of our great God and Saviour Jesus Christ, who gave himself for us to redeem us from the power of all lawlessness, and to purify us

> as a special people for himself, a people eager for all
> fine works.

THERE are few passages in the New Testament which so vividly set out the moral power of the incarnation as this does. Its whole stress is the miracle of moral change which Jesus Christ can work.

This miracle is repeatedly expressed here in the most interesting and significant way. Isaiah once exhorted his people: 'Cease to do evil, learn to do good' (Isaiah 1:16–17). First, there is the negative side of goodness, the giving up of that which is evil and the liberation from that which is low; second, there is its positive side, the acquisition of the shining virtues which mark the Christian life.

First, there is the renunciation of all godlessness and worldly desires. What did Paul mean by worldly desires? The early Church father, John Chrysostom, said that worldly things are things which do not pass over with us into heaven but are dissolved together with this present world. People are very short-sighted if they set their hearts and expend all their energies on things which they must leave behind when they quit this world. But an even simpler interpretation of *worldly desires* is that they are for things we could not show to God. It is only Christ who can make not only our outward life but also our inward heart fit for God to see.

That was the negative side of the moral power of the incarnation; now comes the positive side. Jesus Christ makes us able to live with the *prudence* which has everything under perfect control, and which allows no passion or desire more than its proper place; with the *justice* which enables us to give both to God and to our neighbours that which is their due; with the *reverence* which makes us live in the awareness that this world is nothing other than the temple of God.

The dynamic of this new life is the expectation of the coming of Jesus Christ. When a royal visit is expected, everything is cleaned and decorated and made fit for royal eyes to see. Christians are men and women who are always prepared for the coming of the King of Kings.

Finally, Paul goes on to sum up what Jesus Christ has done, and once again he does it first negatively and then positively.

Jesus has redeemed us from the power of lawlessness, that power which makes us sin.

Jesus can purify us until we are fit to be the special people of God. The word we have translated as *special* (*periousios*) is interesting. It means *reserved for*, and it was used for that part of the spoils of a battle or a campaign which the king who had conquered set apart especially for himself. Through the work of Jesus Christ, Christians become fit to be the special possessions of God.

The moral power of the incarnation is a tremendous thought. Christ not only liberated us from the penalty of past sin; he can enable us to live the perfect life within this world of space and time; and he can so cleanse us that we become fit in the life to come to be the special possession of God.

THE THREEFOLD TASK

Titus 2:15

> Let these things be the substance of your message. Deal out encouragement and rebuke with all the authority which your royal commission confers upon you. Let no one regard your authority as cheap.

HERE, Paul succinctly lays before Titus the threefold task of every Christian preacher, teacher and leader.

It is a task of *proclamation*. There is a message to be proclaimed. There are some things about which argument is not possible and on which discussion is not relevant. There are times when the only thing to say is: 'Thus says the Lord.'

It is a task of *encouragement*. Any preacher who reduces an audience to bleak despair has failed. People must be charged with their sin, not so that they may feel that their case is hopeless, but that they may be led to the grace which is greater than all their sin.

It is a task of *conviction*. The eyes of sinners must be opened to their sin; the misguided must be led to realize their mistakes; the hearts of the inconsiderate must be pricked into awareness. The Christian message is no drug to send us to sleep; it is rather the blinding light which shows us our true selves as we really are and God as he is.

CHRISTIAN CITIZENS

Titus 3:1–2

> Remind them to be duly subject to those who are in power and authority, to obey each several command, to be ready for every work so long as it is good, to slander no one, not to be aggressive, to be kindly, to show all gentleness to all men.

HERE is laid down the public duty of all Christians; and it is advice which was particularly relevant to the people of Crete. The Cretans were notoriously turbulent and quarrelsome and impatient of all authority. Polybius, the Greek historian, said of them that they were constantly involved in 'insurrections, murders and internecine wars'. This passage lays down six qualifications for good citizens.

Good citizens are *law-abiding*. They recognize that, unless the laws are kept, life becomes chaos. They give a proper respect to those who are set in authority and carry out whatever command is given to them. Christianity does not insist that people should cease to be individuals, but it does insist that they remember that they are also members of a group. 'Man', said Aristotle, 'is a political animal.' That means that we best express our personalities not in isolated individualism but within the framework of the group.

Good citizens are *active in service*. They are ready for every work, as long as it is good. The characteristic modern disease is boredom, and boredom is the direct result of selfishness. As long as people live on the principle of 'Why should I do it? Let someone else do it', they are bound to be bored. The interest of life lies in service.

Good citizens are *careful in speech*. They must slander no one. We should never say about other people what we would not like them to say about us. Good citizens will be as careful of the words they speak as they are about their actions.

Good citizens are *tolerant*. They are not aggressive. The Greek word is *amachos*, which means *not a fighter*. This does not mean that good citizens will not stand up for the principles which they believe to be right, but that they will never be so opinionated as to believe that no other way than their own is right. They will allow to others the same right to have their own convictions as they claim for themselves.

Good citizens are *kind*. The word is *epieikēs*, which describes someone who does not stand upon the letter of the law. Aristotle said of this word that it denotes 'indulgent consideration of human infirmities' and the ability 'to consider not only the letter of the law, but also the mind and intention of the legislator'. Someone who is *epieikēs* is always ready to avoid the injustice which often lies in being strictly just.

Good citizens are *gentle*. The word is *praus*, which describes the person whose temper is always under complete control. Such people know when to be angry and when not to be angry. They patiently bear wrongs done to them but are always ready to spring to the help of others who are wronged.

Qualities like these are possible only for those in whose hearts Christ reigns supreme. The welfare of any community depends on the acceptance by the Christians within it of the duty of demonstrating to the world the nobility of Christian citizenship.

THE DOUBLE DYNAMIC

Titus 3:3–7

> For we too were once senseless, disobedient, misguided, slaves to all kinds of desires and pleasures, living in maliciousness and envy, detestable ourselves, and hating each other. But when the goodness and the love to men of God our Saviour appeared, it was not by works wrought in righteousness, which we ourselves had done, but by his own mercy that he saved us. That saving act was made effective to us through that washing, through which there comes to us the rebirth and the renewal which are the work of the Holy Spirit, whom he richly poured out upon us, through Jesus Christ our Saviour. And the aim of all this was that we might be put into a right relationship with God through his grace, and so enter into possession of eternal life, for which we have been taught to hope.

THE dynamic of the Christian life is twofold.

It comes first from the realization that converts to Christianity were once no better than their non-Christian neighbours. Christian goodness does not make people proud; it makes them supremely grateful. When Christians looked at others, living life by the standards of Roman society, they did not regard them with contempt; they said, as the Methodist George Whitefield said when he saw the criminal on the way to the gallows: 'There but for the grace of God go I.'

It comes from the realization of what God has done for us in Jesus Christ. Perhaps no passage in the New Testament more concisely, and yet more fully, sets out the work of Christ for us than this. There are seven outstanding facts about that work here.

(1) Jesus put us into a new relationship with God. Until he came, God was the King before whom people stood in awe, the Judge before whom they cringed in terror, the Ruler whom they could regard only with fear. Jesus came to tell men and women of the Father whose heart was open and whose hands were stretched out in love. He came to tell them not of the justice which would pursue them forever but of the love which would never let them go.

(2) The love and grace of God are gifts which no one could ever earn; they can only be accepted in perfect trust and in awakened love. God offers his love to us simply out of the great goodness of his heart, and Christians never think of what they have earned but only of what God has given. The keynote of the Christian life must always be wondering and humble gratitude, never proud self-satisfaction. The whole process is due to two great qualities of God.

It is due to his *goodness*. The word is *chrēstotēs* and means *graciousness*. It means that spirit which is so kind that it is always eager to give whatever gift may be necessary. *Chrēstotēs* is an all-embracing kindliness, which produces not only warm feeling but also generous action at all times.

It is due to God's *love to men and women*. The word is *philanthrōpia*, and it is defined as *love of someone as a human being*. The Greeks thought much of this beautiful word. They used it for the kindliness of good people to their equals, for a good king's graciousness to his subjects, for a generous individual's active pity for those in any kind of distress, and especially for the compassion which made someone pay the ransom for another who had fallen into captivity.

Behind all this is no human merit but only the gracious kindliness and the universal love which are in the heart of God.

(3) This love and grace of God are mediated through the Church. They come through the sacrament of baptism. That is not to say that they can come in no other way, for God is not confined within his sacraments; but the door to them is always open through the Church. When we think of baptism in the earliest days of the Church, we must remember that it was the baptism of grown men and women coming directly out of the ancient idolatrous religions. It was the deliberate leaving of one way of life to enter upon another. When Paul writes to the people of Corinth, he says: 'You were washed, you were sanctified, you were justified' (1 Corinthians 6:11). In the letter to the Ephesians, he says that Jesus Christ took the Church 'in order to make her holy by cleansing her with the washing of water by the word' (Ephesians 5:26). In baptism, there came the cleansing, re-creating power of God.

In this connection, Paul uses two words.

He speaks of *rebirth* (*paliggenesia*). Here is a word which had many associations. After baptism, converts who were received into the Jewish faith were treated as if they were little children. It was as if they had been reborn and life had begun all over again. The Pythagoreans used the word frequently. They believed in reincarnation and that people returned to life in many forms until they were fit to be released from it. Each return was a rebirth. The Stoics used the word. They believed that every 3,000 years the world was destroyed in a great fire, and that then there was a rebirth of a new world. When people entered the mystery religions, they were said to be 'reborn for eternity'. The point is that when we accept Christ as Saviour and Lord, life begins all over again. There is a newness about life which can be likened only to a new birth.

He speaks of a *renewing*. It is as if life were worn out and, when someone discovers Christ, there is an act of renewal, which is not over and done with in one moment of time but repeats itself every day.

CAUSE AND EFFECT

Titus 3:3-7 (*contd*)

(4) THE grace and love of God are mediated to men and women within the Church, but behind it all is the power of the Holy Spirit. All the work of the Church, all the words of the Church, all the sacraments of the Church have no effect unless the power of the Holy Spirit is there. However well a church is organized, however splendid its ceremonies may be, however beautiful its buildings, all is ineffective without that power. The lesson is clear. Revival in the Church comes not from increased efficiency in organization but from waiting upon God. It is not that efficiency is not necessary; but no amount of efficiency can breathe life into a body from which the Spirit has departed.

(5) The effect of all this is threefold. It brings forgiveness for past sins. In his mercy, God does not hold our sins against

us. Once a man was mourning gloomily to St Augustine about his sins. 'Man,' said Augustine, 'look away from your sins and look to God.' It is not that we should live our lives without being perpetually repentant for our sins; but the very memory of our sins should move us to wonder at the forgiving mercy of God.

(6) The effect is also new life in the present. Christianity does not confine its offer to blessings which shall be. It offers us here and now life of a quality which we have never known before. When Christ enters into our lives, for the first time we really begin to live.

(7) Last, there is the hope of even greater things. Christians are men and women for whom the best is always still to be; they know that, however wonderful life on earth with Christ may be, the life to come will be greater still. Christians are people who know the wonder of the forgiveness of past sins, the thrill of present life with Christ, and the hope of the greater life which is yet to come.

THE NECESSITY OF ACTION AND THE DANGER OF DISCUSSION

Titus 3:8–11

This is a saying which we are bound to believe – and I want you to keep on affirming these things – that those who have put their faith in God must think and plan how to practise fine deeds. These are fine things and useful to men. But have nothing to do with foolish speculations and genealogies and contentious and legalistic battles, for they are no good to anyone and serve no useful purpose. Avoid a contentious and self-opinionated man, after giving him a first and a second warning, for you must be well aware that such a man is perverted and stands a self-condemned sinner.

THIS passage stresses the need for Christian action and the danger of a certain kind of discussion.

The word we have translated as *to practise* fine deeds is *proistasthai*, which literally means *to stand in front of* and was the word used for a shopkeeper standing in front of the shop and calling out to advertise the produce. The phrase may mean either of two things. It might be a command to Christians to engage only in respectable and useful trades. There were certain professions which the early Church insisted that people should give up before they were allowed even to ask for membership. More probably, the phrase has the wider meaning that Christians must practise good deeds which are helpful to others.

The second part of the passage warns against useless discussions. The Greek philosophers spent their time on their oversubtle problems. The Jewish Rabbis spent their time building up imaginary genealogies for the characters of the Old Testament. The Jewish scribes spent endless hours discussing what could and could not be done on the Sabbath, and what was and was not unclean. It has been said that there is a danger that people might think themselves religious because they discuss religious questions. It is much easier to discuss theological questions than to be kind and considerate and helpful at home, or efficient and conscientious and honest at work. There is no virtue in sitting discussing deep theological questions when the simple tasks of the Christian life are waiting to be done. Such discussion can be nothing other than avoidance of Christian duties.

Paul was certain that the real task for Christians lay in Christian action. That is not to say that there is no place for Christian discussion; but the discussion which does not end in action is very largely wasted time.

It is Paul's advice that contentious and self-opinionated people should be avoided. The Authorized Version calls that kind of person the *heretic*. The Greek is *hairetikos*. The verb *hairein* means *to choose*, and *hairesis* means a party, or a school or a sect. Originally, the word carried no bad meaning. This creeps in when someone sets private opinion against all the teaching, the agreement and the tradition of the Church. Heretics are simply people who have decided that they are right and everybody else is wrong. Paul's warning is against those who have made their own ideas the test of all truth. We should always be very careful of any opinion which separates us from the fellowship of our fellow believers. True faith does not divide people; it unites them.

FINAL GREETINGS

Titus 3:12–15

> When I send Artemas or Tychicus to you, do your best to come to me at Nicopolis, for I have decided to spend the winter there.
>
> Do your best to help Zenas the lawyer and Apollos on their way. See to it that nothing is lacking to them.
>
> And let our people too learn to practise fine deeds, that they may be able to supply all necessary needs, and that they may not live useless lives.
>
> All who are with me send you their greetings. Greet those who love us in the faith.
>
> Grace be with you all. Amen.

As usual, Paul ends his letter with personal messages and greetings. Of Artemas, we know nothing at all. Tychicus was one of Paul's most trusted messengers. He was the bearer of the letters to the Colossian and the Ephesian churches

(Colossians 4:7; Ephesians 6:21). Nicopolis was in Epirus and was the best centre for work in the Roman province of Dalmatia. It is interesting to remember that it was there that Epictetus, the great Stoic philosopher, later had his school.

Apollos was the well-known teacher (Acts 18:24). Of Zenas, we know nothing at all. He is here called a *nomikos*. That could mean one of two things. *Nomikos* is the regular word for a *scribe*, and Zenas may have been a converted Jewish Rabbi. It is also the normal Greek for a *lawyer*; and, if that is its meaning, Zenas has the distinction of being the only lawyer mentioned in the New Testament.

Paul's last piece of advice is that the Christian people should practise good deeds, so that they themselves should be independent and also able to help others who are in need. Christian workers work not only to have enough for themselves but also to have something to give away.

Next come the final greetings; and then, as in every letter, Paul's last word is grace.

The Letter to Philemon

INTRODUCTION TO THE LETTER TO PHILEMON

The Unique Letter

In one respect, this little letter to Philemon is unique. It is the only *private letter* of Paul which we possess. Doubtless Paul must have written many private letters; but, of them all, only Philemon has survived. Quite apart from the grace and the charm which pervade it, this fact gives it a special significance.

Onesimus, the Runaway Slave

There are two possible reconstructions of what happened. One is quite straightforward; the other, connected with the name of the American scholar E. J. Goodspeed, is rather more complicated and certainly more dramatic. Let us take the simple view first.

Onesimus was a runaway slave and very probably a thief into the bargain. 'If he has wronged you in any way', Paul writes, 'or owes you anything, charge that to my account' (verses 18–19). Somehow the runaway had found his way to Rome, to lose himself in the crowded and busy streets of that great city; somehow he had come into contact with Paul, and somehow he had become a Christian, the child to whom Paul had become a father during his imprisonment (verse 10).

Then something happened. It was obviously impossible for Paul to go on harbouring a runaway slave, and something brought the problem to a head. Perhaps it was the coming of Epaphras. It may be that Epaphras recognized Onesimus as a slave he had seen at Colosse, and at that point the whole wretched story came out; or it may be that, with the coming of Epaphras, Onesimus' conscience moved him to make a clean breast of all his discreditable past.

Paul Sends Onesimus Back

In the time that he had been with him, Onesimus had made himself very nearly indispensable to Paul; and Paul would have liked to keep him beside him. 'I wanted to keep him with me', he writes (verse 13). But he will do nothing without the consent of Philemon, Onesimus' master (verse 14). So he sends Onesimus back. No one knew better than Paul how great a risk he was taking. A slave was not a person but a living tool. A master had absolute power over his slaves. 'He can box their ears or condemn them to hard labour – making them, for instance, work in chains upon his lands in the country, or in a sort of prison-factory. Or, he may punish them with blows of the rod, the lash or the knot; he can brand them upon the forehead, if they are thieves or runaways, or, in the end, if they prove irreclaimable, he can crucify them.' The Roman lawyer and satirist Juvenal draws the picture of the mistress who will beat her maid servant at her whim and of the master who 'delights in the sound of a cruel flogging, deeming it sweeter than any siren's song', who is never happy 'until he has summoned a torturer and he can brand someone with a hot iron for stealing a couple of towels', 'who revels in clanking chains'. Slaves were continually at the mercy of the whims of a master or a mistress.

What made it worse was that the slaves were deliberately repressed. There were in the Roman Empire 60,000,000 of them, and the danger of revolt was constantly to be guarded against. A rebellious slave was promptly eliminated. And, if a slave ran away, at best he would be branded with a red-hot iron on the forehead, with the letter F – standing for *fugitivus*, *runaway* – and at the worst he would be put to death by crucifixion. Paul was well aware of all this and that slavery was so ingrained into the ancient world that even to send Onesimus back to the Christian Philemon was a considerable risk.

Paul's Appeal

So Paul gave Onesimus this letter. He makes a pun on Onesimus' name. *Onesimus* in Greek literally means *profitable*. Once Onesimus was a useless fellow, but now he is useful (verse 11). Now, as we might say, he is not only Onesimus by name, he is also Onesimus by nature. Maybe Philemon lost him for a time in order to have him forever (verse 15). He must take him back, not as a slave but as a Christian brother (verse 16). He is now Paul's son in the faith, and Philemon must receive him as he would receive Paul himself.

Emancipation

Such, then, was Paul's appeal. Many people have wondered why Paul says nothing in this letter about the whole matter of slavery. He does not condemn it; he does not even tell Philemon to set Onesimus free; it is still as a slave that he would have him taken back. There are those who have criticized Paul for not seizing the opportunity to condemn the slavery on which the ancient world was built. The New Testament scholar J. B. Lightfoot says: 'The word *emancipation* seems to tremble on his lips, but he never utters it.' But there are reasons for his silence.

Slavery was an integral part of the ancient world; the whole of society was built on it. Aristotle held that it was in the nature of things that certain men should be slaves, hewers of wood and drawers of water, to serve the higher classes. It may well be that Paul accepted the institution of slavery because it was almost impossible to imagine society without it. Further, if Christianity had, in fact, given the slaves any encouragement to revolt or to leave their masters, nothing but tragedy could have followed. Any such revolt would have been savagely crushed; slaves who took their freedom would have been mercilessly punished; and Christianity would itself have been branded as revolutionary and subversive. Given the Christian faith, liberation was bound to come – but the time was not ripe; and to have encouraged slaves to hope for it, and to seize it, would have done infinitely more harm than good. There are some things which cannot be achieved suddenly, and for which the world must wait, until the leaven works.

The New Relationship

What Christianity did was to introduce a new relationship between individuals in which all external differences were abolished. Christians are one body whether Jews or Gentiles, slaves or free (1 Corinthians 12:13). In Christ there is neither Jew nor Greek, slave or free, male or female (Galatians 3:28). In Christ there is neither Greek nor Jew, circumcised or uncircumcised, barbarian, Scythian, slave or free (Colossians 3:11). It was as a slave that Onesimus ran away, and it was as a slave that he was coming back; but now he was not only a slave, he was a beloved brother in the Lord. When a relationship like that enters into life, social grades and classes cease to matter. The very names, master and slave, become irrelevant. If masters treat slaves as Christ would have treated them, and if slaves serve the masters as they would serve Christ, then the terms *master* and *slave* do not matter; their relationship does not depend on any human classification, for they are both in Christ.

In the early days, Christianity did not attack slavery; to have done so would have been disastrous. But it introduced a new relationship in which the human divisions in society ceased to matter. It is to be noted that this new relationship never gave slaves the right to take advantage of it; rather, it made them better slaves and more efficient servants, for now they had to do things in such a way that they could offer them to Christ. Nor did it mean that the master must be soft and easy-going, willing to accept bad work and inferior service; but it did mean that he no longer treated any servant as a thing, but as a person and a brother or sister in Christ.

There are two passages in which Paul sets out the duties of slaves and masters – Ephesians 6:5–9 and Colossians 3:22–4:1. Both were written when Paul was in prison in Rome, and most likely when Onesimus was with him; and it is difficult not to think that they owe much to long talks that Paul had with the runaway slave who had become a Christian.

On this view, Philemon is a private letter, sent by Paul to Philemon, when he sent back his runaway slave; and it was written to urge Philemon to receive back Onesimus, not as a master who was not a Christian would, but as a Christian receives a brother.

Archippus

Let us now turn to the other view of this letter.

We may begin with a consideration of the place of Archippus. He appears in both Colossians and Philemon. In Philemon, greetings are sent to Archippus, *our fellow soldier* (verse 2); and such a description might well mean that Archippus is the minister of the Christian community in question. He is also mentioned in Colossians 4:17: 'And say to Archippus, "See that you complete the task that you have received in the Lord."' Now, that instruction comes after a whole series of very definite references, not to Colosse, but to *Laodicaea* (Colossians 4:13, 4:15, 4:16). Might not the fact that he appears among the messages sent to Laodicaea imply that Archippus must be at Laodicaea too? Why in any event should he get this personal message? If he was at Colosse, he would hear the letter read, as everyone else would. Why has this verbal order to be sent to him? It is surely possible that the answer is that he is not in Colosse at all, but in Laodicaea.

If that is so, it means that Philemon's house is in *Laodicaea* and that Onesimus was a runaway *Laodicaean* slave. This must mean that the letter to Philemon was, in fact, written to Laodicaea. And, if so, the missing letter to Laodicaea, mentioned in Colossians 4:16, is none other than the letter to Philemon. This indeed solves problems.

Let us remember that in ancient society, with its view of slavery, Paul took a considerable risk in sending Onesimus back at all. So, it can be argued that Philemon is not really only a personal letter. It is indeed written to Philemon *and to the church in his house*. And, further, it has also to be read at Colosse. What, then, is Paul doing? Knowing the risk that he takes in sending Onesimus back, he is mobilizing church opinion both in Laodicaea and in Colosse in his favour. The decision about Onesimus is not to be left to Philemon; it is to be the decision of the whole Christian community. It so happens that there is one little, but important, linguistic point, which is very much in favour of this view. In verse 12, the Revised Standard Version makes Paul write that he has *sent back* Onesimus to Philemon. The verb is *anapempein*; this is the regular verb – it is more common in this sense than in any other – for officially referring a case to someone for decision. And verse 12 should most probably be translated: 'I am referring his case to you' – that is, not only to Philemon but also to the church in his house.

There is a lot to be said for this view. There is only one difficulty. In Colossians 4:9, Onesimus is referred to as *one of you*, which certainly looks as if he is a Colossian. But E. J. Goodspeed, who states this view with such scholarship and persuasiveness, argues that Hierapolis, Laodicaea and Colosse were so close together, and so much a single church, that they could well be regarded as one community, and that, therefore, *one of you* need not mean that Onesimus came from Colosse, but simply that he came from that closely connected group. If we are prepared to accept this, the last obstacle to the theory is removed.

The Continuation of the Story

Goodspeed does not stop there. He goes on to reconstruct the history of Onesimus in a most moving way.

In verses 13–14, Paul makes it quite clear that he would very much have liked to keep Onesimus with him. 'I wanted to keep him with me, so that he might be of service to me in your place during my imprisonment for the gospel; but I preferred to do nothing without your consent, in order that your good deed might be voluntary and not something forced.' He reminds Philemon that he owes him his very soul (verse 19). He says, with charming wit: 'Let me have this benefit from you in the Lord!' (verse 20). He says: 'Confident of your obedience, I am writing to you, knowing that you will do even more than I say' (verse 21). Is it possible that Philemon could have resisted this appeal? Spoken to in such a way, could he do anything other than send Onesimus back to Paul with his blessing? Goodspeed regards it as certain that Paul got Onesimus back and that he became Paul's helper in the work of the gospel.

The Bishop of Ephesus

Let us move on about fifty years. Ignatius, one of the great Christian martyrs, is being taken to execution from Antioch to Rome. As he goes, he writes letters – which still survive – to the churches of Asia Minor. He stops at Smyrna and writes to the church at Ephesus, and in the first chapter of that letter he has much to say about their wonderful bishop. And what is the bishop's name? It is *Onesimus*; and Ignatius makes exactly the same pun as Paul made – he is Onesimus by name and Onesimus by nature, the one who is profitable to Christ. It may well be that, with the passing years, the runaway slave had become the great Bishop of Ephesus.

What Christ did for Me

If all this is true, we have still another explanation. Why did this little slip of a letter, this single papyrus sheet, survive; and how did it ever get itself into the collection of Pauline letters? It deals with no great doctrine; it attacks no great heresy; it is the only one of the letters universally accepted as having been written by Paul that is addressed to an individual. It is practically certain that the first collection of Paul's letters was made at *Ephesus*, about the turn of the century. It was just then that Onesimus was Bishop of Ephesus; and it may well be that it was he who insisted that this letter be included in the collection, short and personal as it was, in order that all might know what the grace of God had done for him. Through it, the bishop tells the world that once he was a runaway slave and that he owed his life to Paul and to Jesus Christ.

Did Onesimus come back to Paul with Philemon's bless-ing? Did the young man who had been the runaway slave become the great Bishop of Ephesus? Did he insist that this little letter be included in the Pauline collection to tell what Christ, through Paul, had done for him? We can never tell for certain; but it is a lovely story of God's grace in Christ – and we hope that it is true!

PHILEMON

A MAN TO WHOM IT WAS EASY TO APPEAL

Philemon 1–7

> This is a letter from Paul, the prisoner of Jesus Christ,
> and from Timothy, the brother, to Philemon our well-
> beloved and our fellow worker; and to Apphia, the sister,
> and to Archippus, our fellow soldier, and to the church
> in your house. Grace be to you and peace from God,
> our Father, and from the Lord Jesus Christ.
>
> I always thank my God when I make mention of you
> in my prayers, for I hear of your love and your faith,
> which you have to the Lord Jesus, and to all God's
> dedicated people. I pray that the kindly deeds of charity
> to which your faith moves you may be powerfully
> effective to increase your knowledge of every good thing
> that is in us and that brings us ever closer to Christ.
> You have brought me much joy and encouragement,
> because, my brother, the hearts of God's people have
> been refreshed by you.

THE letter to Philemon is remarkable, for in it we see the
extraordinary sight of Paul asking a favour. No one ever asked
fewer favours than he did; but in this letter he is asking a
favour, not so much for himself as for Onesimus, who had
taken the wrong turning and whom Paul was helping to find
the way back.

The beginning of the letter is unusual. Paul usually identifies himself as Paul *an apostle*; but on this occasion he is writing as a friend to a friend, and the official title is dropped. He is writing not as Paul *the apostle* but as Paul *the prisoner of Christ*. Here at the very beginning, Paul lays aside all appeal to authority and makes his appeal to sympathy and to love alone.

We do not know who Apphia and Archippus were, but it has been suggested that Apphia was the wife and Archippus the son of Philemon – for they, too, would be very much interested in the return of Onesimus, the runaway slave. Certainly, Archippus had seen Christian service with Paul, for Paul speaks of him as his fellow campaigner.

Philemon was clearly a man from whom it was easy to ask a favour. He was a man whose faith in Christ and love towards the Christian community was well known, and the story of his faith and love had reached even Rome, where Paul was in prison. His house must have been like an oasis in a desert – for, as Paul puts it, he had refreshed the hearts of God's people. It is a lovely thing to go down in history as someone in whose house God's people were rested and refreshed.

In this passage, there is one verse which is very difficult to translate and about which much has been written. It is verse 6, which the Revised Standard Version translates: 'I pray that the sharing of your faith may promote the knowledge of all the good that is ours in Christ.' The phrase translated as *the sharing of your faith* is very difficult. The Greek is *koinōnia pisteōs*. As far as we can see, there are three possible meanings. (1) *Koinōnia* can mean *a sharing in*; it can, for instance, mean partnership in a business. So this may mean *your share in the Christian faith*; and it might be a prayer that the faith in which Philemon and Paul share may lead Philemon deeper and deeper into Christian truth. (2) *Koinōnia* can mean *fellowship*; and this may be a prayer that *Christian fellowship* may lead Philemon ever more deeply into the truth. (3) *Koinōnia* can mean the *act of sharing*; in that case, the verse will mean: 'It is my prayer that your way of generously sharing all that you have will lead you more and more deeply into the knowledge of the good things which lead to Christ.'

We think that the third meaning is correct. Obviously, Christian generosity was a characteristic of Philemon: he had love for God's people, and in his home they were rested and refreshed. And now Paul is going to ask the generous man to be even more generous. There is a great thought here, if this interpretation is correct. It means that we learn about Christ by giving to others. It means that by emptying ourselves we are filled with Christ. It means that to be open-handed and generous-hearted is the surest way to learn more and more of the wealth of Christ. The one who knows most of Christ is not the intellectual scholar, not even the saint who spends all day in prayer, but the one who moves among others in loving generosity.

THE REQUEST OF LOVE

Philemon 8–17

> I could well be bold in Christ to give you orders as to where your duty lies, but for love's sake I would rather put it in the form of a request, I, Paul, such as I am, an old man now, a prisoner of Christ. My request to you is for my child, whom I begat in my bonds – I mean Onesimus, who was once useless to you, but who is now useful to you and to me. I am sending him back to you, and that is the same as to send you a bit of my own heart. I could have wished to keep him beside myself, that he might serve me for you in the bonds which the

gospel has brought to me; but I did not wish to do anything without your approval; so that the boon which I
ask might not be forcibly extracted but willingly given.
It may be that he was parted from you for a time that
you might get him back forever; and that you might get
him back, no longer as a slave, but as more than a slave
– a well-beloved brother, most of all to me, and how
much more to you, both as a man and a Christian. If
you consider me as a partner, receive him as you would
receive me.

PAUL, being Paul, could have demanded what he wanted from
Philemon; but he will only humbly request. A gift must be
given freely and with goodwill; if it is forced, it is no gift at
all.

In verse 9, Paul describes himself. The Authorized Version
translates – and we have retained the translation – as Paul *the
aged*, and a prisoner of Christ. A good number of scholars
wish to substitute another translation for *aged*. It is argued
that Paul could not really be described as an old man. He
certainly was not sixty years old; he was somewhere between
that and fifty-five. But, on this basis, those who object to the
translation *aged* are wrong. The word which Paul uses of
himself is *presbutēs*; and Hippocrates, the great Greek medical
writer, says that a man is *presbutēs* from the age of forty-
nine to the age of fifty-six. Between these years, he is what
we might call *senior*; only after that does he become a *gerōn*,
the Greek for an old man.

But what is the other translation suggested? There are two
words which are very like each other; their spelling is only
one letter different, and their pronunciation exactly the same.
They are *presbutēs*, *old*, and *presbeutēs*, *ambassador*. It is
the verb of this word which Paul uses in Ephesians 6:20,
when he says: 'I am an *ambassador* in chains.' If we think

that the word ought to be *presbeutēs*, Paul is saying: 'I am an ambassador, although I am an ambassador in chains.' But it is far more likely that we should retain the translation *old*, for in this letter Paul is appealing all the time, not to any office he holds or to any authority he enjoys, but only to love. It is not the ambassador who is speaking, but the man who has lived hard and is now lonely and tired.

Paul makes his request in verse 10, and it is for Onesimus. We notice how he delays using the name of Onesimus, almost as if he hesitated to do so. He does not make any excuses for him; he freely admits he was a useless character; but he makes one claim – he is useful now. Christianity, as the theologian James Denney of Glasgow Free Church College used to say, is the power which can make bad men good.

It is significant to note that Paul claims that in Christ the useless person has been made useful. The last thing Christianity is designed to produce is vague, inefficient people; it produces people who are of use and can do a job better than they ever could if they did not know Christ. It was said of someone that 'he was so heavenly-minded that he was no earthly use'. But it is true that Christianity makes people heavenly-minded and useful upon earth at one and the same time.

Paul calls Onesimus the child to whom he has become a father in his imprisonment. A Rabbinic saying runs: 'If one teaches the son of his neighbour the law, the Scripture reckons this the same as though he had begotten him.' To lead someone to Jesus Christ is as great a thing as to bring that person into the world. Happy are the parents who bring a child into life and who then lead that child into life eternal, for then the child will be theirs twice over.

As we have noted in the introduction to this letter, there is a double meaning in verse 12. 'I am sending him back to you', writes Paul. But the verb *anapempein* does not mean only *to send back*, it also means *to refer a case to*; and Paul is saying to Philemon: 'I am referring this case of Onesimus to you, that you may give a verdict on it that will match the love you ought to have.' Onesimus must have become very dear to Paul in these months in prison, for he pays him the great tribute of saying that to send him to Philemon is like sending a bit of his own heart.

Then comes the appeal. Paul would have liked to keep Onesimus; but he sends him back to Philemon, for he will do nothing without his consent. Here again is a significant thing. Christianity is not trying to help people escape from their past and run away from it; it is aiming to enable them to face the past and rise above it. Onesimus had run away. Well, then, he must go back, face up to the consequences of what he did, accept them and rise above them. Christianity is never escape; it is always conquest.

But Onesimus comes back changed. He went away as a slave who did not know Christ; he comes back as a brother in Christ. It is going to be hard for Philemon to regard a runaway slave as a brother, but that is exactly what Paul demands. 'If you agree', says Paul, 'that I am your partner in the work of Christ and that Onesimus is my son in the faith, you must receive him as you would receive me.'

Here again is something very significant. Christians must always welcome back those who have made a mistake. Too often, we regard with suspicion people who have taken the wrong turning and show that we are never prepared to trust them again. We believe that God can forgive them; but we, ourselves, find it too difficult. It has been said that the most uplifting thing about Jesus Christ is that he trusts us on the very field of our defeat. When someone has made a mistake, the way back can be very hard, and God cannot readily forgive

anyone who, through self-righteousness or lack of sy
makes it harder.

THE CLOSING APPEAL AND THE
CLOSING BLESSING

Philemon 18–25

> If he has done you any damage or owes you anything,
> put it down to my account. I, Paul, write with my own
> hand – I will repay it, not to mention to you that you
> owe your very self to me. Yes, my brother, let me make
> some Christian profit out of you! Refresh my heart in
> Christ. It is with complete confidence in your willingness
> to listen that I write to you, for I know well that you
> will do more than I ask.
>
> At the same time get ready a lodging place for me;
> for I hope that through your prayers it will be granted
> to you that I should come to you.
>
> Epaphras, my fellow prisoner in Christ, sends his
> greetings to you, as do Mark, Aristarchus, Demas and
> Luke, my fellow workers.
>
> The grace of the Lord Jesus Christ be with your spirit.
> Amen.

IT is one of the laws of life that someone has to pay the price
of sin. God can and does forgive, but not even he can free us
from the consequences of what we have done. It is the glory
of the Christian faith that, just as Jesus Christ took upon
himself the sins of all, so there are those who in love are
prepared to help pay for the consequences of the sins of those
who are dear to them. Christianity never entitled anyone to
default on debts. Onesimus must have stolen from Philemon,
as well as run away from him. If he had not helped himself to
Philemon's money, it is difficult to see how he could ever

have covered the long road to Rome. Paul writes with his own hand that he will be responsible and will repay in full.

It is interesting to note that this is an exact instance of a *cheirographon*, the kind of acknowledgment met in Colossians 2:14. This is *a handwriting against Paul*, an obligation voluntarily accepted and signed.

It is of interest to note that Paul was able to pay Onesimus' debts. Every now and again, we get glimpses which show that he was not without financial resources. Felix kept him prisoner, for he had hopes of a bribe to let him go (Acts 24:26); Paul was able to rent a house during his imprisonment in Rome (Acts 28:30). It may well be that, if he had not chosen to live the life of a missionary of Christ, he might have lived a settled life of reasonable ease and comfort on his own resources. This may well have been another of the things which he gave up for Christ.

In verses 19–20, we hear Paul speaking with a flash of humour. 'Philemon,' he says, 'you owe your soul to me, for it was I who brought you to Christ. Won't you let me make some profit out of you now?' With an affectionate smile, Paul is saying: 'Philemon, you got a lot out of me – let me get something out of you now!'

Verse 21 is typical of Paul's dealings with people. It was his rule always to expect the best from others; he never really doubted that Philemon would grant his request. It is a good rule. To expect the best from others is often to be more than half-way to getting it; if we make it clear that we expect little, we will probably get just that.

In verse 22, Paul's optimism speaks. Even in prison, he believes it possible that, through the prayers of his friends, freedom may come again. He has changed his plans now. Before he was imprisoned, it had been his intention to go to far-off Spain (Romans 15:24, 15:28). Maybe after the years in prison, two at Caesarea and another two at Rome, Paul felt that he must leave the distant places to younger men and that for him, as he drew near the end, old friends were best.

In verse 23, there is a list of greetings from the same comrades whom we meet in Colossians; and so there comes the blessing, and both Philemon and Onesimus are commended to the grace of Christ.